STRENGTH
FOR THE
JOURNEY

STRENGTH
FOR THE
JOURNEY

A Pilgrimage of Faith in Community

Diana Butler Bass

FOREWORD BY PHYLLIS TICKLE

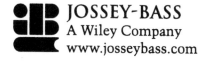

JOSSEY-BASS
A Wiley Company
www.josseybass.com

Published by Jossey-Bass
A Wiley Imprint
989 Market Street, San Francisco, CA 94103-1741   www.josseybass.com

Jossey-Bass books and products are available through most bookstores. To contact Jossey-Bass directly call our Customer Care Department within the U.S. at (800) 956-7739, outside the U.S. at (317) 572-3986 or fax (317) 572-4002.

Jossey-Bass also publishes its books in a variety of electronic formats. Some content that appears in print may not be available in electronic books.

AUTHOR'S NOTE: Unless otherwise referenced, the liturgical passages are from The Episcopal Book of Common Prayer, 1979 Edition. As a memoir spanning two decades, the reader should realize that some of the dialogue is reconstructed. The name Burt Thomas is a pseudonym.

Credits are on page 293.

Library of Congress Cataloging-in-Publication Data

Bass, Diana Butler, date.
    Strength for the journey: a pilgrimage of faith in community /Diana Butler Bass; foreword by Phyllis Tickle.—1st ed.
      p. cm.
    Includes bibliographical references.
    ISBN 0-7879-5578-7 (alk. paper)
    ISBN 0-7879-7425-0 (paperback)
    1. Bass, Diana Butler, date. 2. Episcopal Church—United States.
3. Episcopalians—United States—Biography. I. Title.
BX5995.B377 A3 2001
283'.092—dc21   2001003791

Printed in the United States of America
FIRST EDITION
HB Printing   1 0   9   8   7   6   5   4   3   2
PB Printing   1 0   9   8   7   6   5   4   3   2   1

CONTENTS

CONTENTS

FOREWORD

The book you are holding in your hands is as much an amazement as a book. Though it may be—and is—gentle and unassuming, the tale told on these pages spreads in one's soul over time like a powerful music heard or a rich brandy well savored.

Spiritual journals, spiritual autobiographies, spiritual confessionals. Call them by whatever name we may, there will always be myriad labels remaining for books that record a spirit's movement toward its consummation. Many of those travelogues of the soul are excellent aids to the spiritual wayfaring of others, and almost all the published ones are worthy of some greater or lesser readership. *Strength for the Journey* does not fall within their precise category, however.

I say this with some reservations, of course, for I am writing in total ignorance of all the blurbs and market-driven words with which publishers feel obliged to decorate the backs and side flaps of every book these days, even the good ones. That is to say that if, as you read what I have written here, you can also see or remember an opened flap or a review or even a bit of front jacket copy that calls this book a spiritual memoir, please both forgive me and understand why I beg to differ.

I beg to differ because *Strength for the Journey* is a *sui generis,* a thing unto itself, a one-of-a-kind book. The best I can tell, in fact, is that it comes close to constituting a wholly new, albeit one-book-only, category of books. (Suffice it to say also that I most devoutly hope that there will be many more examples of this new subgenre before my time on earth is over and done.)

By her own admission, Bass is a churchgoer, and that is a dangerous thing to lay claim to in contemporary Western culture— dangerous not because of political oppression, as is the case in many parts of the world, but because of scorn. To claim churchgoing as central to one's being is almost to invite the diminishment of one's intellectual stature and social worth among one's associates and even sometimes among one's intimates. The assumptions made about self-proclaimed churchgoers, as Bass herself says, are ones either of a stifling religiosity and arrogance or else of social ambition and a self-serving hypocrisy. Long gone among our general populace (if indeed it was ever present), is the notion that a Christian may go to corporate worship as earnestly and naturally as he or she may go to table or to bed, or even as he or she may choose to make love while in bed. What Diana Butler Bass has given us in *Strength* puts the lie to the readiness of those assumptions, just as it also exposes, by simplicity and sometimes wrenching story, the ancient truth of the notion, especially of the part about lovemaking.

In their aggregate, the tales told here are the story of the religious soul in general and of one such rare soul in particular. Together, they are the memoir of one woman's passionate engagement, not with spirituality (though that is certainly patent in Bass's work) but with formal faith and its tradition-drenched, corporate exercise. These chapters are an assertion beyond refute and by example of the individual believer's calling into full life as a member, however small, of the body of Christ.

Because Bass is an academic deeply schooled in American religion, she enjoys what many another raconteur might not. She knows how to interpret her own story as a piece and part of the larger story. That is, she can, and does, make of herself an example as well as a proof text for the roiling landscape that has been established religion in America for the last four decades. This very rootedness lends to her explications and her confessionals a richness of breadth, interest, and credibility that they would otherwise not have. But it is Bass's intimacy with and love of the fathers and mothers of the church that carry this story of the religious traveler to its fullness of texture. Embroidering her commentary with the intricate knots and binding strands of the church's history among us, Bass renders for us a new fabric of many colors and invites us to shelter ourselves within its triumphant folds. She also, as I have said from the very beginning, thereby creates something of a postmodern amazement.

Lucy, Tennessee   PHYLLIS TICKLE
Ascension 2001

TO RICHARD, JONAH, AND EMMA BASS,
A PILGRIM FAMILY

ACKNOWLEDGMENTS

For several years, when I wrote a religion column for the *Santa Barbara News Press,* faithful readers kept asking that I write a book about my experiences as a contemporary churchgoer. Since I was writing about controversial subjects like religion and politics, it surprised me that they were interested in me as a person of faith. As a trained academic, however, I shied away from the prospect, fearing that it might undermine my vocation as a scholar of American religion.

The idea, however, would not go away, as both friends and colleagues urged me to take on the project. Still too reticent to write a spiritual autobiography in the strictest sense, I decided to use my life as "data" to tell the larger story of the last twenty years of mainline church life. During those two decades, I was a member of eight Episcopal congregations whose corporate stories taught me much about the inner texture of mainline churchgoing, the outer upheavals of a religious tradition in the throes of change, and the nature of contemporary American spirituality. Thus, this book is part autobiography, part cultural analysis, and part congregational studies. It is personal, journalistic, and scholarly. And it is the interlaced stories of a single churchgoer, eight congregations, the Episcopal Church, and mainline Protestantism.

Because of this scope, I hardly know how to thank the multitude of people involved in the telling of these stories. Each of the congregations—including their current secretaries and clergy—put up with me probing their past, asking questions, and requesting endless stacks of materials from their files and archives. Although I worked carefully to get the facts right and provide solid sociological and theological background, their stories are told from my perspective, enmeshed with my experience, feelings, and spiritual struggles. Because of this personal angle, not everyone involved with these events may agree with my interpretation of them.

Further, with the exception of Christ Church in Alexandria, Virginia, where I end this journey, each congregation will be different today than how I described it.

It should be clear that I am writing as honestly as possible about past events—and how I experienced those events at the time—and not the state of affairs at any place today. The willingness of all of the congregations to let themselves become characters in this story reveals a spiritual maturity and level-headedness that seems to have emerged in the wake of the events described. For the good people of All Saints Pasadena, All Saints-by-the-Sea, Christ Church (Hamilton), St. Stephen's, Holy Family, Christ the King, Trinity, Grace–St. Luke's, and Christ Church (Alexandria), you all witness to God's love in extraordinary—and extraordinarily different—ways. I am deeply grateful for your faithfulness, fellowship, and community. Thank you for letting me sojourn in your midst. And I hope that in some way my words do you justice.

Many people mentioned in these pages spent time helping me and some read some portion of the manuscript while it was in progress, making comments along the way. I particularly want to thank Rebecca Adams and Robin Collins, Linnae Himsl Petersen, Steven Hayward, Richard Yale, Gethin Hughes, Melinda Menoni, Anne Sutherland Howard, Barry Howe, Titus Presler, Tom Morton, Chip and Carol Nix, Dan and Kathleen Willey, Sam Mason, Loren Mead, Todd Granger and Jill Martin, Timothy Kimbrough, David Frauenfelder, Michelle Woodhouse, Ann Jaqua, Mark Asman, Nora Gallagher, Clark and Terry Roof, Dodie Little, David Fikes, John Baker, Virginia Dabney Brown, Cathy Cox, Anne Carriere, Noel Schwartz, and James and Patti Newsom.

In addition, a number of people not mentioned by name in the text gave support, direction, or advice to this project. They include Dorothy Bass, Bill and Courtenay Bass, Marcia Hochstedt, Jonathan and Marti Wilson, Patrick Henry, Patrick Vance, Mark Tauber, Phyllis Tickle, Bob Abernethey, Martha Horne, Tim Sedgwick, Bill Sachs, Bill Craddock, Stephanie Cheney, Bill Anderson, Clay Matthews, Guy Lytle, Pierce Klemmt, Bev Weatherly, Carol Pinkham Oak, Lee Ramsey, Steve Haynes, John Planchon, Susan Crawford, Julie Ingersoll, Stacia Brown, Ted and Dale Campbell, Allen Parsons, my Spiritual Autobiography class at Rhodes College, the people of Christ Church in Springfield, Missouri, and the library staff at Virginia Theological Seminary. All of these readers, students, colleagues, and friends helped make this a better book. Whatever mistakes remain are mine alone.

The Louisville Institute/Lilly Endowment provided a grant enabling me to revisit the congregations in the book, conduct interviews and research, and enjoy a reduced course load while writing. In addition, thanks go to Jim Lewis, the director of the Louisville Institute, for his continued interest in and support of my work.

Rhodes College, where I taught when I began the book, generously agreed to that reduced teaching load and provided additional financial resources. Some of the ideas in the story were first explored as columns in the *Santa Barbara News Press* and distributed by the New York Times Syndicate. In 1999, the Episcopal Church Foundation invited me to participate in the Zacchaeus Project, a major sociological study of the Episcopal Church. Insights from that research inform this narrative at several points. In late 2000, Bob Abernethey, Arnie Labaton, and Gail Fendley of the PBS program, *Religion and Ethics Newsweekly,* generously allowed me to try out some of my ideas about mainline religion on their show.

I deeply appreciate Virginia Theological Seminary for inviting me into their community as an adjunct professor and providing space in their wonderful preschool for my daughter. I also thank the people, staff, and clergy of Christ Church in Alexandria, where I work and worship. You teach me far more than I could ever teach you.

In the early stages of this project Sarah Polster helped clarify and shape the ideas and the narrative. She often understood what I wanted to say more than I did myself and pushed me to be as transparent and personal as I possibly could as a storyteller. In the process, she became a friend as well as an editor. When she was diagnosed with cancer halfway through the writing of this book, it became difficult to proceed without thinking of her, her insights, and her struggle. Although my work is dedicated to my family, in a very real way, this is Sarah's book as well, a tribute to her joy and wisdom and a reminder that she lives on in the words she birthed into the world. I thank all those at Jossey-Bass, especially Sheryl Fullerton, who share the sadness over her death but pressed on with amazing fortitude and professionalism to fulfill Sarah's vision for my work.

Finally, there are no words to adequately thank my husband, Richard Bass. He is my soul mate, friend, partner in life and ministry, live-in editor, computer fix-it guy, an incisive cultural critic, a born theologian, and the world's best baby-sitter. That he can make me laugh at 6 A.M. is nothing short of a miracle. We found each other as pilgrims on this journey—a gift of grace-filled companionship that continues to awe both of us. To him, to Jonah Bass, my stepson, and to Emma Katherine Bass, my theologically precocious three-year-old, this book is dedicated with all my love.

Alexandria, Virginia   DIANA BUTLER BASS
Easter 2001

STRENGTH
FOR THE
JOURNEY

INTRODUCTION

Resurrection

ALL SAINTS CHURCH

Pasadena, California, 1996

I am a churchgoer. Even at the rather traditional Southern college where I recently taught this was not an easy public confession to make. In the minds of many Americans, churchgoing conjures either negative or nostalgic images. Church people are dull, narrow, anti-intellectual, and unimaginative. They live by a list of do's and don'ts. And everything fun is on the don't side. More positively, they might be considered solid, old-fashioned, or traditional. A family praying around the dinner table, women wearing hats and gloves, a clapboard building on the prairie, a pie supper—all these images represent the comforting faith of an earlier, simpler America. A vision of Norman Rockwell religion.

That simpler America—if it ever existed at all—certainly exists no longer. These days, churchgoers rarely fit the old stereotypes. I certainly do not. Forty-something, a twice-married "older mother," a professor and writer, I grew up in the waning days of what seemed a simpler time. It was Baltimore in the early 1960s. As a girl, I attended Hamilton Elementary School—the school where

Miss Lillian Springfield taught two generations of my family to read. My great-grandfather laid its cornerstone when he served as captain of the local volunteer fire department.

Uncle Eddie, Aunt Doris, and the cousins lived across the street from us. Everyone in the neighborhood knew my family; they simply referred to me as "Bobby's oldest girl." The whole Hochstedt clan—grandparents, parents, uncles, aunts, and cousins—worked together in a florist shop that we had owned for more than a century. Like our forebears, we left the store at noon and gathered around the family table for a dinner of sausages, sauerbraten, and German potato salad. Although he was a successful businessman, Grandpop Hochstedt missed Miss Springfield's academic ministrations and could neither read nor write. His father recruited him to work in the shop from age six onward. When he died, in 1985, he had worked in that florist shop for nearly seven decades and had never traveled more than sixty miles from his birthplace.

Late in the 1960s, it all changed—Baltimore, our neighborhood, the florist shop, and my family. Unlike Grandpop Hochstedt and the generations preceding me, I would eventually live in nine different states and trek three continents. My life has played out against the tableau of the baby boom generation, with all its doubts, seeking, and questions. Although every generation faces change, we grew up during a time of particularly challenging social ferment. As we came to adulthood, a global revolution of economic and technological change opened possibilities for us that even our parents often failed to grasp. Our nation no longer seemed a safe, homogeneous "Christian America," as we instead embraced religious pluralism as an ordering principle. The world seemed relative and revolutionary at the same time. Living in such days, our lives were filled with change and changes—plunging us into a near-constant quest for meaning and authenticity amid the chaos.

For me, however, one thing has remained the same throughout: nearly every Sunday in the last forty years I have been in church. Most of those years have been spent in mainline Protestantism—a tradition that has suffered under the weight of change. Having lost millions of members in the last two decades, the old mainline denominations are usually depicted as "the empty church," a spiritual dead end. Secular critics, when they paid any attention at all, gleefully predicted the demise of these irrelevant institutions. And when the denominations themselves attempted to be relevant, other critics assailed them for agenda-driven political liberalism and theological radicalism.

In spite of this catch-22, the old mainline is still around and finally stabilizing after the long descent. It is not, however, the same old church. Although diminished in size and prestige, it often possesses an unexpected and underestimated vitality. In the last twenty years, mainline churchgoing has been anything but dull as these churches have struggled to understand their identity and vocation in a changed world. In many places, they have succeeded in reinventing themselves, and old Protestant congregations are coming alive again. There has been a quiet resurrection in the mainline tradition, unnoticed and unreported by most observers of American religion. Those of us who have been around for the journey—and there are more of us than is generally suspected—know that mainline churchgoing is not like living in a Norman Rockwell painting.

One Sunday in September 1981, I visited All Saints Episcopal Church in Pasadena. I cannot remember the exact date. I do, however, remember the day. It was very warm, more like summer than autumn. September in southern California is hard on those of us who grew up in the East and long for real fall weather once school has started.

That autumn, I missed both crisp northern air and classes. The previous spring I had graduated from college. For the first time since I was five, I did not start school in the fall. I had just moved to Pasadena to start my first job. I felt dislocated and I worried whether I could find my way in the world.

All Saints was new to me, as was the Episcopal Church of which it is a part. I grew up Methodist but left that church as a teenager under the influence of some conservative evangelical friends. From fifteen onward, I attended a number of "nondenominational" churches usually bearing such words as "Bible Church" or "Christian Fellowship" in their monikers. During my senior year in college, I began attending an Episcopal parish near my college campus in Santa Barbara and had become transfixed by the liturgy. Although I wondered if the denomination might be too theologically liberal for me, I sensed I had found a spiritual home. Upon graduation, I asked my priest, the Rev. Gethin Hughes, where I might go to church when I moved in the fall.

Gethin, who eventually became the Episcopal bishop of San Diego, recommended two churches: St. Luke's in Monrovia and All Saints in Pasadena. St. Luke's, he assured me, was a "good church" whose theology would resonate with my own conservative views. "And then there's All Saints," he said in his lilting Welsh accent. "That's a very interesting place. The rector, George Regas, is doing very interesting things. Very interesting things. Yes, yes, I think you should go to All Saints."

I knew nothing about All Saints, but I respected Gethin and trusted his advice. Three months later, I stood nervously at its doors with my then-boyfriend, Steve. He grew up in Pasadena, was a neoconservative, and was highly skeptical of the whole venture. "You won't like it," he warned. "It is very liberal."

"Why then," I insisted, "would Gethin tell me to come here? He knows what I think. He said it is a good church. I want to go."

We walked into the neo-Gothic building and sat on the left side of the church. Even to a new Episcopalian like myself it felt familiar—the architecture, the flowers, the music were all very Anglican.

But something else felt strange.

As the party processed to the altar, I noticed that one robed man did not appear, well, quite heterosexual. My imagination? The church seemed traditional enough. I tried not to worry because I wanted to enjoy the service.

My no-worry attempt failed when George Regas began to preach. Unlike Gethin, who preached almost exclusively from the Bible, Regas launched into a political speech railing against involvement in Latin America. Years earlier, my parents left the Methodist church because of the left-wing politics they heard preached from the pulpit. They did not like it; neither did I. I wanted theology, spirituality, and scripture. I was mad. Steve grinned, "I told you so."

"At least they can't ruin the liturgy," I whispered back. "It is always the same—very orthodox. It is in the Prayer Book."

In 1981 I did not know that the Prayer Book we used was a "new" one. The church had recently replaced an older Prayer Book with one written in the 1970s. The change had created quite a controversy in the church and many people disliked the new liturgies. But even this book, the only Prayer Book I have known as an Episcopalian, reverberated with biblical theology and historical orthodoxy. In only a year I had come to love it.

"The Lord be with you," Regas began.

"And also with you," we responded.

The liturgy moved through its now-familiar paces. I had learned what to expect, where to respond, what words came next. My spirit rose as we pressed on to Sunday's climax: the weekly celebration of the Eucharist. No leftist preacher can ruin this, I thought.

As is the practice for Episcopalians, Steve and I went forward for communion. Wincing, I recognized that the man whose apparent sexual orientation troubled me would be serving us the chalice. Not a problem—I reminded myself that St. Augustine had taught that the validity of the sacrament did not depend on the morality of the minister. "Thank you, St. Augustine," I thought as I held out my hands to receive. "The Body of Christ," said the priest, "the Bread of Heaven."

The lay chalice bearer approached next. I eagerly anticipated the words, "The Blood of Christ, the Cup of Salvation." Christ's blood shed for my sins—the theological centerpiece of orthodox Christianity. Jesus' death on the cross saved me, even me, a sinner. The cup, full of sacrificial symbolism, summed up everything I believed about God and God's grace. The Gospel of John proclaims, "For God so loved the world that he gave his only Son, so that everyone who believes in him may not perish but may have eternal life." Jesus' blood. God's cup of salvation.

Reaching toward me, the chalice bearer smiled. I reached out, guiding the cup toward my lips, and tentatively smiled back. "The Blood of Christ," he said softly. "Strength for the Journey."

Strength for the journey? What? No cup of salvation? What kind of sentimental nonsense was this? Where was the bloody sacrifice? Where was the heart of Christian faith? Was this some sort of heresy?

Nothing could have shocked or hurt me more. "How could they do that?" I asked angrily. "How could they change the liturgy?"

"Had enough?" asked Steve.

"I will never go back," I vowed.

Fifteen years later I had all but forgotten that vow. Perhaps part of me wanted to forget that Sunday when, with all the hubris of a new college graduate, I judged All Saints and found it spiritually wanting. In 1996 I was still an Episcopalian and was living again in Santa Barbara. Theologically, however, I was now closer to All Saints than I was to the small Christian college where I had been a student, and later, for a short time, a professor. I no longer divided the world into "orthodox" and "heretical" camps. I had grown weary of theological nitpicking and religious right politics dictating church life. Increasingly I distanced myself from the world of conservative evangelicalism and I felt pretty sure I was a healthier Christian for having done so.

In April of that year I returned to All Saints, accompanied by my soon-to-be husband, Richard. Although he was new to the Episcopal Church, Richard had heard of All Saints—by this time a very well-known and successful liberal parish that had even been written about in *Time* magazine. Curious, he wanted to see it for himself. One weekend, I needed to research a story in Los Angeles and asked him to join me. On Sunday we planned to attend All Saints.

Only when we took our seats in the church did I recall my earlier vow. I found myself sitting in nearly the same place I had fifteen years before! The pew may have been the same, but everything else seemed different. In the intervening years, All Saints had renovated the sanctuary. The old rood screen—a kind of decorative "fence" separating the congregation from the high altar in

Victorian Anglican architecture—was gone. The communion table had been moved forward, the choir stalls rearranged. The church seemed less forbidding than I remembered and much more open and inviting.

The processional was "Love Divine, All Loves Excelling," a beautiful Methodist hymn I have sung since childhood. Still in the church's Easter season, the service began with the acclamation: "Alleluia. Christ is risen. Christ is risen indeed. Alleluia." I felt God's presence.

The words were familiar, but like the building itself, the liturgy had been altered. Although the traditional liturgical structure of word and sacrament remained, All Saints no longer used male pronouns to refer to God. They had replaced some words in the creed and used a new version of the eucharistic prayer. Responsive to concerns raised by feminist theology, All Saints was attempting to be more inclusive in worship and theology.

The morning's scriptural passages were from the book of Acts and the book of Luke. The Episcopal Church places special emphasis on Matthew, Mark, Luke, and John, and most sermons are based on these Gospel texts. We listened to Luke's account of the resurrected Jesus meeting two of his disciples on the road to Emmaus. Even though they walked and talked together, the disciples failed to recognize their teacher until they sat down to share a meal. Most of the sermons I had heard on this passage depicted this as symbolic of Christians meeting Jesus in the Eucharist.

But All Saints' new rector, the Rev. Ed Bacon, said that the passage revealed the disciples' conversion from "a faith based in fear to one based in love." Jesus' followers failed to recognize him because they were mired in fear. They feared the authorities that had killed Jesus; they feared the rumor that his body was gone from the tomb; they feared they might be next to die. Only when they broke bread with this stranger did their fears abate. At that moment "their eyes were opened and they recognized him." Bacon said that this story encapsulated the meaning of Christian faith: Christ invites humanity to reject the fear that separates us from God and to embrace God's love that empowers us to serve others. Fear drives us from God; only love opens the way to wholeness, relationship, and compassion.

For several years, my spiritual director and I had explored the same idea. My adolescent faith was filled with fear—fear of the world, fear of hell, fear of punishment, fear of disobeying God's will. As a result of this background, I did not really comprehend God as Love. I could say it, and believe it intellectually, but I could not live into the reality of a God who is completely Love. It took a protracted struggle to convince me emotionally and spiritually that God did, indeed, love humanity and all creation. And that God loved me.

From the pulpit, Bacon described the theological twists and turns of my own spiritual journey; it was as if he had sat in the room and listened to my story. I sat amazed, inwardly laughing and crying at the same time: "Okay, God. I get it. I get it!" The years leading to this moment had been as Ed Bacon depicted it—a journey from fear-based religion to the love-based faith celebrated that morning. I went from thinking I knew who Jesus was but failing to recognize him, to finally seeing him in the breaking of bread. It was the journey of a rigid, judgmental kid, who had feared heresy at All Saints fifteen years earlier, to an adult who felt safely cherished by God in that same pew.

After the sermon and prayers, we sang as we waited for communion:

The strife is o'er, the battle done,
The victory of life is won;
The song of triumph has begun. Alleluia!
The powers of death have done their worst,
But Christ their legions hath dispersed;
Let shout of holy joy outburst. Alleluia!
Lord! by the stripes which wounded Thee,
From death's dread sting Thy servants free,
That we may live and sing to Thee. Alleluia!

As I walked down the aisle, the words buoyed me with a sense of triumph, telling both Jesus' story and my own at the same time. It was Easter. The Resurrection. It was over. The long battle with childhood faith, the suffering of Holy Week, the dark night of the soul, the fear—all vanquished in the victory of Christ. I knelt at the altar and held out my hands. "The body of Christ," the priest said, "the Bread of Heaven."

The chalice bearer followed. As she served those ahead of me, I listened to those familiar words: "The Blood of Christ, the Cup of Salvation; the Blood of Christ, the Cup of Salvation." How much more I understood now than the first time I visited All Saints—the cup of life, God's own life, drawing me into the divine mystery, united with Love. She served Richard: "The Blood of Christ, the Cup of Salvation." Finally, she stood in front of me, lifted the cup to my lips and said, "The Blood of Christ, Strength for the Journey."

The tears streamed down my face—I was joyful, awash with the spirit. As I walked back to the pew, Richard asked, "Are you okay?" Through the sobs, I laughed, unable to say anything more than "God has such a sense of humor."

During the fifteen years between those two Sundays, we had been on a journey, All Saints and me. My story is not all that unusual. I grew up. I passed from adolescence to adulthood—spiritually as well as physically, emotionally, and intellectually. Mine was a spiritual coming-of-age story in which my understanding of God and faith deepened and matured through life experience and personal struggle.

My spiritual journey differs only slightly from the journeys of my peers. In recent years, many baby boomers have come of age spiritually. A number of fine authors, such as Kathleen Norris and Anne Lamott, have written of renewing faith at midlife and have articulated a kind of generational spiritual longing. Psychologists say that our newly kindled concern with religion has to do with aging. Our middle-aged developmental task is to figure out the nature of existence and to be reconciled to it. Thus, millions of Americans—a generation reaching midlife at the beginning of a new millennium—are exploring faith and spirituality at the same time.

Sociologist Wade Clark Roof dubbed us a generation of seekers. Since we were children, we have done most things together—our individual stories are often personal expressions of corporate and generational ones. So it is not surprising that our "seeker" stories often follow similar plots. A person grew up in a particular religious tradition, but that tradition failed to answer significant questions during the college years. As a result, he or she rejected organized religion. Finally, after finding a modicum of personal fulfillment through work or family, the person still feels oddly dissatisfied. So he or she returns to religion (sometimes, but not necessarily, to the same one as in childhood) and discovers that spirituality is the way to deeper meaning and inner fulfillment.

These seekers, sometimes dubbed returnees, have been credited with spurring much of the current interest in spirituality. They are filling American pews, retreat centers, and seminaries once again.

While I find that this plot resonates with my experience, my story differs at a significant point: I am not a returnee. I am a stayer. Baptized as an infant in the Methodist Church, I never left the Christian faith. Not even the Protestant faith. Indeed, I never stopped going to church. Sure, I had questions, struggles, and doubts, but I never left. I just kept hanging around. Maybe I did not know where else to go.

When I was a child, my family participated in the Methodist congregation in which my grandparents had been members. My mother taught Sunday school and organized the yearly Vacation Bible school. My Girl Scout troop met in the church basement, where photographs of the Men's Bible Class—stretching back to the early twentieth century, hung in the hallways. Everything about St. John's United Methodist Church of Hamilton bespoke family, neighborhood, and continuity of faith. I was baptized there shortly after Easter in 1959, when I was barely three months old. I loved the sermons, the Wesley hymns, Holy Communion, the dark wooden pews, and the way the sunlight fell in colored patterns across the red carpet in the sanctuary. My fondest childhood memory is of singing "Holy, Holy, Holy," standing next to my mother in the balcony looking down over the whole congregation one spring morning. At that moment, she embodied God to me—joy and hope incarnate in a yellow dress and pillbox hat. Nothing, I was convinced, could ever go wrong with her by my side. The comforting, motherly Methodist God of childhood did not teach me fear.

Despite the gifts it gave me, I stopped attending the Methodist church when I was fifteen. My family followed the sun-belt migration of the early 1970s and moved from Baltimore to

Scottsdale, Arizona. I did not like our new Methodist church. I made friends with a number of evangelical teenagers from my high school, who convinced me that I was a sinner going to hell and needed to be saved. Perhaps I was just scared and lonely, missing my childhood home. But I believed them and the Bible they preached. I got "born again" and joined their church. For the next six years, that congregation formed me and served as my home church while I attended an evangelical Christian college. I studied the Bible and theology, attended prayer meetings, went on mission trips, and usually attended church on Sunday. I dreamed of being a missionary or Bible teacher.

In 1980, as a college senior, I first stepped inside an Episcopal church. Although it felt almost spiritually defiant to do so, I let myself be seduced by the church's beautiful architecture and historic liturgy. But parts of me held out—the Episcopal Church's notorious theological liberalism worried me. My home church, my evangelical friends, and my college professors warned that mainline liberalism was not true Christianity. One professor was a member of a denomination whose founder, J. Gresham Machen, had argued that mainline Protestantism was "a religion which is so vastly different from Christianity as to belong in a distinct category." To embrace mainline religion, to even flirt with it, was a sure route to damnation. In American evangelicalism, theological orthodoxy and eternal salvation were spiritual twins. If that was not enough to scare me, the Episcopal Church was a "denomination," a religious institution with which few of my evangelical friends had patience. As far as they were concerned, denominations were all liberal, dangerous, and spiritually dead.

Despite these reservations, however, I fell in love with the Episcopal Church. While praying for direction whether to join the denomination, it occurred to me that the Episcopal Church could be renewed if infused with evangelical theology. All that beauty and orthodoxy, too? Why, I mused, the institutional church would come alive with fresh spirit if enough people like myself joined! I became convinced that God wanted me to become an Episcopalian so that I might help save the church.

Thus recommenced my mainline spiritual journey. I frequently joke that, other than that with my immediate family, my relationship with the Episcopal Church has lasted longer than any other relationship in my life. Whereas my returnee friends tell exotic tales of experimenting with alternative lifestyles and Eastern religions before coming back to faith, stayers like me have no such adventures. Instead, our spirituality grew in conversation with the Bible and tradition, with hymnody and theology, with parish life and church suppers, with fights over church organs and stained glass windows. On the face of it, it seems a bit dull. But staying is not necessarily boring. As many of us have discovered, we have ended up in a much different place than where we began. In 1996, on my knees at All Saints, I realized that I had not saved the church; rather, it had saved me.

I had not saved the church—at least not in the way I imagined as a college student. But over the last two decades, the Episcopal Church has changed—as have its cousin mainline churches. On that Sunday morning in 1996, I realized that All Saints had been on a journey, too. It was not the same place it had been. And, although unaware of it, I had been part of their journey even as they had been part of mine.

Since colonial days, the Church of England, later re-created as the Episcopal Church, has been considered part of America's Protestant mainline, a church at the culture's center—tolerant, traditional, moneyed, and powerful. For many generations, Episcopalians, Presbyterians, Congregationalists, Methodists, Lutherans, and northern Baptists served as an informal church establishment in a nation where religion had been formally disestablished. They shaped education and politics, the media, and morality. Until recently, the great majority of Americans belonged to one of these denominations.

Beginning in the 1960s, the mainline churches began to lose prestige and power. For a host of debated reasons, people stopped coming. What began as a steady numerical decline turned into a hemorrhage as these denominations lost anywhere from a quarter to a third of their members. In particular, the baby boomers, whose parents had swelled the ranks of mainline membership since World War II, deserted their childhood churches, finding their worship tedious and their theology out of touch. When the churches tried to be more relevant and attempted to change, many older members protested by withdrawing financial support or by leaving themselves. The old mainline, it seemed, could not please anyone. Congregations moved, combined, or closed in an effort to save money and resources. As the membership decline progressed, internal conflict increased, and bitter denominational battles ensued. Observers nicknamed them old-line, or sidelined, churches.

At the same time, evangelical Protestants, the mainline's long-ignored Protestant cousins, experienced a resurgence. Quietly at first, but with increasing public attention after 1976, conservative Christians took the religious center stage. Their once-small congregations, like the one I attended in Scottsdale, Arizona, grew into megachurches. Having previously eschewed politics, they entered into the political arena with amazing savvy and professionalism. They proved themselves adept with the media, new technologies, and contemporary worship styles. As a result, for most contemporary Americans the word *Christian* conjures images of Billy Graham, Jerry Falwell, and Pat Robertson—not of some learned theologian at Union Seminary in New York or the minister of the local Congregational church. In the last two decades of the twentieth century, *Christian* became equated with *evangelical* in the popular mind. Mainline Protestants seemed not to exist at all.

All this created an identity crisis in the old mainline churches. Over the course of the last twenty years, while I sat in its pews struggling through my own internal battles, the Episcopal Church itself was struggling. Although unaware of it at the time, I did not enter into a static institution. In the 1970s, the church ordained its first female priests, revised its prayer book (and shortly thereafter, its hymnal), and opened the discussion regarding gay and lesbian persons in the church. As a result, the church has struggled—and is struggling—with its theological identity, the nature of ordained and lay ministries, and the scope of its mission and spirituality in what many are calling a post-Christian society. In a generation, the church has essentially reinvented itself, with many of its members and congregations still grappling with the implications of the changes. I have often heard older clergy friends remark, some happily and some with regret, "This is not the same church to which I was ordained."

Although some mainline churchgoers suffer from a sort of establishment hangover and hanker for the old days when they were in charge, it is impossible to go back. It is not the same old Episcopal Church. And it never will be again. However frightening these permutations seem to some people, I believe that the crisis has brought forth previously hidden spiritual vitality and creativity. The old style of the culturally privileged institution has been replaced with a new vision of spiritually vital, networked congregations seeking meaningful ways to *be*—and not just go to—the church. Mainliners are much more self-conscious and purposeful about doing God's work in the world. Denominational identity is shifting away from professionally organized religious institutions to being communities that embody God's presence in, among, and for God's people.

I know little of All Saints' journey during those fifteen years. However, their renovated sanctuary proclaimed how much they had changed. The service no longer focused on a clergyman performing a sacred task at a holy altar; rather, the emphasis was now on the whole people of God joined in celebration around a family table. The new liturgies made overt All Saints' commitment to inclusion and justice. The language welcomed men, women, and children into communal expressions of praise and lifted up a variety of biblical images to communicate God's presence. The clergy— male and female, white and black, gay and straight—modeled a new vision of full personhood—everyone is invited to God's banquet. By design or providential accident, All Saints no longer felt like a theological performance by a radical preacher or professional sacramental magician. It felt like a community joined in worship and service—a community committed to being together on a spiritual journey.

Perhaps all these things were present at All Saints fifteen years ago, but if so, they were there only in words or in quieter, more implicit ways. By 1996, All Saints was clearly working to make such commitments explicit in the lives of its people. The vision proved itself compelling: the church had grown dramatically in the intervening years. From my new perspective, it appeared that they had moved away from the fear of upsetting ecclesiastical apple carts into fully expressing their love for all God's people. Maybe they, too, had come to terms with their own identity and had grown up.

On my more optimistic days, I sense that the old mainline is slowly coming to terms with its identity—that of a culturally marginalized institution—and trying to face this new calling with love and not fear. That does not mean that all mainline churches will embrace All Saints' theological commitments or program of social justice. But it does mean that mainline churches must abandon old ways of doing business in favor of creating authentic Christian community and empowering God's people to do God's work in the world. Mainline churches must understand that they are no longer America's chapels. Instead, having lost their cultural hegemony, mainliners now sit on America's sidelines. Because of this change, it is impossible to be a casual churchgoer anymore. We will survive—and perhaps thrive—only if we can communicate the joy, pain, struggle, courage, energy, and reward of intentional spiritual commitment and purposeful Christian living.

Thus this book is the story of intertwined journeys—how one woman observed and experienced the shifts and struggles of mainline religion as she lived her own journey in eight Episcopal congregations over two decades. And it is the story of each congregation at a particular moment in its history. Each experienced some degree of ferment about its identity, about the denomination, about its vocation and mission in the world, and about the nature of faith community. Those conflicts have changed me, have changed the congregations, and, I believe, are changing the nature of mainline churchgoing.

These eight stories depict often tense, and sometimes desperate, struggles. The Episcopal Church often forced me to come to terms with ideas and people I would rather have avoided. But throughout the process, the church was being quietly transformed by the experiences of stayers like myself who demanded different visions and practices of churchgoing than the institution had traditionally offered. Many of the changes came too slowly. Some came too quickly. Along the way, I felt like quitting. I suspect others did, too. But churchgoers stay with it. And therein lies the journey.

Perhaps not surprisingly, my own journey with mainline religion recommenced with a theological argument. On one warm Santa Barbara spring night in 1978, I sat outside the college library with Rich Yale, a classmate nicknamed "The Archbishop," who wanted to become an Episcopal priest. He was complaining about the bishop's office, church bureaucracy, and the whole process of ordination. "Why would you want to do that anyway?" I harangued. "Just join a different one. The Episcopal Church is dead. Why, they even believe in infant baptism. How could anyone be saved and believe in that?"

"Well, I do." He laughed as my mouth fell open. I didn't know what to say. That was the beginning of my journey home.

CHAPTER ONE

Coming Home

ALL SAINTS-BY-THE-SEA

Santa Barbara, California, 1980–1981

Years after I found my way back to mainstream Protestantism, someone asked what attracted me to the Episcopal Church. With only a moment's pause I replied, "The wood."

I am convinced that wood is holy. Cut from living things, it takes on new life when used as beams and columns and pews in traditional church architecture. It is as if the trees continue to grow as they absorb generations of candle smoke, incense, and prayer. The rings no longer measure age. Rather, they measure decades of spirituality and faithfulness. When colored light from stained glass windows falls across this holy patina, the wood itself seems to breathe God's spirit.

All Saints-by-the-Sea in Santa Barbara, California, was built in 1900. Although the small Arts and Crafts–style building sits two blocks from the Pacific Ocean, it appears as if it were transplanted from an English country village. Its wooden doorway is framed by an ivy-covered porch, where a sign, "Bide a Wee and Pray," invites both the curious and the faithful to enter. The sanctuary smells faintly of California redwood. Intricate carvings decorate arched beams; handcrafted millwork graces the pillars, rails, and church furniture. No matter where one looks, the eye falls upon holy wood carved more than a century ago and worn through one hundred years of prayer.

The late 1970s, when I was a college student, were not an architectural highpoint in church history. An odd mid-century devotion to functionality stripped churches down to an artistic minimalism. In the evangelical circles where I spent my high school and college years, sanctuaries were plain, often massive, multipurpose rooms with basketball hoops overhead. For most evangelicals, such sensible simplicity is a prerequisite to holiness. Of American Protestants, we most imbibed the spirit of Puritanism—the plainer the building, the clearer God's Word. Decoration, considered a kind of spiritual crutch, distracted the faithful from the real business of hearing the sermon. Architectural beauty detracted from God's beauty—and might lead some misguided soul to worship the building instead of divine majesty.

The college I attended required daily chapel attendance, but we had no chapel building. Instead, we met this requirement in a gym, seated on plastic chairs and metal risers with a broken-down piano to accompany our hymns. A large lectern served as the chapel's focal point, backed only by a plain white movable wall. The whole thing was so dull I used to keep track of imaginary theological basketball games on the scoreboard: Arminians 72–Calvinists 60. Lots of students did homework. Although school officials insisted that the gym was a practical necessity—the entire student body could not fit elsewhere—they seemed to take pride in the fact that there was no specifically set-aside, or, to use the theological term, *sanctified,* worship space on campus. One even commented to me that "the college did not want to mislead students to think God could only be found in a particular building."

I would, however, find God in a building. All Saints shocked my spiritual senses. Wood and windows, icons and organ—it was as if I had stumbled into God's own house. Here was holiness, robust and physical, passed down through generations. It was the Christian tradition embodied in architecture, music, and liturgy. But it was not a "wooden tradition," stilted and moribund. Like All Saints' glowing woodwork, here, tradition was vital, a living thing, crafted in the faithfulness and vision of God's people present and past. I felt as if I had stumbled into some great secret world and found the biblical pearl of great price. Although I could scarcely name it myself, I was seeking God, incarnated in dynamic tradition, and God was there—at All Saints-by-the Sea during the autumn of my senior year in college.

It was odd that I ever found my way to All Saints. As a teenager I had embraced a particularly theologically rigid form of evangelical Protestantism with the zeal of a youthful convert. When it came time to attend college, I feared both heterodoxy and secularism and rejected offers from several fine universities. Instead, I chose to attend Westmont College in Santa Barbara, an evangelical college, a school similar to its more famous institutional cousin, Wheaton College in Illinois. I wanted to pursue my faith intellectually, but I also wanted to be safe. Evangelical Protestants extol the virtues of theological and moral purity, and they built these colleges to ensure the safety of their young people in the midst of a sinful world. Although Westmont's ethos at the time was not as narrow as its history might suggest, it still possessed a kind of spiritual certainty— the evangelical way was the surest way to God.

Evangelicals generally believe that other forms of Christian belief and practice are, at best, incomplete; some are misguided, dangerous, or wrong. Being "born again" is the litmus test for true Christianity. Denominations—and historic traditions—are all judged by this rubric. Thus, a Roman Catholic might be a "real" Christian if he or she could testify to a personal conversion experience. But if a Catholic spoke of papal authority, the saints, or the stain of original sin being removed at baptism, that person would not be regarded as a true Christian. Acceptable piety matters as well: serious evangelical young people do not smoke, drink, take drugs, go to "R"-rated movies, or engage in sexual intercourse before marriage. These things are sins, to be eschewed or repented of. To be cool as an evangelical young person, it helped if you wanted to be a preacher, a preacher's wife, a missionary, or a Bible teacher. Under the appropriately humble circumstances, you could admit to your friends that you got up at 6 A.M. for your "quiet time" and prayed for an hour for lost souls in Africa.

Westmont had a statement of faith and behavioral standards to which all members of the community were required to adhere. All of my professors and almost all of my classmates were evangelicals and accepted such restrictions with only minimal complaint. Some people, however, wanted to go to Westmont because it was so beautiful—and near the beach in Santa Barbara. Located in the hills above the ocean, we called it the Garden of Eden. A few charismatic Roman Catholics or theologically skillful agnostics fooled admissions counselors and made it through the gates of this evangelical paradise. But there were no Jews or Muslims or Buddhists or overt atheists at the school. Most of my classmates were Baptists or "nondenominational" Christians from California megachurches like Calvary Chapel. A coterie of Presbyterians provided theological ballast and a sense of the historic church—well, going back to

John Calvin at least. I remember only a couple of Methodists (I worried over whether they were "really Christians") and do not think I ever met a Lutheran among the student body.

At a Christian college I figured I would date the right boys and learn right doctrine. Like other evangelical girls my age, I was more concerned with falling in love and reading the Bible than building a career. So Westmont seemed the perfect place. And it would turn out to be so—but for reasons I never expected. For as romantic and dogmatic as I was at eighteen, college would broaden both my character and my intellect. To my surprise, the school provided an environment more conducive to friendship than romance and it challenged my beliefs rather than confirmed them. When I went off to college in the fall of 1977, I expected to find a boyfriend and get all my questions answered. Instead, I got life-long friends and all my answers questioned.

During my first month on campus, I noticed one group that did not fit in and who reveled in their distinctiveness. They were Episcopalians, some of whom had grown up in the tradition and reclaimed it in college and some of whom were converts. They appeared odd and artsy, less a clique than a collection of characters from Chaucer's *Canterbury Tales*. In the dining hall they actually performed Broadway-like songs such as "I Am an Anglican" (sung to the tune of "God Bless America") and a musical take-off of "Fiddler on the Roof," entitled "Archbishop on the Cathedral." Two of the women actually made the sign of the cross when they prayed! They spoke some exotic language—they used mysterious-sounding words like "communion of saints," "eucharist," and "liturgical spirituality." They would talk about "needing" the sacraments and professed openly their belief in infant baptism. They dressed up in costume on All Saints Day (November 1) instead of on Halloween.

They said they were Protestants, but they looked Catholic to the rest of us. They were art, theater, English, and theology majors who extolled "Christian humanism" and a "sacramental worldview." Most people had no idea what they were talking about and few Westmonters could figure why they attended an evangelical college. Westmont's hardcore cared more about saving souls and studying the Bible than the humane traditions of the liberal arts. But the Anglican types took culture and learning seriously—albeit with a playful edge. Many students dismissed them; others, like myself, viewed them with curious suspicion. Some people snidely referred to them as the "Anglican Mafia." I was pretty sure they smoked and drank. I was equally sure that they were not quite theologically orthodox.

The most colorful character in this colorful group was Rich Yale, a religious studies major who felt called to the priesthood. At Westmont no one wanted to become a *priest*—men got calls to be preachers. My college roommate, Becca Adams, whose spiritual journey resembles my own, jokes that we all became "Rich's groupies." Rich was a "cradle Episcopalian," a person born, baptized, and raised in the Episcopal Church.

As a boy, however, he felt that the "liberal church had failed him" when his parents went through a painful divorce. "They offered nothing but platitudes," he remembered. "Certainly not the Christian community I wanted and needed." Only after joining Young Life, an evangelical high school fellowship group, did Rich find spiritual support, friendship, and theological answers to his questions. He came to Westmont to study theology and prepare for the ministry. He had only the most tenuous ties to the Episcopal Church. He was naturally attracted to the campus Episcopalians and would later remark upon the influence they had had on his own life. "At Westmont," he observed, "I found committed young

Episcopalians who were in community and were intentional and serious about it." They helped him reclaim his familial faith.

Eventually Rich realized that Anglicanism was his "native language." Together, he and his friends followed the time-honored practices of Anglican spirituality. They prayed from their prayer books, followed the daily office, studied early Christian theology, held an alternative liturgical chapel, went to church regularly (more regularly, by the way, than the Baptists), kept Lent, and dabbled in medieval spirituality. As college students, they were not doing this because their parents made them. Rather, they practiced a way of faith in community that they freely chose. And they freely recruited others to join them, as well.

Rich and I met during our first week at Westmont, and somehow, despite how very different we were, we became friends. His artsy Anglican friends probably thought I was uptight; my zealously evangelical friends thought he was spiritually lax. Whatever our differences, Rich and I loved to talk about theology—about Calvin and Luther and Karl Barth, about whether or not the gift of tongues was still valid and whether God predestined people to hell, about the theology of the Lord's Supper and baptism. We talked theology into many late nights in dorm lounges, at local coffee shops, and on benches along Westmont's wooded paths.

By my junior year, our friendship served as an anchor in my own rather chaotic life. Rich took me out to celebrate my twenty-first birthday, despite my evangelical reservations, and introduced me to gin and tonic. Much to my surprise that night, he had romantic designs in mind. My response to those affections was a decidedly unsubtle rebuke, and I later fell in love with his best friend. He accepted it all with humor and grace. I was never sure how we managed to do it, but we stayed friends—almost like brother and sister.

One of the most doggedly held lines of analysis regarding contemporary religious practice is that Americans are resolutely atheological. According to researchers, historians, and sociologists, evidence of this tendency can be found everywhere—even in the churches themselves, where theology is muted in favor of spiritualized self-help and secularized leadership. Although current scholarship seems to indicate that this is a relatively new trend, this tendency runs deep in the American past. Inasmuch as the United States has been a religiously diverse nation from the outset, we Americans have often downplayed theological particularity in public discourse. Our national identity schools us to temper distinctive theology in favor of generalized faith. Thus, even fervent churchgoers will usually invoke this ideological minimalism with such statements as "Theology does not matter; being a good person is what counts" or "Theology divides, faith unites."

For whatever reasons, most scholars accept this cultural mantra as a fundamental given about American spirituality. However, my experience as both a historian and a churchgoer suggests another story. Whereas the United States has been historically shaped by public toleration of religious diversity, theological particularity has often challenged the national soul. American churches have divided and divided again on issues that seem quite petty to those outside the arguments. For example, the issue of baptism: should it be adult or infant, sprinkled or immersed, once or multiple times, in the name of the Trinity or of Jesus alone?

Many of our greatest national struggles have been shaped by underlying theological disagreements. Can a Christian rebel against a king? Does baptism make a slave equal to a master? Did God establish one race as superior to all others? Should wives submit in all cases to their husbands? Whose prayer can be officially sanctioned by the state? Where are the lines to be drawn between church and state? American theology—stretching back to the arguments between Puritans and Anglicans over whether or not to celebrate Christmas, or the Puritans and the Baptists over who constitutes the true church—is pragmatic and practical. Although we often disguise it with different names, Americans argue theology in church, at home, and in the public square. We are a deeply theological people who, tempered by the discord over our myriad divisions, fear to admit that we are.

Westmont encouraged the students in its care to address theological questions in community—essentially letting young adults loose in a theological hothouse. We were besieged daily by the kinds of theological questions with which many Americans struggle: Who is God? How can we know God? Are human beings innately good or sinful? Does God choose us or do we choose God? Is human will free? What does God require of humankind? What is our responsibility toward our neighbor? Does God speak through one religion or many? What happens after we die? What constitutes the true church?

Attempting to find answers to our questions, my friends and I read voraciously. At first we wanted answers from the Bible or popular evangelical preachers. By our junior year, however, we had developed more sophisticated theological tastes: we read the works of early church theologians like St. Augustine and St. Irenaeus, medieval mystical writers like St. Benedict, St. Francis, and Julian of Norwich, Renaissance humanists like Dante and Erasmus, the Protestant Reformers Luther and Calvin, and modern thinkers like Karl Barth, Sören Kierkegaard, Dietrich Bonhoeffer, and Rudolph Bultmann. For fun, we read C. S. Lewis, J.R.R. Tolkien, Dorothy Sayers, and the English mystical poets John Donne and George Herbert.

In chapel, speakers challenged us—liberation theology, pacifism, feminism, racism, environmentalism, and other issues of social justice became the stuff of everyday conversation. Our reading expanded, eventually, to radicals like Gustavo Gutierrez and Rosemary Ruether. Long before most churchgoers cared, we argued about what it meant to be "global Christians," "stewards of creation," and to "live simply" in intentional community. We sponsored forums on poverty and peacemaking. With a growing global consciousness, we studied Islam and Buddhism for ourselves because the college offered no courses in world religions. We talked, argued, and debated in class, after chapel, in the dining hall, and in our dorms. I earned a certain reputation for passion in theological debate when I tearfully exhorted the student government to give money to world missions and not to waste it by funding a campus golf club.

After having been a college professor myself, I realize now that we were a student body dream team. We read everything our professors assigned and more. I turned down a date one Friday night because I wanted to read Martin Luther's *Table Talk,* and I wrote a very bad poem commemorating the occasion. Becca says that we "learned that theology was joyful and sensuous and it made sense."

As an evangelical college, Westmont's trustees and faculty members surely had answers they hoped we would accept. Strangely enough, they did not force them upon us. Instead, they gave us room to explore and try to find our own. Anyone who doubts that young adults are interested in theology should spend some time around such places—Christian colleges, Inter-Varsity Christian Fellowship groups, seminaries. By the time we were twenty-two we had explored many of the major classical questions of Christian theology and were concerned with a host of contemporary social issues.

Looking for answers did not make any of my friends more narrow or rigid (except maybe for a time, as part of a process of change). It did the opposite—it opened both our minds and our hearts. At that time in its history, Westmont's liberal spirit of inquiry unintentionally schooled many students out of evangelicalism. Most of my friends eventually rejected the simplistic answers offered by their evangelical churches back home. Many joined mainline denominations (usually the Presbyterians); a few rejected Christianity altogether. My own quest for theological certainty led to a spiritual pilgrimage on which questions would vastly outnumber the answers—until I realized that the questions were themselves a kind of answer.

Meanwhile, Rich and I talked and argued about theology. His commitment to the Episcopal Church fascinated me. I just could not figure out how he could be "born again" (as he had been in Young Life) and want to be a minister, a *priest,* in a denomination that baptized infants. Baptism was more than a theoretical issue for me. Since high school, evangelical friends had pressured me to reject my own infant baptism in the Methodist church as inadequate and to be baptized as an adult believer. As a theologically precocious teenager, I had gotten the impression that I was not quite saved until I professed salvation through the public act of adult baptism. According to my Baptist friends, infant baptism was an empty ritual without personal faith. To trust its efficacy could be spiritually dangerous and might place one in danger of eternal damnation. After all, the Bible directs us to "repent, and be baptized," not the other way around. At Westmont, almost all of my friends had been baptized in conjunction with their conversion experiences.

However, I was reluctant to be rebaptized, fearing that it might further complicate my relationship with my parents, who expressed concern about my "fundamentalism." My friends prodded me with Jesus' words: "I came to set mother against daughter and father against son." At Westmont, adult baptism–types were in the majority. With my reluctance to see things their way, I began to wonder if I really was a Christian. Secretly, I longed for a place where my own infant baptism counted as a sign of God's grace in my life.

So I argued with Rich, hoping that he could convince me that my own infant baptism was a sign of God's love toward me, because I could not readily believe that there existed a gentle theological world in which Jesus embraced tiny children—loving them without threat of damnation. Baptism, Rich explained, was God's gift to children in the Christian community. In those sanctified waters, God made each of us a member of the church, Christ's body, instilling in us grace by which we grew to be like God. This gift, like circumcision for the Jews, marked us as God's own forever. We could accept or reject the gift, but the gift of being part of God's people was always there. Sometimes our acceptance of it was accompanied by a dramatic conversion; more often, it was a growing realization, a process of faith.

I listened. I was intrigued. I read C. S. Lewis and Martin Luther, neither of whose "real" Christian faith could be denied and both of whom believed in infant baptism. Sometime around my twenty-first birthday, I walked along East Beach in Santa Barbara, alone in the winter fog. As the waves touched my toes I realized I had been touched by the grace of God's waters since birth. Baptism was a gift—one that I had opened long ago—years before any dramatic teenage "conversion." At three months old, in the font at St. John's United Methodist, God's saving love had washed over me. God was the deep sea in which I had always swam, and, like the fourteenth-century saint Catherine of Siena, who I would later learn also likened God to the sea, "into which the deeper I enter the more I find, and the more I find, the more I seek," God's waters would carry me home.

Through my junior year I still attended a nondenominational church. Whatever its attractions for Rich and his friends, the Episcopal Church seemed too exotic and foreign for me. It frightened me.

However, I felt growing theological discontentment with popular evangelicalism. During the spring semester of 1980, I took a class in Reformation theology and struggled with Calvin and Luther. The Reformers were supposed to be our heroes. I had a sneaking suspicion that if they walked into the evangelical church I attended they would find both the theology and the worship shallow. They certainly would not be welcomed by most of the evangelical preachers I knew.

Luther particularly gripped my imagination. I loved his doubts, his bluster, and his vision of a God hidden in the suffering of humanity. I started to skip Sundays at the acceptable churches and quietly visited the Methodists, Presbyterians, and Lutherans, in hopes of finding richer worship. But even the Lutherans did not seem as theologically robust as their founder. In chapel at school, I could barely disguise my growing disdain for the spare worship of evangelical pietism. Singing revivalist hymns in the gym did not draw me into the wonder and mystery of God. A few of us started our own small group, where we sang old hymns and new choruses, read the Bible, shared our theological insights, prayed for each other's needs, and weekly fed one another bread and grape juice. The little group grew to almost thirty people and we thought of ourselves as our own church.

In the summer of 1980, Rich and I, along with friends Linnae Himsl and Steve Hayward (Rich's best friend whom I had not yet met), planned to travel through Europe together. I spent several weeks working in Holland as a summer missionary as I explored whether or not God wanted me to pursue missions as my vocation. Rich and Steve had been in England and Linnae had been in Eastern Europe with her mother. We arranged to meet in Switzerland and travel through the Alps and then go on to Italy together.

The trip took on the air of a pilgrimage. Rich insisted we pay homage at the gravesite of his great theological hero, Karl Barth. We talked about Francis Schaeffer and thought about staying at the Christian Swiss youth retreat of L'Abri. We visited churches, monasteries, and Christian youth hostels. In Florence, art galleries and museums became church history classrooms. We visited Dante's house and read from his *Divine Comedy*. We went to Rome feeling spiritually indignant and very Protestant as we walked its ancient Catholic streets. We touched monuments where Christian martyrs had spilt their blood. We drank wine while sitting on great Baroque fountains and talked philosophy, art, history, politics, and theology into the night. And there was always music in the background—chamber music, organ recitals, opera. It stirred in me deep intellectual and emotional connections of culture and faith. I understood for the first time the complex splendor of the European world that I had inherited.

Like Lucy Honeychurch in E. M. Forster's *A Room with a View*, I felt I had found "the primal source whence beauty gushed out to water the earth." I experienced my first European journey with a mixture of fear and wonder—and with all the winsome innocence of a heroine in a Henry James novel. Art, music, culture, beauty, history, literature—the whole thing was a joyful discovery of imagination, mystery, sacredness. It was as if I had been blind but could now see. Like other provincial college students, it swept me away and made me question nearly everything I thought I had understood. Mostly, I learned that tradition is not carved in stone, and it does not die. Rather, tradition, like the Law given to the ancient Hebrews, is carved on the tablets of human hearts. It continues to live, passed down through the generations who inherit it, embraced or rejected, being made and remade—consciously or unconsciously.

This ancient and wildly cosmopolitan world called forth emotions and ideas outside my experience. And on its passionate stage I fell in love. As my train pulled into Basel, Switzerland, for the arranged meeting with Rich and Linnae, I spotted my friends across the station. Standing near them, I noticed a good-looking, tall, dark-haired man reading the *International Herald Tribune.* He looked up. We stared at each other and became immediately infatuated. It was Rich's best friend, the "Steve" about whom I had heard for two years. After a week or so, flirtation led to romance. I suppose it could be blamed on Italy. As even Lucy Honeychurch discovered, "all feelings grow to passions in the South." It must have been hell for Rich and Linnae.

On August 16, Steve and I parted at the Rome train station. Linnae and I headed north to Vienna, Paris, and London; Rich and Steve went south to Greece. I alternately sobbed and indulged in romantic daydreams on the train. I saw Paris for the first time through the eyes of summer love. I moped through its streets thinking about the thwarted medieval affair of Abelard and Heloise. I threw rose petals into the Seine. I was not very good company.

When we arrived in London I was a different girl from the one who had arrived in Europe just ten weeks before. Everything was unhinged. What once was, back in Santa Barbara, could no

STRENGTH FOR THE JOURNEY

longer be; of what lay ahead I had no idea. Anthropologists have a name for such times: *liminal periods.* During a liminal period, old systems of meaning and belief break down and no new system has yet emerged. In the liminal space, a person experiments with things outside of normal experience. Backpacking through Europe often served as liminal space for baby boomers like myself. Removed from the familiar, we let go of inherited manners and morals to explore new paths. When faced with so many new possibilities, lots of my generation opted out of old traditions—including the church and Christian faith.

I opted out, too. But not out of faith. Although it took a while to admit it, I opted out of evangelical Protestantism and chose instead to opt into a denomination closely related to the one of my childhood. I opted back into mainline church. A day or two before we left England, Linnae and I were visiting Westminster Abbey. As we ambled around its great aisles and chapels, an announcement came over the loudspeaker: "Ladies and gentlemen, Westminster Abbey is primarily a church, a place of prayer. We welcome all visitors to join us and partake Holy Communion in the chapel at 2 P.M." Linnae, herself one of Westmont's Anglican crowd, grabbed my arm saying, "Let's go. I've not taken the Eucharist all summer and feel as if I am starving."

Unable to say no, I followed her into the small side chapel. There were five of us: Linnae and me, a tourist couple from either Australia or New Zealand, and a homeless man. Linnae immediately knelt down and prayed. I had never knelt in a church before. But the others were doing the same, and feeling the liturgical pressure, I did as well.

As we prayed, the most decrepit and rumpled-looking Church of England minister came through the sacristy door. He stood in front of us, looked warily at his tiny congregation, and opened the Prayer Book. After the Lord's Prayer he began to read: "Almighty God, unto whom all hearts be open, all desires known, and from whom no secrets are hid, cleanse the thoughts of our hearts by the inspiration of thy Holy Spirit, that we may perfectly love thee and worthily magnify thy holy Name. Through Christ our Lord, Amen." We read the Ten Commandments, prayed for God to bless the queen, listened to the exhortation to repent, and confessed our sins. As we continued to kneel, the priest pronounced God's absolution of our sins and read comforting scripture.

Finally, we stood. The priest turned toward the table and started speaking to God: "It is very meet, right, and our bounden duty that we should at all times and in all places give thanks unto thee, O Lord, Holy Father, Almighty, Everlasting God.

"Therefore with Angels and Archangels, and with all the company of heaven, we laud and magnify thy glorious Name; evermore praising thee, and saying, 'Holy, holy, holy, Lord God of hosts, heaven and earth are full of thy glory: Glory be to thee, O Lord most High.'"

I felt like crying but do not remember if I did or not. I do remember that I was stunned. Completely and utterly. Years later, I would understand the dimensions of the moment much better. The words of the Prayer Book were those from which the Methodist liturgy of my youth had been drawn; I am sure I felt at home with my Methodist childhood God. The words also resonated with the Lutheran theology that had spiritually confounded me in class.

At the time, however, I was only vaguely aware of the historical connections between Lutheranism and Anglicanism or Methodism and the Church of England. As the priest rehearsed the liturgy, I only felt its beauty, its ancient, simmering spiritual passion—passion only recently awakened by Steve and Italy—and an earthy, human longing to be consumed by love. Inwardly, I heard Martin Luther's confession upon first understanding faith: "Here I felt that I was altogether born again and had entered paradise itself through open gates." The chapel became luminous with grace. For a brief moment, all my longings abated and I was, as C. S. Lewis has written, "united with beauty." I stumbled forward to the altar rail, knelt on a worn pillow, held my hands out, and received the food and drink of God. Until that moment, I never knew that I had been spiritually starving for years.

All Saints-by-the-Sea Episcopal Church sits at the ocean in Montecito, California, about a mile downhill from Westmont. Through the years, a small number of Westmont students had found their way to the Episcopal Church through its doors. The parents of my roommate Becca had lived in the caretaker's cottage at the church while they were a young married couple in college. Through the 1960s and 1970s an occasional curious or theologically deviant student would brave All Saints biblical liberalism and moneyed reputation to experience liturgical worship. When I was a student, however, most of the Westmont Anglicans went to Christ the King, a small charismatic Episcopal mission across town.

But I did not want to go to a charismatic church. It would be too much like worship in the school chapel at the gym. I wanted to touch the "otherness" of Westminster Abbey. I wanted to be overwhelmed by God's beauty. Some other friends hungered for the same. One September morning during our senior year, about a dozen of us piled into our cars and drove to All Saints. I suspect that the gray-haired congregation was surprised when we invaded their sparsely attended service that Sunday morning. Not including us, some forty or so people, all over sixty, were seated scatter-shot throughout the sanctuary. My friends and I came in, sat down together in a pew near the front, and, as the organist played, waited for the liturgy to begin.

I looked around the church and delighted in the wood and windows—especially the Annunciation window close to our pew. For all its beauty and tradition, All Saints was very intimate. The pews seemed closer together than in some buildings, the ceiling was cozily low, and the stained-glass windows could be touched. Becca described All Saints as "like going to a foreign country" and remembers "the smell, an incense wood smell, like a redwood grove." It was familiar and exotic at the same time; that sense I had experienced in Westminster Abbey was palpable.

I have the impression that the opening hymn that morning was "Immortal, Invisible, God Only Wise." My friends sang very loudly—as did the priest as he walked down the aisle. He stood, faced us, and began, "Blessed be God: Father, Son, and Holy Spirit."

I could barely respond with the traditional "And blessed be his kingdom, now and forever," because the priest's voice so surprised me. Gethin Hughes was from Wales and had been educated at Exeter and Oxford, had been ordained in the Church of England, and had served Welsh parishes before coming to the United States. When he sang the service, the liturgy seemed to be the language of angels. It lifted me out of my immediate realm of experience. I felt connected to all God's people—past, present, and future. In a single moment, time collapsed into a mysterious whole. I was part of the sea of God, touching the shores of life and death and life hereafter. It was as it had been in Westminster Abbey. I had come home.

Gethin Hughes had only just arrived at All Saints. For thirty-two years previously, from 1948 to 1980, the Rev. George Hall, an old-fashioned liberal, had virtually reigned over All Saints. For years, All Saints had been like a family, with Hall serving as its personable and pastoral "Father." Like other Episcopal churches in the decades following World War II, All Saints celebrated Morning Prayer, a simple service of prayer and a sermon, on three Sundays and the Holy Communion once a month. This pattern of worship was established in the 1928 Book of Common Prayer.

Hall's congregation comprised much of the wealthy Santa Barbara Anglo-upper class, whose religion was measured, reasonable, and private. Baptisms were family affairs held behind the gates of tony estates. To those who "fit in" at All Saints, George Hall and his wife, Sally, could be quite welcoming. The rectory was always open, they served breakfast immediately following the service, and they never forgot to send anniversary and birthday cards to parishioners. George Hall had molded a successful, culturally relevant postwar congregation whose vision matched its time. And whose time had come and gone. Membership was declining and the congregation was aging. There were not many young families. By the time he retired in 1980, Hall's old-time liberalism seemed dated and failed to resonate with a new generation. The place was clearly in need when Gethin Hughes arrived.

In the 1970s the Episcopal Church faced several difficult issues: the Civil Rights movement, the war in Vietnam, the call for women's ordination, the role of homosexual persons in the church, and liturgical reform. Although all these social, political, and theological concerns affected local congregations, few had such emotional power and none had greater immediate impact than did liturgical renewal.

In 1976, when the church debated use of a new Book of Common Prayer in national meetings, sincere Episcopalians fretted that their spiritual and mental health would suffer if they were forced to surrender the familiar 1928 prayer book. They worried over the loss of Shakespearean cadences and complained that the new language seemed "too modern." Despite resistance, the denomination mandated use of the 1979 Prayer Book for all services. For years, individuals and parishes might dodge certain issues of social justice or refuse to hire a female priest. To remain in good standing within the national church, however, parishes had to switch from the 1928 Prayer Book to the new 1979 book within the proscribed adjustment period. Only certain local exceptions would be provided.

When Gethin Hughes arrived in 1980, and when I first worshiped at the church, All Saints was using the new Prayer Book. Throughout the 1970s, Hall, who was theologically liberal and liturgically progressive, encouraged use of the "green book," a trial version of what became the new Prayer Book. Unlike most Episcopal priests at that time, Gethin did not have to struggle with the congregation to put the new books in the pews. They were already there—although some people wanted them gone.

As attested to by the national opposition, the 1979 book marked a significant change for many Episcopalians. But the change had been brewing for some time and was not a denominationally isolated phenomenon. For much of the twentieth century, and with increasing urgency since the end of World War II, Christians have embarked on an international and interdenominational theological project for liturgical renewal. Sometimes clearly expressed and sometimes only implied, Christians of all persuasions realized that the world had become numb or hostile to the message of Jesus and that they had to speak God's message in a new tongue.

Like the situation of first-century Christians, believers found themselves aliens in a non-Christian world. Not since the decades prior to Emperor Constantine's legalization of the Christian religion had the faithful felt so at odds with the societies in which they lived. Beginning with World War I, the remnants of Christian political empires—and the vision of Christendom itself—began to dissolve into historic memory. Church leaders hoped that renewed Christian worship, modeled on that of earliest Christianity, would renew the churches, focus their distinctive identity as Christ's body, and strengthen them to do God's mission of bringing about love and justice in the world. As was the case in early Christian communities, the sacraments of baptism and Eucharist regained center stage as the very life of Christian identity, spirituality, and witness.

For Roman Catholics the highpoint of the change occurred in 1963, when the Second Vatican Council endorsed the liturgical renewal movement and revised the liturgy of the Mass. Lacking institutional and sacramental unity, Protestants were somewhat slower than Catholics in liturgical reform. In 1982, however, the World Council of Churches issued its seminal document, *Baptism, Eucharist and Ministry,* which summarized much of the century's theological work regarding the nature of the church and firmly established liturgical renewal among its member denominations. The new Episcopal Prayer Book reflected these new liturgical understandings and expressed more clearly the prayer of a pilgrim church. Liturgically, it shifted from the establishment center of American culture to its sojourning edges. Gethin Hughes, I am quite sure, understood that.

When I was a girl my Methodist mother would rouse us from bed every Sunday saying, "It's time to go church." Church was a place you went, a sort of religious club you joined. By the time I found my way into All Saints, a new understanding was permeating American Protestantism—an understanding summed up in *Baptism, Eucharist and Ministry:* "In a broken world God calls the whole of humanity to become God's people. . . . Belonging to the Church means living in communion with God through Jesus Christ in the Holy Spirit. . . . The Church is called to proclaim and prefigure the Kingdom of God."

Such language, although profoundly biblical and theologically orthodox, would have sounded strange to my mother's ears. And it was certainly foreign in the Sunday school world of my childhood. "Belonging to the church" meant being born to a Christian family, being baptized, believing in God and Jesus, and living a good, moral life. The Church prefigures the Kingdom of God?

Although I loved the Lord's Supper, the sermons, and the hymns at church, much of church—especially Sunday school— struck me as boring. Methodism was dull; Protestantism, uninteresting. I secretly wished I had been born in a Catholic or Jewish family. I envied the little Catholic girls at the church across the street because they wore pretty lace veils to their service. I envied the Jewish children at my elementary school because they celebrated interesting holy days like Passover and read the Bible in Hebrew. I wanted religion to be special, to set the faithful apart from the world, and to hold out some sort of mythic and mystical quest into the heart of God. Whereas it was loving, kind, and gentle, my girlhood Methodism was neither exotic nor heroic. It was white bread religion for middle-class white children. It was meant to maintain order, not spark the spiritual imagination; it embodied American civil religion and did not prefigure God's Kingdom. It was all terribly socially acceptable and routine.

About 1967 or so, the preachers at St. John's United Methodist seemed to understand that the religion they offered was dull and appeared to embark on a campaign to stir things up. I remember that one minister got us all riled up, preaching that "the Negroes" were our brothers and sisters and that Jesus would never go to Vietnam and fight the Communists, because he was a pacifist. The nice Methodists I knew were shocked to hear that their black servants and the Vietnamese did not think they were nice at all. The grown-ups, with the exception of my mother's saintly friend Miss Jean, got very upset. I can even recall my parents talking in hushed tones about how much the church had changed. They murmured words like "Communist" and "World Council of Churches" when they talked about the Methodist Church.

About the same time, I began to sense that they were afraid. Their world was changing; they did not understand draft protesters or why black people were so unhappy. One day, when my mother took us children to lunch at a downtown cafeteria, a man came into the building and started shooting. She pushed us under the table, where we sat huddled together and shaking until the police came. We never went downtown as a family again. Then in 1968, terrible riots ripped the city apart. My grandfather, sad and worn from his battle with lung cancer, held my little sister on his lap one day and said, "I fear for these children and the world they are inheriting." I was not quite ten, but I felt it. I felt all his raw fear. I think my mother went to church to feel safe, but even there, with the minister challenging her childhood values, she felt threatened.

My parents joined the white exodus from Baltimore City to the distant suburbs and our Methodist churchgoing became erratic. I missed it and still wanted to go. Instead of attending Sunday services, I would take the Revised Standard Version of the Bible given me upon second-grade church school graduation and sneak off to the woods to read it. If preaching from it at St. John's could cause so much trouble, I figured the Bible must be pretty interesting.

Sitting on piles of soft pine needles and old leaves, hidden from sight and shaded from the steamy Maryland summer sun, I taught myself the stories of the Old Testament, tried to memorize the Psalms, and read Jesus' teachings.

After we moved to Arizona in 1972, my parents began attending the Methodist Church once again. Nothing drifts leftward in Scottsdale, so we were able to settle back into middle-class respectable religion once again. In the eighth grade I dutifully subjected myself to confirmation. After that ritual, however, it would be the last time I would attend a mainline congregation for nearly ten years. The only thing I remember from the confirmation classes was a story about John Wesley, a Church of England clergyman and the founder of Methodism, who would daily walk around Oxford at the exact same time and pray.

Despite the tedium of the church he had founded, Wesley excited my theological imagination. I could not imagine any Methodist I knew praying so much. Wesley, like the Catholic girls and Jewish school children I envied, evidently thought faith was special and demanded spiritual courage. I liked him. He would prove a pivotal figure in my own spiritual development as I came to understand the way he combined Anglican tradition, Catholic piety, and evangelical fervor. I now know myself as one of his spiritual offspring. But understanding that was in the future.

Shortly after my Methodist confirmation, Scottsdale Bible Church, a local evangelical congregation, would reap the spiritual harvest the Methodists had sown. The left-wing Methodist ministers had awakened my spiritual conscience. I could not let go of the questions they raised. They made church interesting—everybody was talking about big issues and not just the theme for the Ladies' Bazaar or the next Vacation Bible school. Although my parents found those Methodist ministers unsettling, I am sure that these ministers were trying to get us to understand that the church was called to be different from the world—however imperfectly and insensitively they tried to do that. The church was called, in the words of *Baptism, Eucharist and Ministry,* to "proclaim and prefigure the Kingdom of God" and to be "the body of Christ." Church was not a place to go to find comfort; church was something we were supposed to be for the sake of a broken and unjust world. Church was not about safety. Rather, church freed us from fear of the world to a powerful, prophetic love for the world. Maybe those Methodist ministers did not get their point across to my parents' generation, but I heard the echoes of the gospel.

In Arizona, the Methodists were still mired in the 1950s. Only evangelical churches like Scottsdale Bible preached that the body of Christ was fundamentally different from the spirit of the world. After attending a student-led youth group for months, I sensed a powerful call to serious Christian discipleship during a Sunday evening service in the summer of 1975. It was monthly communion and I was sitting two chairs away from my friend Phil Thorne. I greatly admired and respected Phil. He was intelligent, compassionate, and deeply spiritual, and, as a teenager himself, he led our Bible study group. After the ushers passed the broken crackers and tiny grape juice glasses, he held the elements, staring at them, and I suspect he was earnestly praying for forgiveness of his sins. As I watched him take it so seriously, I understood that Jesus invited us to feast with God, to be one in fellowship with all the company of the church in service to the world.

At that moment, which my evangelical friends interpreted as a conversion, I finally inwardly understood all that I knew about God. Much of that was the legacy of St. John's United Methodist Church. I am willing to bet that I was the only person to get born again at Scottsdale Bible Church, because I first heard the call of the gospel from a leftist Methodist preacher and felt the sacramental power of the Lord's Supper. But Scottsdale Bible depicted faith as an adventure with God and I willingly signed up. I gulped down the Saltines and Welch's saying, "Yes, God, yes."

Of course, faith is an adventure to evangelicals—but only within boundaries established by a fairly narrow reading of the Bible. Pushing back those boundaries led me to All Saints several years later—home to the very church that had formed John Wesley—and into a denomination that was intent on pushing its own traditional boundaries for the sake of God's kingdom in the world.

Gethin Hughes pushed back boundaries. The new Book of Common Prayer was in the pews, but that did not mean that the congregation liked it. A 1980 parish survey found that "a large majority" of All Saints parishioners "still favored the 1928 Prayer Book." But Gethin was deeply committed to liturgical renewal. He loved the new Prayer Book and believed in its theological vision. He was determined to make All Saints into a "1979 Prayer Book Church" in all aspects of its life.

The Episcopal Church was learning to live into its new liturgical identity and was trying to find its way in a rapidly changing culture. The theological vision of the 1979 book was grounded in the fundamental idea of the church as Christ's body engaged in the work of God's Kingdom. As Vatican II did for Roman Catholics, the new Episcopal liturgy reversed the old understanding of Christian ministry. In the past, the clergy ministered and the people supported the ministry. Now, the people minister and the clergy support, empower, and equip them for ministry. An individual is not called to "the ministry"; rather, at baptism, all of God's people are called as Christ's ministers. Weekly, they are strengthened to do God's work through the grace of God's table, the bread and wine of the Eucharist. Church is not a building, a place you go. Church is the body of Christ; it is who you are.

This theology was expressed in a number of liturgical changes in the Book of Common Prayer. The language was simplified for ease of access and congregational participation. The clergy actually said less and the people responded more often. God was no longer addressed with the archaic "Thee" and "Thou" but with the plain modern counterpart of "you." Episcopalians would no longer refer to themselves as "miserable sinners" but would simply confess that they had sinned. Christ now offered salvation to both sexes— instead of the traditional "us men." Words were changed to clarify God's call to all persons for ministry, and ecumenical accommodations were made to express the unity of all Christians in God's mission. Eucharist replaced Morning Prayer as the weekly Sunday service. And, in the middle of it, parishioners would "pass the peace," an ancient practice in which Christians would actually bless one another with God's peace.

Those Episcopalians who objected to the new liturgy generally did so on three grounds: (1) the new language lacked majesty and reverence for God, (2) weekly Eucharist would undermine the solemnity of a monthly Lord's Supper, and (3) they hated touching one another during the peace. The old liturgy had kept God at a distance from the people and the people at a distance from one another. It was private, personal, and inwardly meaningful. The new liturgy sounded wrong, made old-timers feel lost, forced everyone to participate, and caused some stranger to stick his or her hand in your space during communion. While I was still new at All Saints, I heard an older woman behind me mutter with disdain, "You mean they expect me to actually shake hands with someone in this pew?"

After George Hall introduced the new Prayer Book, some unhappy parishioners stayed at All Saints out of personal loyalty to him. But upon his resignation, unsure of the direction of the parish under new clergy, and disgruntled about the changes, many just disappeared. They felt no loyalty to the new priest who came in September 1980. As the Old Guard left, however, the church began to attract new people—people like myself, who were eager for the theological vision embodied in the liturgy and the church's willingness to trust the Spirit to lead it to new places. As evangelism, it began to work. Although the denomination was still shrinking, by 1984 a startling 60 percent of all Episcopalians were adults who had been raised in another church. The church was finding a new audience.

I only witnessed his first year at the church, but Gethin Hughes would continue at All Saints for another dozen years. In the mid-1980s he spearheaded a campaign to renovate the sanctuary so that the church's interior would reflect the eucharistic vision of the 1979 Book of Common Prayer. The altar was pulled away from the back wall and the chancel area was redesigned in order for the people to gather around the table. Old walls were moved to improve lines of sight, old carpet was ripped up and homey wooden floors were revealed, and old woodwork was scrubbed and polished. Gethin commissioned a portable baptism font to enable him to perform baptisms at the altar instead of by the back door. This symbolized baptism as a public event of communal faith rather the entry of a single individual into the church. He began to refuse to do private baptisms, insisting instead that all baptisms be part of congregational worship.

Melinda Menoni, who also arrived at All Saints in September 1980 and eventually became a staff member, recalls, "People were going crazy about ripping up the carpet. But it wasn't about the carpet, it was really about the Prayer Book, baptism, and Eucharist.

But it all came out around the carpet. They finally understood all the implications of it all." They understood that God called them as a distinct people to practice their faith in the world. That church was not a social gathering or a time of private prayer. Rather, the church fed God's people to do God's mission. And that, of course, is exactly what Gethin Hughes intended. By 1989, weekly Sunday attendance topped 600, and more than 850 people were engaged in some sort of lay ministry. "By the end of the decade," Melinda says, "All Saints was a new church. We'd completely changed the place."

On that Sunday in the fall of 1980, I think Gethin was pleased to see an entire pew full of college students enthusiastically fumbling through that new Prayer Book. Although we made many liturgical mistakes, we loved the tradition that we had only recently discovered, and we represented the first fruits of a generation who would eventually come home to mainline faith. Not only did we love that book, but we also loved Gethin, who proved himself a tolerant and welcoming host to a bunch of evangelical interlopers. On that first Sunday he preached a low-key but theologically moving sermon about Christ. He would prove to be a profoundly Christocentric person. Early in his ministry he urged the parish, "May we give our whole hearts and lives unhesitatingly to the Christ who lives among us."

It was a vision tailored for eager evangelical converts. He came right up to us after the service and asked who we were. No minister had ever asked my name before. Becca says that "Gethin had a certain 'evangelical' warmth and faith. He spoke a language that was not too foreign. But it was not culturally and ideologically evangelical. It was Anglican." Over the months to come, we would never miss church. We were on a sort of honeymoon with the worship service. Everything excited us. We watched, we participated, we read, and we discussed. Gethin was schooling us in the tradition—a tradition that was changing even as we entered its stream. It was a unique moment of spiritual confluence: the Episcopal Church was discovering new expressions of its identity even as we, as college students, were finding ours for the first time.

Back in class, we taught ourselves Anglicanism and openly evangelized other students. The "Anglican mafia" grew. Some of our evangelical professors worried. One quizzed Becca, "How do you know that this just isn't an aesthetic experience?" She remembers that his comment confused her until she realized that "aesthetic experience and religious experience are essentially the same thing." The college chaplain laughed at me: "You'll get over it. Everyone does. Ten years from now you'll be a Presbyterian."

Eventually some professors went for themselves—some out of curiosity, a few for the same reasons we had for going, and a number stayed. We discovered that we were not alone in our quest back to the mainline. We heard rumors that something similar was happening at other evangelical colleges—like Gordon College in Massachusetts and Wheaton College in Illinois. In 1981 we did not know what to call the movement of which we were a part. But four years later, Robert Webber, an Episcopal convert and theology professor at Wheaton, published a little book about like-minded seekers, called *Evangelicals on the Canterbury Trail.* We at last had a name.

Identity and vocation are often related. When you know who you are, what you are to do becomes more obvious. At twenty-two, in 1981, I graduated from college committed to my new church and with a passionate interest in serving God. I had no idea, however, how the details would work out. In the next few months, after a short stint working for a mission organization in Pasadena, I decided to pursue my interests in theology and church history. I thought I might become a missionary and teach overseas. At seminary, I figured, I could further explore vocation and calling.

And, after many tempestuous months, Steve and I broke up. He planned to stay in Pasadena for graduate school; I knew I had to leave California. The year before, Linnae had gone to Gordon-Conwell Theological Seminary, north of Boston. She liked one of her church history professors a great deal, the Rev. Mark Dyer, who was also the priest at the Episcopal Church near the campus. And she needed a roommate. In May 1982 I flew east to embark upon graduate studies in religion.

CHAPTER TWO

Competing Authorities

CHRIST CHURCH

South Hamilton, Massachusetts, 1982–1987

On Boston's North Shore, locals refer to the highest spot in Essex County as "Holy Hill." On an autumn day, the vista from the hill is a postcard New England scene, a vast expanse of red and yellow trees punctuated by white clapboard steeples as the land undulates to the sea. The hill does not get its moniker from those steeples, however. Since 1969, an evangelical Protestant school, Gordon-Conwell Theological Seminary, has occupied the hill.

Before that, reaching back to the nineteenth century, it was home to Roman Catholic monks, members of the Carmelite Order. The men's dorm had served as monastic cells; the women's dorm had previously housed spiritual retreatants. The woods hid unused grottoes where the Catholic faithful had once prayed to the Virgin Mary. In the chapel, pews faced each other around a large marble altar on which had been performed the miracle of the Mass.

The evangelicals tried to erase the signs of Catholic habitation. The Virgin's statue was long gone. Dried flower arrangements filled the niches in the chapel where the saints had stood as witnesses to the faith. Simple crosses replaced all crucifixes, icons, and images of

Jesus. The Protestant administration erected a massive neon cross on the steeple as a testimony to their reform of the faith on the hill. At night, this yellow, glowing cross guided pilots on their approach to Logan Airport. Above the old confessionals, discreet signs announced, "Prayer Booth," lest any ignorant visitor enter in begging forgiveness from some long-departed priest.

While I was a student there, school officials took jackhammers to the altar and turned the once-sacred space into a plain Protestant multipurpose room. As the desecration proceeded, one of my Episcopal friends stood outside the door with tears running down her cheeks. Caught in the competing theological visions of Protestant and Catholic, I sometimes imagined that I heard the mournful echoes of monks chanting Psalm 15 in the chilly halls at night: *Domine, quis habitabit?* "Lord, who may dwell in your tabernacle? Who may abide upon your holy hill?"

At the base of the hill sits the small town of Hamilton, Massachusetts, home to the surprisingly large Episcopal parish of Christ Church. At Christ Church, Catholic and evangelical do not usually compete. Rather, they inform, shape, and act upon each other. For Christ Church sees itself as truly Anglican—both Catholic and Protestant, the Reformation's *via media,* inclusive and welcoming of a variety of faith practices and theological views. While the evangelical Protestants on Holy Hill still warred against Rome, much as their forebears had done in the sixteenth and seventeenth centuries, Christ Church tried to follow a different path— that of a comprehensive church.

In part, at least, I went to Gordon-Conwell to join Christ Church. The other part was that I wanted to study church history. Despite my new commitment to the Episcopal Church, mainline seminaries like Yale and Princeton seemed too liberal and intimidated me. No faculty member at Westmont recommended them. One professor advised, "Young evangelicals need grounding in the Bible and theology. You can go to a more liberal place for a doctoral degree." So I settled for the intellectual safety of another evangelical school. Gordon-Conwell had a strong tradition of church history and a good Episcopal parish nearby. It appeared to be the right choice.

Christ Church served both the seminary and Gordon College, an institution related to Westmont. Christ Church attracted a sizable number of the college faculty members—many of whom had grown up in fundamentalism or evangelicalism and had since become Episcopalians. Malcolm Reid, professor at the college and member of Christ Church, who grew up Pentecostal, remembers that finding the Episcopal Church was like an "epiphany." At Christ Church he discovered worship that embodied—in the weekly celebration of the Eucharist, the historic creeds, the liturgical setting of the Scripture, and the church's musical tradition—much of the theology he had believed as an evangelical. His journey, like those of his colleagues, was not unlike mine.

The most famous of Christ Church's evangelical converts was Thomas Howard, an English professor at the college. While I was a student at Westmont, I had read his most popular book, *Christ the Tiger,* a youthful spiritual autobiography about growing up fundamentalist and finding poetry and God and beauty and passion in ancient Christian liturgy. For a time, it was my favorite book. I read it until it was more dog-eared than my Bible, writing comments like "That's it *exactly*" in the margins. My friends considered Howard a kind of American C. S. Lewis, born out of time and place. When it came time to go to seminary, a few of us chose Gordon-Conwell because Howard taught at the college and worshiped at Christ

Church. Being a literary groupie, I later realized, is not exactly the best way to pick a seminary. But my only other option was Fuller Seminary in Pasadena, with the offensively liberal All Saints across the street. It made sense at the time to go to Massachusetts.

Linnae spoke of Christ Church with great enthusiasm. She admired the rector, Mark Dyer, who also taught early Christian history and medieval spirituality at the seminary. He was so popular with the evangelical students—whose own theological tradition typically rejected the notion that anything important happened in Christian history between the Apostle Paul and Martin Luther— that they endured long waiting lists to enroll in his courses. His reputation attracted some Episcopal students, who came to the seminary expressly to study with him. A good number of non-Episcopalians—particularly the Presbyterians—were attracted to his vision of a monastic-type spirituality that combined a love of learning and the desire for God. Despite the denominational differences, they thronged to Christ Church to sit under him and be mentored in liturgical worship and medieval spirituality.

Until I went to Christ Church, I do not think I ever heard the word *spirituality* used in a positive sense. In my adolescent evangelical circles, we spoke of "piety," "holiness," "sanctification," and "giving it all to Jesus" in describing a serious life of prayer and discipline. *Spirituality* sounded frivolous and even suspiciously like spiritualism, witchcraft, and the like. Spirituality was certainly not something a committed evangelical young person would fool around with. It bordered on religious flakiness.

But Mark Dyer introduced this word into my world and into the world of the evangelicals of South Hamilton. *Spirituality* is, of course, a word Roman Catholics have long used to talk about the life of faith, of prayer and intentional Christian practice. Unbeknownst to me, Catholics had *liturgical spirituality, spiritual theology,* and *his-*

tory of spirituality. It was the Catholic way of talking about lively faith, that mix of personal piety and theological rigor—belief invigorated by true holiness—also prized by evangelicals. Catholics traditionally spoke of spirituality in relation to monasticism, but, by the early 1980s, Catholics had begun to speak about spirituality outside the walls of the monastery and in the lives of Christians working in the world. Despite some reservations, when Dyer taught or preached or modeled classical spirituality in this evangelical world, it commanded respect. His version of spirituality resonated with evangelical Protestant virtues of true Christian faith.

"His version" was not really his, of course. Before he became an Episcopal priest, Mark Dyer had been a Roman Catholic brother, a Benedictine monk. His wife, Marie Elizabeth, had been a nun. Mark had left Catholicism because he rejected papal claims to authority. But Mark and Marie Elizabeth brought with them to Christ Church lives formed in prayer and scripture, in service and community, in the Benedictine marriage of heart and head. Although no longer Roman Catholic, Mark's faith was *small c catholic,* meaning "universal," in its scope. He was not parochial in theology or piety; he obviously understood himself, and his ministry connected to the whole of the Christian tradition through time. At Christ Church, Dyer's spirituality proved compelling. His congregation began moving away from the more rationalistic piety common among evangelicals and experienced a growing desire for the mystery of God. Thus, he imbued both his parish and the seminary classrooms with a kind of catholic Anglican sensibility of spirituality.

Founded in 1914 by New England landed gentry, the old Boston Brahmin establishment, Christ Church embodied the ethos of much of twentieth-century mainstream Protestantism. Like other churches, Christ Church grew rapidly in the years following World War II. By 1962, they replaced their tiny neo-Gothic building with a massive, modern, and very plain sanctuary. As the decade progressed, the congregation grew more slowly and the native conservatism of Hamilton's hunt club set maintained a cautious distance from the social changes around them. It was not a place one would expect to find either evangelical enthusiasm or catholic spirituality.

In 1968, in a somewhat surprising move, Christ Church called the Rev. Jim Hampson, a graduate of the theologically liberal Episcopal Theological Seminary, to be their new rector. Hampson was, as one Gordon College professor remembers, "a mild Tillichian" (a devotee of the liberal theologian Paul Tillich), who was "kind of spiritually uptight." At about the same time, Tom Howard, who had converted to Episcopalianism in New York, arrived in Hamilton to teach at Gordon College. Within a couple of years, a number of Gordon professors, proselytized by Howard, began to attend Christ Church.

Aided by his colleagues, Howard pressed Hampson regarding his spiritual life. Hampson experienced an evangelical conversion and was "born again." He quickly herded his flock down the same theological path. In 1974 the parish adopted a new motto: "To Know Christ and Make Him Known." They supported missions and evangelism, emphasizing personal religious experience and biblical preaching. Under the new theological regime, and with the help of Hampson's assistant, the Rev. Ted Schroder, who also served as dean of Christian life at Gordon College, students and seminarians began filling Christ Church's pews. Within a decade, evangelical students from the two schools made up more than a third of the congregation. Christ Church had become a successful evangelical Episcopal congregation.

Something, however, was missing. Many of Gordon's evangelicals did not become Episcopalians in order to embrace some Anglophile version of their own tradition. John Skillen, a member of Christ Church, has written that they wanted "the recovery of authority, catholicity, and ceremony in the liturgy and the sacraments." They had discovered, along with Tom Howard, who gave words to their longings, that "evangelical is not enough." They wanted the *mysterium tremendum*—not Billy Graham in a cassock. After Hampson left in 1977, Mark Dyer's Benedictine-tinctured Anglicanism meshed with their spiritual longings. The parish turned toward Mark's distinctly small c catholic direction.

Episcopalians pride themselves on one particular aspect of their tradition: they are the church of the *via media,* the middle way. Forged in the decades following the Protestant Reformation, Anglicanism defined itself as Protestant in its theology and Catholic in its worship. Its two foundational documents—the Thirty-Nine Articles, with their Protestant doctrines, and the Book of Common Prayer, with its medieval liturgical practices—present the vision of a comprehensive church. Christ Church self-consciously understood itself as the *via media.* Much of the congregation remained intellectually committed to historic Protestant doctrines, but under the leadership of Mark Dyer they experienced a wider range of catholic worship than ever before. For some of the parishioners, catholic spirituality opened the doors for theological experimentation with Roman Catholic and Eastern Orthodox doctrines. Christ Church's *via media,* as it has been for centuries of Anglicans, amounted to a kind of orthodox pluralism—an amazing number of theologies existed in one sanctuary. Christ Church was often surprisingly eclectic and diverse.

Although Episcopalians are relatively aware of the theological pluralism in their congregations, other mainstream Protestant churches live with similar diversity. Whereas Methodists, Lutherans, Congregationalists, and Presbyterians had started out as distinctive protest movements with clear theological commitments, by the twentieth century, all had become more pluralistic than particular and comprised a variety of theological positions within their boundaries. Theological inclusiveness created some huge problems for mainliners—notably a loss of identity and authority. In the short run, at least, pluralism seemed to make mainline Protestantism pointless.

Christ Church would teach me, however, that theological diversity is not a bad thing. I have come to believe that a truly comprehensive church—an inclusive community of faith, one not defined by the boundaries of a dogmatic and singular theological stance—best incarnates God's ever-present mercy and love for humankind and creation. But it would be a while before I would understand that.

Gordon College professors seemed more pleased with Christ Church's small c catholicism than those at the seminary. With only two or three exceptions, no one at the seminary spoke well of the *via media* or comprehension or theological pluralism. When I matriculated in 1982, certain professors in the institution had just begun a sort of theological crusade to turn the seminary toward what the students would eventually call the hard Calvinist right.

Calvinists are followers of the sixteenth-century Protestant Reformer John Calvin. Their theology emphasizes God's glory and sovereignty, human sinfulness, salvation by faith alone, the primacy of scripture, and ecclesiastical order and discipline. They are infamous for their belief in double predestination—the doctrine that God elects some people to heavenly bliss and others to eternal damnation. Calvinism influenced Anglicanism at a number of historical junctures, but there was also a certain theological antipathy between strict Calvinists and mainstream Anglicanism. Anglicanism, always a less rigid form of Protestantism, was more open to both divine mystery and human goodness than was Calvinism.

In the seventeenth century, those tensions contributed to the English civil wars. When the Calvinists briefly ruled England in Oliver Cromwell's Puritan Commonwealth, they outlawed Anglicanism, the consecration of bishops, and worship from the Book of Common Prayer. Although Anglicans returned to power after a scant dozen years of Puritan government, they neither forgot nor forgave the persecution. Relations between the two remained strained for generations.

As an institution, Gordon-Conwell combined warm evangelical piety and fundamentalist mores while allowing for a variety of conservative theological positions—including a high regard for Calvinism. By the 1980s, Gordon-Conwell had transformed itself into a temperate version of American evangelicalism—culturally aware, theologically vigorous, and biblically open—in contrast to the separatist fundamentalism of its earlier days. On paper at least, Gordon-Conwell espoused views resonant with the kind of social justice concerns that I had embraced at Westmont. Several well-respected New Testament scholars and ecumenically minded church historians served on its faculty. It resembled Fuller Theological Seminary in Pasadena, a school marked by its willingness to experiment theologically and break some of the rules of the evangelical subculture. At the time, Fuller and Gordon-Conwell shared leadership of what seemed to be an emerging progressive evangelical coalition.

This relative progressiveness attracted many students to Gordon-Conwell. At that time, mostly mainline Protestants—Episcopalians, Presbyterians, United Methodists, Congregationalists, and American Baptists—thronged to the school. Many were raised in these denominations and, like me, had been born again during the Jesus Movement of the 1970s. We wanted to infuse traditional Protestantism with evangelical zeal. We saw ourselves as reformers. Gordon-Conwell seemed a good place for idealistic young evangelicals.

But we had no idea that theological warfare was about to break out on Holy Hill. Unbeknownst to the entering class, certain faculty members were uncomfortable with what they perceived to be theological squishiness and a "slippery slope" toward liberalism. They did not want to be identified as Fuller East. A strong dose of Calvinism, they felt, would correct the school's intellectual course and make it the flagship of conservative—not progressive—evangelicalism.

Episcopal students were at the front line of this holy war. In the fall of 1982, a number of my classmates still held a grudge against a particular professor who had tried to get their service of weekly Eucharist—and along with it the Episcopal student fellowship—kicked off campus. The complaint was that some Episcopalians appeared to hold "catholic" ideas about the Lord's Supper—that Christ was actually present in the bread and wine. This clearly violated the school's Protestant heritage and proved offensive to other members of the community. The administration intervened and allowed the Episcopal fellowship to remain on campus. But bad feelings remained and an informal persecution persisted.

It may have been informal, but it was real. About this time, the school began to more vigorously de-Romanize its liturgical space and it planned to build a new, plain, and very Protestant chapel. Even the tiny prayer chapel where we held our Friday Eucharist was stripped bare. One day someone emptied out all our bottles of communion wine. Episcopal students were treated to a near daily barrage of insults regarding their tradition—mostly by the Calvinist faculty members and students who bought into the views of their party. The student body divided into pro- and anti-Calvinist factions. But Episcopalians were not simply targets. With their tradition of *via media,* the Episcopal students were unwilling combatants—caught emotionally in the theological crossfire. We wanted to stand in the middle and hold our historic ground. No one, however, would let us. Faculty members and other students wanted us to pick sides. It hurt.

Mark Dyer's classes appeared to irritate conservative members of the faculty. Before Mark served on the faculty, the seminary had few classes on early Christianity or the medieval church. The curriculum skipped—in good Protestant fashion—from the Bible to the Reformation. Shortly after I arrived, Mark left Christ Church to become the bishop of Bethlehem, Pennsylvania. The seminary simply canceled his classes and offered no replacement. Some students speculated that he was about to be let go anyway. The Calvinist faculty members were clearly relieved by his departure. My friends and I, however, were heartsick.

In church history classes, the Puritans—the radical Calvinists who had nearly destroyed the Church of England in the seventeenth century—were considered the towering heroes of Christian history. One professor even remarked to me that had he been in Oliver Cromwell's army, he would have been "the first to smash the stained glass windows in every Anglican parish in the countryside." With no Catholics around, Episcopalians took the full brunt of evangelical anxiety about Roman Catholicism. The *via media* was held up to scorn and ridicule. Classical forms of Christian expression, such as the Benedictine rule and traditional church music and architecture, were derided. Because we liked these things, Episcopalians were viewed as quasi-Catholics and theologically suspect. When one of my friends complained, an administrator told him that if the Episcopal students did not like it, "they could go elsewhere."

Some of this evangelical anxiety was based in a very particular crisis over the nature of theological authority. In 1976, Harold

Lindsell, a noted evangelical leader, published a controversial book entitled, *Battle for the Bible*. In it, he claimed that evangelicals had subtly undermined—or rejected outright—the doctrine of biblical inerrancy, the belief that the Bible is free from error in *all* that it teaches. "The battle that rages over the Bible today," Lindsell claimed, "centers around the question of infallibility—whether the Bible is fully or partially trustworthy."

In particular, he accused Fuller Seminary of rejecting inerrancy. Its president, Daniel Fuller, son of the seminary's founder, believed that the Scriptures contained errors—mistakes attributed to historic or literary problems in the text that pertained only to "nonrevelational" matters. The Bible was without error only in regard to salvation—not in matters of history, science, or culture. Fuller Seminary issued a new doctrinal statement replacing the strong word *inerrant* with the more flexible term *infallible*. Lindsell warned: "Down the road, whether it takes five or fifty years, any institution that departs from belief in an inerrant Scripture will likewise depart from other fundamentals of the faith and at last cease to be evangelical."

The threat sent other evangelical institutions scurrying to reassure worried trustees, donors, and conservative churches. *Battle* dropped like a bombshell at Gordon-Conwell, linked as it was in the mind of the evangelical public with Fuller Seminary. Harold Ockenga, then president of Gordon-Conwell, even wrote the foreword to Lindsell's book, hoping, I suspect, to forestall any populist inquisition.

On campus, in the years immediately preceding my arrival, however, inquisition became inevitable within the faculty. As a group, the New Testament professors were noticeably more liberal than the increasingly powerful and reactionary theology department. Within three years of my arrival at the school, these conservatives effectively silenced the more liberal faculty voices by filling open positions with new scholars whose views matched their own. A couple of progressive professors remained—disheartened and isolated in marginal departments.

Although we could not see it then, Gordon-Conwell was somewhat typical of the trend during the 1980s. During that decade, after a brief flirtation with a more progressive style in the 1970s, American evangelicalism turned back to the right. The Southern Baptists, for example, fell victim to a self-styled fundamentalist takeover. Denominational conservatives, worried about the erosion of biblical inerrancy in their churches, slowly repositioned the governing boards and theological seminaries to limit theological diversity. Inerrancy became the litmus test of Southern Baptist orthodoxy. Throughout major evangelical institutions, biblical inerrantists forged a political and theological coalition that would eventually have a profound effect on American life as a whole. Some of my Gordon-Conwell classmates, especially the ones who embraced the Calvinist agenda, eventually became leaders in a number of religious right causes and organizations. I would see them again when I covered the 1996 Republican National Convention for the *New York Times* regional newspapers.

Evangelical worries over authority are nothing new. Whenever the larger culture faced a crisis of authority—such as the Civil War or the theological crisis around Darwinism—evangelicals reasserted doctrines of biblical authority to bolster their intellectual and political position in society. Not surprisingly, *Battle for the Bible* appeared about the same time my high school classmates put bumper stickers on their cars reading, "Question Authority." And *Battle* was not an arcane, in-house theological text. It was a jeremiad, a kind of spiritual call to arms, for evangelicals to get their act together and attack immorality. Harold Lindsell's book naturally led to Jerry Falwell's Moral Majority and Pat Robertson's Christian Coalition.

On the heels of the 1960s cultural crisis, when every kind of authority—political, moral, religious, and legal—was questioned and, as some argue, completely and finally undermined, evangelicals insisted on the absolute authority of an inerrant Scripture. Some powerful Gordon-Conwell professors deeply objected to the political and social movements of the 1960s. That the school would reassert biblical authority, wrapped in a dogmatically precise Calvinist package of classical evangelical piety and the politics of the religious right, should have surprised no one. By 1984 they had made their position clear. No Catholics or liberals—and no one suspected of being either—were welcome on Holy Hill.

Anglicanism was born in an earlier crisis of questioning authority— in the sixteenth and seventeenth centuries. Then, Protestants questioned a thousand years of Catholic tradition and insisted that authority lay elsewhere—outside the magisterium of the Catholic Church. Richard Hooker, a leading theologian in the Church of England, developed a different take on authority than did his Lutheran and Calvinist peers. Hooker formally assented to the Protestant principle of "the Bible alone," but he also articulated the notion that Christian authority was a three-legged stool. Scriptures reveal God's will but they should be interpreted by human reason with the guidance of Christian tradition. Scripture, reason, tradition.

Although Hooker depicted the Bible as the thickest leg of the stool, his followers would emphasize the balance between the three supports. Anglicanism would eventually insist on both Protestant individual conscience and Catholic dependence on tradition. In time, the three-legged stool became foundational to the Anglican *via media,* its "middle way" between extreme Protestantism and

Roman Catholicism. Anglicanism would develop a reputation of being moderate, reasonable, and tolerant.

Historically, middle ways have a tough time holding. In the seventeenth century, both extreme Protestantism (the Puritans) and a nostalgic yearning for Roman Catholicism (the High Church party) pulled Anglican comprehensiveness to the breaking point. Although Christ Church looked to the theological shenanigans upon the hill with disdain, a different problem regarding authority was beginning to arise in its midst. For the most part, Christ Church was a happy place in the early and mid-1980s. There were no major conflicts in the parish during those years. But there were tensions—tensions that were often centered around the nature of authority in a comprehensive church. For extreme Protestants and for Roman Catholics, authority is not much of a problem. You know what authority is, the content of what you are supposed to believe, and how to act. The only question is whether or not you obey it. But for centrist traditions like those of mainstream Protestantism, answers can be more difficult to discern.

Although the clergy and many of the parishioners at Christ Church embraced the creative ambiguities of the middle way, others were not always happy with Anglicanism's lack of clarity. Extremists within the congregation began to question the basis of theological authority within the Episcopal tradition. There were four major interest groups in the church: the Old Guard "hunt club" set, progressive evangelicals, conservative evangelicals, and Anglo-Catholics.

The Old Guard, the heirs of the church's founders, maintained a certain stabilizing presence in the church. Linnae noted that "everything swirled around them but nothing swayed them." The progressive evangelicals were generally liberal in their politics and broadly orthodox in their theology, and they expressed support for the policies and ideals of the denomination. The conservative evangelicals were usually related to the college and seminary and sometimes were not even Episcopalians—they were often long-term attendees who maintained ties with Presbyterian or Baptist churches. The Anglo-Catholics were theologically conservative and embraced the "highest" form of churchmanship in the parish. They prayed to the saints, venerated the Virgin Mary, genuflected before the altar, and held to the doctrine of transubstantiation—that the Eucharist was the actual body and blood of Christ.

These diverse groups did hold things in common. With the exception of the Old Guard, Gordon and Gordon-Conwell professors, students, and alumni could be found in every camp. They shared a history of growing up in evangelicalism. A few in the Gordon crowd remained rigorously evangelical in piety and Calvinist in doctrine—many of these people had been quite supportive of the classically Anglican evangelical congregation Jim Hampson had created. They felt uncomfortable with Mark Dyer's catholic Anglicanism, while most of the Gordon people liked and respected the rector.

Despite the huge numbers of Gordon parishioners, the Old Guard were not outcasts in their own church. Like the conservative evangelicals and the Anglo-Catholics, they were politically and socially right-wing. Usually, their conservatism was not theological but was expressed in terms of tradition: "That's not the way we do things at Christ Church."

Thus the hunt club/conservative evangelical/Anglo-Catholic coalition held a tremendous amount of power at the church. Nowhere was it more clearly manifested than around the issue of women's ordination. Mark Dyer's wife, Marie Elizabeth, was ordained to the priesthood, but Christ Church remained largely opposed to women priests. The Old Guard opposed women in ministry on the basis of social traditionalism. The conservative evangelicals opposed it on the basis of their literal reading of the Bible. The Anglo-Catholics opposed it on the basis of historic Christian practice. Only the progressive evangelicals (some who even eschewed the term *evangelical*) and the clergy supported it! For several years, the vestry regularly turned down female aspirants to the ministry, whereas numerous men were admitted as postulants. A number of those women are now Episcopal priests, but they had to go elsewhere to find support.

Women's ordination was an extremely difficult issue at the church. The anxiety around it was palpable. In 1976 the Episcopal Church had officially approved of women in the priesthood, and many traditionalists saw this—along with the new Prayer Book—as an assault on Christian orthodoxy. Throughout the church, parishes refused to let women celebrate the Eucharist—and refused to hire them.

At Christ Church, a leading opponent of women's ordination was Elisabeth Elliot, an evangelical celebrity whose first husband, Jim Elliot, had been killed by a native Indian tribe while serving as a missionary in Ecuador. After his death, she returned to Ecuador and worked among those who had murdered him. She wrote a best-selling account, *Through Gates of Splendor,* about her experiences. By 1982, however, she was best known for her defense of traditional roles for women. She had just published a book, *Let Me Be a Woman,* extolling wifely submission. She based her beliefs on a literal reading of the Apostle Paul: "Wives, submit to your husbands," "I allow no woman to have authority over a man," and "Women are to remain silent in church." To her, women's ordination was clearly unbiblical. Simple and straightforward, just as it says in the inerrant, authoritative Word of God. Elliot was an icon to the Christ Church conservative evangelicals.

She was also Tom Howard's sister. Tom Howard opposed women's ordination as well—but for rather different reasons from those of his better-known sibling. Although he would later say to a reporter, "I'm a fundamentalist when it comes to the Word of God." Howard understood that a simple appeal to scriptures was not enough to forestall women's ordination. Plenty of Episcopalians—some of his fellow parishioners—believed the Bible supported female priesthood. According to them, Paul's directives had to be interpreted within the context in which they had been written. Properly understood, they argued, St. Paul did not forbid women from serving as ministers. Rather, Paul had envisioned a Christian church where, in his words, "there is no longer male or female, but all are one in Christ Jesus." Women are not to be submissive participants but rather full partners in mutual ministry with Christian men.

Instead of appealing to the Bible alone, Howard cited Catholic tradition, the faith that Jesus handed down through the apostles (who were, by God's design, all men) and guarded by the church for two millennia. In its insistence on a male priesthood, the Roman Catholic Church was correct and simply following the ancient church dictum of doing what "all Christians everywhere and at all times" have done. In college I had accepted the progressive evangelical understanding of Paul's theology regarding women's right to preach. At Christ Church, however, Howard's appeal to Catholic tradition shook me. Had the church really been wrong for two thousand years? What gave us the right to overturn two millennia of Christian tradition?

After his own conversion to the Episcopal Church, Howard must have been surprised by the quick succession of changes in the 1970s—first the liturgy, then women priests. What next? Inclusive language? Homosexual marriage and ordination? Where would it stop? In his later spiritual autobiography, *Lead Kindly Light,* Howard writes, "As an Anglican I felt that I was in some sense 'catholic,' but I was unhappy that the church to which I had given my allegiance was reluctant to speak authoritatively, *as a church,* on just what we, the laity, were to believe. This was a state of affairs that would have been unimaginable to our Fathers in Faith in the early days of the Church." Of course, Howard overlooked that the Episcopal Church had spoken authoritatively: Women will be priests. He did not believe the Episcopal Church possessed the authority to, as he saw it, reject two thousand years of Christian practice.

Behind the words of his criticism lay Christ Church's internal struggle regarding authority. Even though Marie Elizabeth Dyer was a priest and would later be quite successful in her ministry, she was so low-key at Christ Church that she was almost invisible. Linnae recalls that "it appeared she had staged a strategic disappearing act, knowing the controversy she could cause." Mark's catholic piety, orthodox theology, and political savvy steadied the parish. As long as he remained in charge, the more extremist elements stayed in line. In the autumn of 1982, however, he left Christ Church and became the bishop of Bethlehem, Pennsylvania.

Christ Church struggled to recover from Mark Dyer's departure. His assistant, the Rev. Titus Presler, who followed him for a year as interim rector, graciously guided Christ Church until a new priest was found. In 1983 the Rev. Barry Howe arrived to serve as the church's new rector. Titus and Barry shared Mark's liturgical sensitivities and catholic sense of prayer and spirituality, but they were both more overtly liberal in their theology and views of the larger Episcopal Church. On a grander theological scale, Barry was rather moderate. But at Christ Church, moderate meant "liberal."

Barry Howe was a gracious man, tolerant and gentle, a fine pastor, and probably the most thoroughly Anglican parson I have known. He always seemed the perfect rector for an English countryside parish. At Christ Church, however, his toleration for diversity made him appear theologically fuzzy—especially in contrast with Mark Dyer's clarity. Even before he was hired, numerous members of the search committee called him and quizzed him on his theological views, asking, "Are you an evangelical?" Barry admits that "I never got a clear picture of what that meant." After he arrived it became clearer: he attests that he never served a parish where so many people were absorbed "by the business of theological certainty." He had never been around evangelicals before. Evangelicals insist on certainty. Even ex-ones or genuflecting ones. I worried he was out of place—an Anglican lamb in an evangelical foxhole.

Tom Howard was looking for theological certainty. He wanted to be as certain of the Truth as was his sister Elisabeth. In that quest, he struggled with both evangelical and Catholic conceptions of authority. He published a book stating his conclusion in the title: *Evangelical Is Not Enough*. We students, some of whom had been his students, watched the twists and turns of his journey and debated his every move. Unnoticed by much of the congregation, he had us in an uproar over the nature of authority—and the issues related to women's ordination. For a time, it was impossible to attend a discussion or have brunch together without someone raising the issues of whether the Bible was the inerrant Word of God, whether the Episcopal Church was orthodox, and whether the Roman Catholic Church was the only true church. The seminarians moved between the Calvinists on the hill, who insisted only that they were right, and the growing discontented Catholic faction at Christ Church. In the midst of it all, Tom Howard found peace. On Easter Vigil, 1985, he joined the Roman Catholic Church. At the time, I envied him his ability to choose.

I wondered what path I would take—Calvinist or Catholic? *Sola Scriptura* or the authority of the Pope? Was there another road?

I remember that Easter Vigil at Christ Church. Surrounded by all these quests for certainty, the Vigil provided a liturgical respite amid the theological stress and gave us all a sense of God's presence. Since the first time I experienced the Vigil at Christ Church in 1983, the Easter Eve liturgy had become the high point of the Christian year for me. In many ways, its breathtaking beauty, its ability to draw me into the heart of God's story, was the power that drew and held me within the Episcopal Church.

With Tom Howard's conversion, it became harder to resist the Calvinist faction at school. Against some of my deepest spiritual sensibilities, I began siding with them. Their arguments seemed so logical. Howard's conversion startled me. Maybe the only two options were Roman Catholicism and Calvinism. I read nearly everything written by John Henry Newman, the great nineteenth-century apologist for Roman Catholicism, but I questioned his theological conclusions. I felt pretty sure I was a Protestant—no matter how unattractive its expression at Gordon-Conwell. I could not become a Roman Catholic. But Newman managed to undermine my confidence in the Anglican *via media*. I was beginning to feel theologically adrift.

Another factor pushed me toward the Calvinist camp. In 1984, still mourning the end of my relationship with Steve, I married Buck Butler, a Californian who had graduated from a Calvinist seminary outside Philadelphia. We met at a mission conference in Edinburgh, Scotland. Five years older than I, Buck possessed intense theological certainty. His clarity served as a refreshing corrective to my confusion. We planned to become missionaries and wanted to teach in an African seminary. The relationship supplied a sense of vision and purpose that I had lacked.

However, Buck only tolerated the Episcopal Church on my behalf. His friends tried to get me to leave the Episcopal Church and join their small, fundamentalist Presbyterian denomination. Whenever I attended his church—which met in an ugly, ramshackle sanctuary—I would weep. The Calvinists in that congregation thought I displayed a remarkable spiritual sensitivity to the preaching of God's word. But I was sobbing because I missed the Eucharist and all the heartbreaking beauty of the liturgy. I missed stained-glass windows. No matter how illogical, I missed the *via media*. I tried, but I could not return to spiritually austere Protestantism. I begged to go back to Christ Church, where we might combine his Calvinism with my need for a more mystical, mysterious sense of God's presence. He eventually agreed.

Despite my continued connection with Christ Church, it appeared to my friends that I was throwing my lot with the Calvinists. I was, however, vaguely aware that I was already following a different path, one springing from the liturgy itself, winding its way through ancient cadences and ritual, which eventually would bring me to the heart of Episcopal understandings of faith. I was following the way of *lex orandi, lex credendi*, "the law of prayer, the law of faith." Put simply, liturgical worship was leading me to a new theological place, and prayer was pointing the way beyond where my intellect could then take me. Or what I could express. Conversely, nascent theological insights were reshaping my entire understanding of worship and prayer. The weekly liturgy, whose meaning and power was summed up in the Easter Vigil, guided me. I could not go back.

Just a few years off into the future, the theological either/or of the Calvinists and Roman Catholics would leave me cold.

Slowly, with no overt understanding, I was rewriting my internal theology on the basis of my experience in worship. I did not fully realize it, but I was beginning to experience God's love, inclusive and embracing in its reach. A love without boundaries, a love without dogma, a love without political agendas and holy wars. God's love. Catherine of Siena's vast sea. No wonder I felt adrift. I was. But I was not, as I feared, lost. I was adrift on the sea of God's love and it scared me. I wanted both to keep going and to find stable ground.

The liturgy was like a lighthouse—a beacon pointing the way. The way started, of course, in the summer of 1980, with that Eucharist in Westminster Abbey. In the spring of 1983, my first Easter at Christ Church—two years before Tom Howard and Buck—the Great Vigil of Easter shined as that beacon.

Lent is serious business for Episcopalians. Although Roman Catholics, Orthodox Christians, Lutherans, and some Presbyterians observe Lent, many Protestants almost ignore it. As a child, I do not remember hearing about Lent from the pulpit of St. John's United Methodist. Growing up in Catholic Baltimore, however, even young Methodists like me noticed something was going on in those weeks leading up to Easter. After all, some of my classmates had dirty smears on their foreheads and refused to eat the food served in the school cafeteria. My Catholic friends said that it was "spiritual preparation" for Easter.

Spiritual preparation for Easter? My Methodist mother prepared for Easter by making new dresses for my sister and me, outfitting us in pretty pastel coats and beribboned hats, and secretly assembling huge baskets of chocolate bunnies and jellybeans. My agnostic freethinking grandfather chalked Lent up to "superstition," a medieval throwback practiced by people who also prayed to statues. Enlightened Methodists went to church twice for Easter—on

Maundy Thursday to remember Jesus' final earthly meal and on Easter Sunday itself.

Although I first experienced Lent at All Saints in Santa Barbara, the full power of it was not evident to me until Christ Church in 1983. For all their insistence on theological certainty, Christ Church parishioners spiritually reveled in the ecclesiastical drama of Lent. Beginning with Ash Wednesday, they clearly understood themselves as a people on a journey through sorrow, suffering, and death to joy. As the season approached, I distinctly remember one of my friends, Ray Graves, saying "I love Lent," extolling its spiritual virtues. Never having experienced it at Christ Church, I thought he was a little nutty. "You love Lent?" I asked. "Just wait," he said, "until the Great Vigil of Easter."

I waited and I went to as many services as I could squeeze into my schedule—especially during Holy Week. Lent's forty-day fast leads to the great liturgical reenactment of Jesus' final days—the Triduum, in which Christians participate in three services in three days: Maundy Thursday, Good Friday, and the Great Vigil of Easter on Saturday night. I remember sitting in shocked silence when, at the end of the Maundy Thursday liturgy, the clergy and altar guild stripped the altar and covered the crosses with black cloth. They removed any signs of God's presence among us. It was as if someone had died—but it was far worse than any funeral I had ever attended. No joy, no hope. Just a cold, empty, white sanctuary. As we departed, no one said a word.

On the next day, Good Friday, the church was hushed and dimly lit. As early as 416 C.E., Christians would not celebrate the Eucharist on Good Friday, and it remains the single day during the church year when the elements cannot be consecrated. Instead, we read long passages of the Bible, including the Passion of Christ, listened to a sermon, and prayed a long litany of requests for the whole state of the church and the world called The Solemn Collects. For three hours we were imaginatively drawn to Calvary, where Jesus hung bleeding, racked in pain, for the sin of the world. The whole thing was so dignified, so spiritually weighty, that even the conservative Presbyterians and Baptists from the seminary who attended could not refrain from sobbing.

But nothing matched the power of Easter Vigil. My friends and I arrived at the church early that Saturday night, chilled by the still wintry wind of a New England spring. It was dark outside. And it was dark inside. All the lights were off and ushers gave us small unlit candles and helped us to the pews. After several minutes in the black silence, I heard a noise from behind. I looked back. To my surprise, Titus Presler stood near the door. Surrounded by the altar party, he was kindling a fire at the baptismal font. It was so quiet that I could hear his robes rustling as the flame flickered and snapped. When he succeeded in making the fire, he looked up and said,

"Dear friends in Christ: On this most holy night, in which our Lord Jesus passed over from death to life, the Church invites her members, dispersed throughout the world, to gather in vigil and prayer. For this is the Passover of the Lord, in which, by hearing his Word and celebrating his Sacraments, we share in his victory over death." He prayed over the fire and lit the huge Paschal Candle with its flame.

Holding the candle, he walked down the aisle, stopped suddenly and chanted, "The light of Christ." We responded, "Thanks be to God." As he resumed walking, others in the party passed the flame throughout the church to light our candles. Slowly, as Titus continued to chant, those candles lit the whole sanctuary, and we held them in intense anticipation. I could see that the congregation was smaller than usual—the parish's hardiest churchgoers. With its plain white walls, the sanctuary resembled a large cavern, a catacomb perhaps, and we, like a holy remnant of the faithful in ancient Rome, were gathered in secret to celebrate the Resurrection of our Lord. It is an ancient service, nearly as old as Christianity itself—one that liturgically dramatizes what it means to be a disciple of Jesus.

In the hours—yes, hours—that followed, we sat in the candlelight and listened to eight lengthy passages of Hebrew scripture recalling God's love toward his people. In response to each, we read a psalm or listened to a choral anthem. After the readings, parents brought their children to be baptized and adult converts submitted themselves to the ancient rite. As it had been nearly two thousand years ago, the priest asked each a sacred litany of questions:

Do you renounce Satan and all the spiritual forces of wickedness that rebel against God?
I renounce them.
Do you renounce the evil powers of this world which corrupt and destroy the creatures of God?
I renounce them.
Do you renounce all sinful desires that draw you from the love of God?
I renounce them.
Do you turn to Jesus Christ and accept him as your Savior?
I do.
Do you put your whole trust in his grace and love?
I do.
Do you promise to follow and obey him as your Lord?
I do.

The responses resounded off Christ Church's white walls. Loud and strong: "I renounce them. I renounce them. I do. I do." Inwardly, I renounced everything, too. I gave myself anew to God.

There, in the semidarkness, the water of God washed clean weary seekers. Together, we renewed our baptismal vows to continue in fellowship, resist evil, proclaim the Good News, seek and serve Christ, and strive for justice and peace. I will, with God's help. I will, with God's help.

And then, with no warning, it happened. Titus shouted: "Alleluia! Christ is risen! The Lord has risen indeed! Alleluia!" A trumpet. The lights broke the darkness. The congregation reached for bells, hidden in purses and pockets, and rang them. "Alleluia! Alleluia! Alleluia!" The choir led us: "All glory be to God on high and peace on earth from heaven." Next to me, Linnae was weeping. Beyond her, Ray Graves was crying. I was crying. Throughout the sanctuary, everyone was crying, singing, hugging, laughing, and ringing bells. The ecclesiastical mayhem went on for five or ten minutes as Christ Church celebrated with spiritual abandon. The Day of Resurrection! Jesus conquered death and the devil. We were free.

Even now, as I remember that night, I still get chills. Christ Church was a brainy group constantly worried about theological certainty, but Easter Vigil was neither an exercise in intellectual assent nor an orthodoxy test. It was a moment when the boundaries between heaven and earth thinned—where we actually knew ourselves to be God's pilgrim people, wanderers following God's way of love and justice. Of that moment, Episcopal theologian Patricia Wilson-Kastner has written, "Liturgy reconnects us with God and with all creation, rekindles in us the vision of the restoration of all in God, and clarifies and nourishes again in us the hope by which we can live now in justice, peace, and love with each other." At Christ Church, we came so close that there were times when you could almost touch God.

That was true in 1985 as well, with Tom Howard gone and Buck at my side, when we walked the same way with Barry Howe. When

I felt so adrift. The beacon of the liturgy, the power of Easter Vigil, was still pointing the way toward a country I could not quite see.

I love theology. But over the years I have begun to think God might not. Too often, Christians have made idols of their own particular theologies, resulting in terrible repression, oppression, and persecution. The problem, however, is not theology per se. It is when the church separates theology from prayer, from its life with God. We forget that *lex orandi, lex credendi*—"the law of prayer, the law of faith"—is the way of a connected life. In an Anglican vision, prayer and faith inform and intertwine with each other in a circle of spiritual wholeness.

Evangelicals honor both prayer and faith, but the two could be—and often are—separated. Prayer is something you do. Faith is something you have. At Gordon-Conwell, people prayed before class and people studied to find truth. But prayer and faith were not truly integrated, not part of a singular vision of God. Prayer and faith were more of a formula, a kind of spiritual math problem. *Heart* plus *mind* equals *good Christian*. Evangelicals argue about heart and mind. Some emphasize prayer over belief; others, theology over piety. While I was at Gordon-Conwell, those who elevated theological certainty over heartfelt devotion won the day. Some professors would actually sneer at "the pietists." When such theologians get the upper hand, crusades are a sure result.

In American evangelicalism, prayer and belief do not spring from a common source and are often at odds. In the Episcopal liturgy, however, they are two aspects of the same thing. Sometimes—most times—Episcopalians cannot tell them apart.

No wonder I felt torn. I was moving between two traditions with exactly opposite approaches to being faithful. Although I was not conscious of the problem at the time, my seminary education was completely at odds with my spiritual formation in worship and prayer. Gordon-Conwell was pushing me toward either pietism or intellectualism. They wanted me to pick which theology I would embrace, which evangelical camp to join, and how I would serve Jesus. Christ Church was pulling me toward experiential theology, a way of living the practices of prayer, loving God, and being the body of Christ in the world. Gordon-Conwell was about choosing. The liturgy was about being formed by something larger than I was myself.

As an Episcopalian, a person being shaped by worship, I was about to be pushed by God into a new and unexpected theological direction. I would glimpse that direction when Bishop David Johnson visited Christ Church in the spring of 1986.

Although the name *Episcopal* is derived from the Greek word *episcopos,* meaning *overseer* and translated as *bishop,* Episcopalians often have a difficult time with their leaders. In the New Testament, this person was a spiritually mature leader who was given authority in the church. Bishops eventually came to be seen as those who administered a diocese, ensured uniformity in Christian practice, and guarded orthodox doctrine. Since that time, bishops have alternated between being a blessing and a curse to the church. Sometimes they interfered too much with local congregations. Sometimes they ignored important matters in the church. Many Protestant churches rejected bishops—partly, I think, because bishops created so much trouble historically.

Most Episcopalians do not see their bishops very often. The bishop comes around once a year to confirm new members or if the parish is celebrating a special event. Once in a while, some trendy one, like Bishop Jack Spong of Newark, New Jersey, will grab headlines by proclaiming the Virgin Birth to be a myth or asserting that the Resurrection never happened. But as religious authorities go, our bishops tend to be a relatively benign group—not like the Roman ones about whom my Catholic friends complain.

Despite the fact that both Mark Dyer and Barry Howe became bishops, Christ Church had much antipathy toward bishops, especially the bishop of Massachusetts, as well as those running the denomination—all of whom they suspected were hopelessly liberal and spiritually deficient. So when, in 1985, the Diocese of Massachusetts elected David Johnson as its new bishop, Christ Church worried whether or not he would be "orthodox" and a "real Christian." Would he allow them to continue to remain aloof from diocesan concerns regarding women's ordination, inclusive language, and the place of gay and lesbian persons in the denomination? Or would he force them down a theological road they did not want to go?

Whatever the congregation's worries, however, David Johnson's election pleased Barry Howe. The two men had been friends for several years and Barry thought highly of the new bishop. This friendship increased the tension between Barry and the more extreme elements in his congregation—quite a few of whom thought their rector was too cozy with the denominational hierarchy and who therefore resented his attempts to bring them into line with diocesan policies. He had managed to get a few parishioners involved with the larger diocese. And he skillfully navigated vestry politics to get support for a Christ Church woman, Dudley Cleghorn, to be the congregation's first female candidate for ordination. He even let her preach in Christ Church's pulpit. Many people were not happy.

Early in his ministry, Bishop Johnson conducted a sort of diocesan listening tour. Christ Church, as one of the largest churches in the diocese, was picked to host one of these events. When the day arrived, Christ Church's long-standing antipathy was exacerbated by worries that their rector might have somehow betrayed them. In the weeks before the bishop's visit, I heard comments like "Perhaps Barry just doesn't fit here" and "Maybe we hired the wrong person." As Buck and I drove to church, I suspected a hostile audience might ambush the new bishop.

The parish hall was full. Other local congregations sent representatives, but most people were from Christ Church. The bishop told a number of stories about settling in the diocese—and some amusing anecdotes about feeling culture shock in New England. He expressed some of his hopes for the diocese and talked of renovating the cathedral center. He made some vague theological statements about inclusion and openness. Finally, he asked for questions.

Lovelace Howard, Tom's wife, who had remained at Christ Church, raised her hand. Smiling, Bishop Johnson called on her. Clearly he did not expect what followed. For the next ten minutes, the two had a heated exchange about moral issues. Johnson argued that women's ordination and homosexuality were complex issues and that the church had to carefully consider its theological position on such things. Lovelace was not satisfied. "What about the church's moral authority?" she protested. "The church must be clear on these issues. What about the Ten Commandments? Are we to teach our children that they are merely suggestions, guidelines? You can't do that. You have to teach children the rules."

Johnson tried to dodge direct theological questions. But the inquisition continued, and that strategy became impossible. A number of parishioners quizzed him on his position regarding controversial issues and theology. They did not like his answers. As the meeting progressed, I noticed that Barry had moved to the back of the room. He looked pained, as if he wanted to escape through the kitchen door. Part of me appreciated the courage of my fellow parishioners, but another part recoiled as their level of theological indignation grew. I wanted to join Barry. Just as I was seriously considering the kitchen door myself, to my complete horror, an emboldened Buck raised his hand.

"Bishop Johnson," he began. "It says in the book of Timothy that the bishop is to guard the gospel. Sir, listening to you, I cannot discern what you are guarding. Can you tell us, please, exactly what you think the gospel is?"

Every person in the room was staring directly at us. I was shaking uncontrollably and deeply embarrassed by this doctrinal exam. Not a person moved. If the bishop thought the question inappropriate, he did not let on.

Instead, he leaned back against the podium, looked first at Buck, and then, slowly, cast his gaze around the entire room. He unfolded his arms—which he had held across his chest—and stretched them out so widely that he almost looked like Jesus hanging on the cross. "God," he said deliberately. "God loves everybody."

"Well, yes," Buck started to protest, "but . . . ."

"God loves everybody," he replied. "That's it."

"But . . ."

"God loves everybody."

To this day, I am not sure what Buck expected. Did he want Bishop Johnson to recite the Apostle's Creed? Some statement affirming the Trinity? A Bible verse? "For God so loved the world that he gave his only begotten son so that everyone who believes in him may not perish, but may have eternal life." I know, however, that he did not expect those three words: "God loves everybody." And I do not think anyone else quite expected it either.

The bishop was, of course, correct. This terse statement summed up Jesus' message and the whole of biblical history. But it was not what a roomful of evangelicals, ex- or otherwise, wanted to hear. It was theologically sentimental; it was tenderhearted liberal mushiness. God loves everybody? Did that mean homosexuals? Notorious sinners? Those who reject scripture and ancient creeds? The liberals down at Harvard Divinity School? Jews, Muslims, Buddhists? God loves everybody was nothing less than a slippery slope. If you start down that road, where will it stop? Who is in God's kingdom and who is out? I knew this was not going to play well at Christ Church.

But I heard it. Suddenly, and quite unexpectedly, I knew that that squishy liberal bishop was right and I was wrong. God really did love everybody—including all the people I thought were excluded from the reach of the gospel. I had limited God's mercy— just like the Calvinists, who insisted that God predestined only some to be saved, and the Catholics, who said that theirs was the only true church. The bishop said no. No limits. God loves everybody. God's love is as vast as the universe and as difficult to comprehend as eternity itself. God's only boundary is love.

In my early twenties I wanted boundaries because I was afraid of a faith with no rules, afraid of spiritual and moral disorder. I felt I needed someone to tell me who God was, what to believe, how to behave, and what to do with my life. I wanted religious authority. And there, on that day in the Christ Church parish hall, I began to understand that orderliness is not faith and certainty is no substitution for grace.

My desire for certainty, for a kind of moral and theological discipline, marked me as a child of my time. In the late 1970s and early 1980s, many people were seeking order and assurance. It was apparent that some people at Christ Church and nearly everyone at the seminary wanted boundaries, too. But not all. Mark Dyer, Titus Presler, and Barry Howe had all tried to push back the boundaries at Christ Church. That, of course, met with resistance. Too many people wanted boundaries.

Mark, Titus, and Barry were, however, aided by the liturgy itself. When we worshiped together, even the most rigid among us felt the boundaries dissolve when—in those thin places like Easter Vigil—heaven and earth conjoined. We may have been uptight evangelicals intent on theological purity, but we were being shaped by a liturgy that weekly reminded us that Jesus had "stretched out his arms upon the cross, and offered himself, in obedience to God's will, a perfect sacrifice for the whole world." The whole world is invited to God's feast. In the liturgy we understood that we were guests at that banquet—not the one who sent out the invitations. God's love had drawn us all. We knew it, but some of us feared its implications.

In an article, Episcopal theologian Urban Holmes would write of that liturgy: "The 1979 Book of Common Prayer, with its emphasis upon God as creator, proclaims a Gospel with public consequences. The spirit of the prayer book is inclusive, not exclusive. This means that it both expects theological differences among those who participate in its rites and provokes those who find it necessary to be sectarian to reject its theological implications. There is no way to insist upon uniformity of belief."

When I read those words in Holmes's essay "Education for Liturgy: An Unfinished Symphony in Four Movements," the evangelical seminarian in me recoiled in horror. I had joined an inclusive church? What did that mean? How could you have a church with no "uniformity of belief"? But the woman at prayer—whose inner life had been schooled for a half decade in liturgy—understood at some deep level. I understood because of Gethin Hughes and Mark Dyer, because of Titus Presler and Barry Howe. I understood because worship was teaching me.

Barry Howe left a year after the Bishop Johnson debacle. Before departing, he told the vestry, "You know, the Episcopal Church isn't a doctrinal church; it is a liturgical one. When you hire a new priest, don't try to get behind his eyes." He was pushing them to recognize the ambiguities and paradox of faith, urging them to get beyond certainty, to understand the liturgy they loved, and to embrace what it was teaching them.

They appeared to ignore his advice. Despite their desire to be Anglican, they too were caught in the tension between competing authorities. In their quest for certainty, they picked sides in the battle between Calvinist and Catholic. The church called a rigidly Calvinist minister who proceeded to dismantle the parish's entire liturgical tradition. In a matter of months, gone was Mark Dyer's catholic spirituality, gone was Titus Presler's passion for social justice, and gone was Barry Howe's Anglican pastoral toleration. The new man was going to make them a model evangelical Anglican parish—Calvinist and clear in its theology.

Christ Church craved theological certainty. But when they got it, it nearly destroyed them. The more pristine their new rector's theological message and the more authority he assumed, the more disheartened they became. It was like the ancient Hebrews who begged God for a king and were eventually destroyed by malevolent monarchs. Christ Church lost its gloriously messy diversity and fell into spiritual despair as the Calvinist rector tried to march them lockstep down the same theological road. Hundreds of people left. The congregation dwindled to a mere shadow of its former self. Brokenhearted over what they had lost, a remnant of the Christ Church faithful finally managed to dismiss him. Maybe they learned that the creative paradoxes of pluralism were their greatest strength. Maybe they are still learning.

I would not be there, however, to witness this struggle. By the time Barry's successor took charge, I had moved to Durham, North Carolina, to pursue doctoral studies at Duke University.

Prompted by Bishop Johnson's proclamation of the gospel, unnerved by Mark Dyer's small c catholicism, and worried about Barry Howe's tolerant comprehensiveness, I was growing inwardly uneasy about both Calvinism and evangelicalism. Outwardly, however, I was still hanging on to both and was hoping to find some place where they would be affirmed. What I did not know was that I, too, was about to learn an unpleasant lesson in the quest for certainty.

CHAPTER THREE

The Establishment

ST. STEPHEN'S EPISCOPAL CHURCH

Durham, North Carolina, 1987–1989

Surrounded by the New South energy of North Carolina's Research Triangle, St. Stephen's sits hidden in the piney woods of Hope Valley, a tony suburb south of Durham and Duke University. Hope Valley was developed in the 1930s, around a country club and golf course, and it still boasts the gracious early-twentieth-century homes that provided Durham's upper class with splendid isolation from the crime and poverty of the working-class tobacco town. Amidst the rolling wooded hills and wide grassy lawns, Durham's early suburban pioneers endowed themselves with an English manorial past—tastefully naming their streets Windsor, Devon, Cornwall, Eton, Stratford, Avon, and the like. The Hope Valley Country Club served as the social mecca for the county's horse-and-debutante set. It was a world unto itself—a wealthy, white enclave far removed from the mostly poor and mostly black city.

In the early years, Episcopal residents of the neighborhood—and there were probably quite a few—drove to the city when they wanted to go to church. By the 1950s, as the Civil Rights movement threatened the historic patterns of segregation throughout the South, these developments had become worrisome for this well-heeled set. The oldest Episcopal congregation in Durham was poised precariously close to the bad side of town. Hope Valley needed a church nearby—code language for a "safe" church. At the annual Christmas Eve party at the Hope Valley Country Club, someone proposed that a new church be built in the neighborhood. On July 5, 1959, after two years of planning, St. Stephen's Episcopal Church held its first services at Hope Valley Elementary School. On Thanksgiving 1961, the congregation moved into its own building at its present location.

Few places in the United States have changed as much as has Durham in the last forty years. Social institutions are more or less integrated, a large and successful black middle class has overcome much of the poverty and exclusion faced by their ancestors, high-tech newcomers have displaced the old tobacco barons, and elegant subdivisions stand where sharecroppers once farmed. Despite all the changes, Hope Valley Road is still a main route out of the city into the county. Driving south past the golf course, St. Stephen's is off Rugby Road, marked by a small, hard-to-spot sign at the wooded intersection. The road curves uphill through the trees to a residential neighborhood. The church sits on the left and is surrounded by pines, a parish graveyard, and a memorial garden. St. Stephen's is a tranquil retreat hidden from the frenzied suburban development at its borders. If not for its modern architecture, visitors could easily believe that they had stepped into Durham's past—St. Stephen's has the feel of another era. As I came to know the parish, I was pretty sure that most of the old Hope Valley Episcopalians wanted it that way.

Despite the internal conflicts of my seminary years, I had done so well academically at Gordon-Conwell that my professors encouraged me to pursue a doctorate. In the summer of 1987 I moved to Durham to begin Ph.D. work in American religion at Duke University. Upon my arrival, I asked around for a "good Episcopal church." My graduate adviser, George Marsden, mentioned that a new rector had recently started at St. Stephen's. George had heard that the fellow was an evangelical Episcopalian. He had also heard that there had been "some trouble" around the rector's new ministry. Undaunted by this warning, Buck and I visited St. Stephen's, where we met Chip Nix and his wife, Carol, sometime shortly thereafter.

I immediately liked Chip and Carol, and we quickly became friends. We had much in common, including a number of mutual acquaintances. Chip was from Pittsburgh, where he had been involved in youth ministry and served as an assistant priest at St. Stephen's, Sewickley, Pennsylvania, a prominent evangelical Episcopal congregation. Although it is not widely known by people outside the denomination, the Episcopal Church comprises a number of overtly evangelical parishes—a network, really, of which Christ Church in Hamilton was a part. Evangelical Episcopalians, like other American evangelicals, stress personal conversion, sincere piety, moral certainty, and a literalist interpretation of the Bible and Christian creeds. Evangelical Episcopalians meld together the culture of American evangelicalism and the traditions of Episcopal prayer book religion. They also believe that their spiritual "take" on Anglicanism is the only biblical one and that most other Episcopalians have undermined true Christian faith—a claim that often puts them at odds with the rest of the denomination. Chip's church in Pennsylvania was a flagship parish in the movement.

Carol Nix was from England. Evangelical Episcopalians revere—and sometimes envy—their spiritual kin in the Church of England. British Anglicanism has a long and glorious history of evangelical religion, and evangelicals there, unlike their American counterparts, do not have to struggle for denominational recognition and legitimacy. Carol graduated from London Bible College and had been a popular and successful lay Bible teacher. Chip and Carol met in England, and both had been influenced by the Church of England's evangelical tradition—books by theologians and popular British writers like C. S. Lewis, J. I. Packer, and John Stott filled their shelves.

Theologically they were "soft Calvinists," believing in God's sovereignty and human sinfulness. But I doubt that either believed in the stricter tenets of that position, such as double predestination. These mysteries were better left in the hands of God. They were also very cultured people with well-cultivated tastes in travel, books, classical music, gardening, and tea. Every Sunday after church, they opened their home to friends, guests, and newcomers for brunch and conversation. The festivities often went on for hours as they entertained the many graduate students whom they had befriended. They were a generous and hospitable couple who knew the Bible, loved theology, and practiced a faithful life in prayer.

And they were passionate about evangelism. Not in an obnoxious stereotypical sort of way—like some street corner preacher shouting at everyone who walks by. Rather, Chip and Carol were quite convinced that without a living relationship with Jesus Christ a person would be doomed to eternal separation from God's presence. They wanted others to know God's love in salvation as they had experienced it themselves. They were like hundreds of other evangelicals I have known who share their faith because it has been important in their own lives and experience—not because other people are mere targets to be proselytized.

Chip and Carol also believed that the church was a "mission station," where those who know Jesus were trained as disciples to go out into the world and bring others into the fold. And it was also the place where the lost might find faith. To them, all churches that preached Jesus were, in a sense, equal. But they cherished their own Episcopal tradition, especially its history and liturgy, and thought it an especially appropriate vessel to carry God's Good News to the world. They also believed that the institutional church suffered a sort of spiritual ennui, a decline brought about by liberal theology and trendy social action. The church was thus in need of reform and renewal. They frequently pointed to the grand history of missionary endeavor in Anglicanism (next to Roman Catholics, Anglicans have sent out more missionaries than any other Christian tradition in the world) as a kind of spiritual precursor to their own ministry of mission and church renewal.

As I got to know them, I discovered that Chip and Carol came to Durham because they believed God had called them to serve Christ "in this strategic location between the universities and close to the Research Triangle Park." Indeed, Chip was well aware of the potential of a wealthy parish in this growing section of the county. In the late 1980s, forests to the east of Hope Valley were being turned into subdivisions. Hope Valley Farms, the largest, was just then breaking ground. Apartments, townhouses, and middle-class homes were slowly ringing the elite enclave. The Triangle, poised as it was on the edge of the high-tech revolution, proved an irresistible missionary venture to Chip as he imagined a congregation of thoughtful, issues-savvy, committed Christians who would be willing to win Durham and Chapel Hill's intellectual elite for Jesus. St. Stephen's, located halfway between Duke and the University of North Carolina (UNC), was perfectly situated to become parish headquarters for a vast network of activist evangelicals.

Although Chip's missionary plan may have seemed grandiose to some, it is a vision grounded in historical reality. Influenced by evangelical religion in the Church of England, Chip and Carol's ideal of an intellectual and socially elite Christian missionary community was modeled, loosely at least, on the Clapham parish church outside London at the beginning of the nineteenth century. There, prominent members of English society—such as MP William Wilberforce, philanthropist Zachary Macaulay, and author Hannah Moore—practiced an intentional and communal life of prayer and Christian discipleship.

As a result of their passionate faith, the Claphamites embarked on a number of missionary causes, including the expansion of British Sunday schools and the abolition of the slave trade. They were conservatives who believed in a divinely ordered society, but they also believed that the best way to preserve order was with measured reform, extending justice to all through charity, education, and incremental political change. Some historians credit the Clapham evangelicals, especially Wilberforce, with ending English slavery. In the wake of the French Revolution, English evangelicals worked to avoid social upheaval through religious conversion, an increase of morality, and good works. Evangelical Episcopalians count the Claphamites among their greatest heroes. I had studied about Clapham in seminary and longed to be part of a community that combined intense spiritual devotion and social justice.

Many evangelicals, good people like Chip and Carol, feel that modern American society is as corrupt and religiously callous as was early nineteenth-century England. Like the Claphamites, they believe the surest course for avoiding violence and complete moral disintegration is that of inward personal change—convert individuals and society will be "converted" as well. According to such evangelicals, America's technology and intellectual, political, and cultural frontiers are key for the conversion of all society. If the elite embrace Jesus and his message, they, like the Claphamites, can change the actual structures of government and social policy so that God's will may be done on this earth as in heaven.

As Chip himself said, the Triangle was "strategic" for the gospel. "I was there," he confesses, "as a domestic missionary." Its pews filled with born-again Episcopal researchers, doctors, lawyers, and professors, St. Stephen's could be a kind of contemporary Clapham in an age of global technological revolution. And in the case of St. Stephen's, the mission would be funded by a multimillion-dollar endowment held in trust by the church's powerful foundation. It was a heady vision.

From the moment of their arrival at St. Stephen's in 1987, Chip and Carol embarked with zeal upon the project to renew the parish. Being an idealist myself, with all my passion for meaningful faith, I threw my lot with them. They combined evangelical piety, Episcopal liturgy, and Calvinist-leaning theology. Maybe I could get Bishop Johnson's disturbing "God loves everybody" out of my mind. It was so theologically wishy-washy. He could not have been right. I concluded that St. Stephen's was an answer to prayer—the place where I could solve some of the dilemmas raised by seminary and Christ Church. It was an easy choice to make.

Chip thought the parish was aware of this vision when they called him. Feeling the pressure from advancing suburban development, St. Stephen's recruited Chip because they "wanted to grow." He interpreted "wanted to grow" as the congregation's desire to do evangelism and mission work. Both rector and congregation would eventually discover that they were speaking different languages. From the outset, Chip's ministry would be troubled by miscommunication and misunderstanding.

Chip's first Sunday had been on Palm Sunday 1987, the day that marks the beginning of Holy Week. In advance of his arrival, he phoned some members of his new congregation and asked if they did "anything special" for Holy Week.

Each replied the same: "No. Nothing special."

Chip proceeded in a standard evangelical Holy Week way—with minimal liturgical fuss and resolutely "low church" piety—completely unlike the more elaborate liturgies Mark Dyer had celebrated at Christ Church. Most evangelical Episcopalians minimize Holy Week's Catholic-leaning spiritual practices in favor of a more Protestant-style Easter celebration. Generally, evangelical Episcopalians reject ritual as "ritualism," implying that it obscures the necessity for personal faith in Jesus Christ for salvation.

Thus, Chip offered the Eucharist on Maundy Thursday and held a simple, solemn service on Good Friday. No foot washing, no Stations of the Cross, no veneration of the cross, no Easter Vigil. When Sunday arrived, St. Stephen's magnificent organ trumpeted the victory of Christ and the St. Stephen's faithful turned out in their finest new clothes on a beautiful spring day. Chip preached about the certainty of Jesus' Resurrection. Both Chip and Carol felt relieved—their first Easter was a success, a portent of good things to come.

By Tuesday, however, the phone was ringing off the hook in the church office. Chip had unwittingly violated local tradition by eliminating services he did not know existed. Evidently, St. Stephen's followed an involved—and distinctively local—Holy Week tradition. Their "nothing special" was, indeed, very special to them. They were angry. Parish leaders had assumed that St. Stephen's liturgical practice was standard across the church. Chip had assumed that the parish was at least vaguely evangelical and that evangelicals did not like elaborate ritual. He only did what he was trained to do in the evangelical parish from which he had come.

The questions began: Why had he canceled all their services? Why had he preached such a long, revivalist-type Easter sermon? Was he really an Episcopalian? Almost immediately, the relationship between new rector and new congregation began to fall apart. Dan Willey, a member of the vestry who hired Chip, remembers: "When Chip came and started messing with the liturgy, they were really thrown for a loop. . . . For most of the people at St. Stephen's, at least the established people, there was no such thing as a minor change in the liturgy."

The Rev. Sam Mason, the current rector at St. Stephen's, later said of these events that the parish had "little or no awareness of evangelical theology or the evangelical subculture." Dan, who continued to support Chip, says that "the basic problem was that St. Stephen's had no idea what they were getting in Chip." Indeed, Chip's call to St. Stephen's was confusing from the outset. In 1986, as the church tried to find their new rector, they knew they needed to grow and they wanted, in some way, to serve the new neighborhoods around Hope Valley. They were vaguely aware of the Rev. John Guest, the well-known priest at St. Stephen's, Sewickley, who had been Chip's mentor. At that time, Guest's parish was one of the largest and fastest-growing churches in the country. Chip's connection with the Sewickley church and his interest in growth seemed to mesh with the parish's less-than-specific desire to increase its membership. They clearly did not expect that they would have to change as a result.

Chip's call to St. Stephen's in Durham was complicated by the fact that a small group of parishioners had been involved in Bible Study Fellowship, a large evangelical organization headed by Anne Graham Lotz, the daughter of Billy Graham, in Raleigh. Some St. Stephen's members had experienced an evangelical conversion through Lotz's ministry. They influenced a small segment of the congregation, who began to embrace evangelical religion. Thus Dan Willey could testify: "St. Stephen's is where I became a Christian and gave my life to Christ." The parish's few evangelicals were relatively discreet about their experiences, but they longed to renew their parish through Bible teaching and discipleship.

Although small in number, St. Stephen's evangelicals dominated the search committee that found Chip and convinced the vestry that he was the man for the job. The church issued him a unanimous call—against the will of the bishop, the Rt. Rev. Robert Estill, who reportedly had great reservations about the match between St. Stephen's and Chip. The congregation evidently took this as political interference from the diocesan office. There existed a long-standing rift between St. Stephen's and the bishop. They had a reputation for political conservatism, and Bishop Estill was a liberal. To the parish, it appeared that he did not want them to have "their kind" of priest. After trying to convince them otherwise, the bishop let them have their way.

Chip made it through that first Holy Week crisis and began to build the kind of congregation he had envisioned. A few people seemed angry and left—a fact offset by the arrival of many like-minded evangelical newcomers. By the summer of 1987, however, the bishop's reservations proved prophetic. While Chip and Carol were on vacation with their children, a group of parishioners started a letter-writing campaign, demanding that the bishop remove their new minister. With half of their vacation still ahead, Chip received a call from a member of the vestry, telling him his job was in danger.

The malcontents expressed anxiety about "all the new people coming." They listed three major objections to Chip's ministry: that he quoted the Bible too much, that he prayed extemporaneously instead of using the forms in the Book of Common Prayer, and that he had contradicted the bishop on issues of sexuality when interviewed by a television reporter. To them, Chip seemed more like a Baptist—a low-class Bible preacher—than a dignified Episcopal parson. Months after the letter, I can still recall some parishioners talking about what "an embarrassment" their new priest was to them. One woman, a well-connected layperson in the church's national governing structure, openly worried that Chip would make *her* church a laughingstock in the broader denomination.

Despite his reservations about Chip, Bishop Estill refused to give in to this pressure and encouraged the congregation to continue the relationship with their rector. After all, they had only recently argued that Chip was the right person for their position. For many months, Chip would try to work things out by attempting to build consensus, explaining his actions and creating his own leadership team in the congregation. He enlisted an assistant, the Rev. Stephen Freeman, a Southerner and a Duke graduate student, to help with liturgical and pastoral skills he lacked—attempting to fill in ministry gaps while he toiled to redirect the vision of the church toward his missionary endeavor.

With the bishop's backing, Chip and Carol hoped the worst had passed. They started Bible studies, a young adult fellowship, and a program for families; the parish hired a youth minister. Dan recalls that "things were great, at least from my standpoint. The preaching was good. I was learning lots from Chip and new people were coming to church, people who talked openly about Jesus and their faith." We were attempting to build up a church and felt a great deal of emotional and spiritual reward in the project. In just eighteen months, Sunday attendance nearly doubled—increasing from 120 to 225 people.

Chip wrote an adult education curriculum to help newcomers understand the Episcopal Church, inviting them to become members and grow in Christian faith. Eventually those materials formed the basis of Chip's Doctor of Ministry thesis, a book for newcomers to the Episcopal Church entitled *Open House*. In it he writes, "Finding the right church home is similar to hunting for a new house. . . . What we need is time and space to look things over as we explore, to walk around a bit, to sense the guidance of God as we walk through these new doors." It may have been a tough beginning, but Chip was pushing open the doors of St. Stephen's— doors long shut to outsiders.

People were walking through the doors of St. Stephen's. People who did not grow up in Hope Valley or Durham or North Carolina. Northerners, even. Californians, too. Like me. Much of the growth came from graduate students from the two universities. Some were young families who had relocated to the Triangle from other parts of the country. A few were former Southern Baptists or Presbyterians—folks looking for theological freedom or liturgical worship. Lots of them had come to the Episcopal Church through reading C. S. Lewis. Many had been active in Duke or UNC Inter-Varsity Christian Fellowship. A couple had seminary degrees. The new people liked Chip and were eagerly exploring Anglicanism. Many of the newcomers willingly joined committees, taught in the Sunday school, and served the urban ministry center downtown. Through fellowship, education, and outreach, Chip and Carol kept us busy.

It was, sadly enough, the energy and high profile of the newcomers that would continue to cause Chip trouble. Although the parish said it wanted to grow, as events unfolded it became clear that it wanted to grow on its own terms. They seemed to think that

Chip would bring in new church members who would simply replace the older, dying generation. But the new people would be just like them—sharing in the manners and mores of the older congregation. What few people realized at the time, however, was that the newcomers would change the church—and that all of us were caught up in vast social and economic change. In her book *A Particular Place,* sociologist Nancy Eiesland writes about change in a Methodist congregation outside Atlanta: "Newcomers were not the only change agents, but their arrival certainly brought significant change in its wake." These evangelical interlopers became the source of continuing conflict in the parish. The more new people Chip brought in, the angrier the locals got. Dan notes that "St. Stephen's was a very provincial place and had a hard time seeing beyond its own doors."

Quite simply, the newcomers and the Hope Valley Episcopalians were from two entirely different worlds.

The newcomers did not live in gracious golf course homes. Most of us lived in cheap graduate student apartments or modest starter homes. We could not share stories about exotic vacations or go out to dinner at expensive restaurants with fellow parishioners. We had never set foot inside Hope Valley Country Club. We did not even play golf. We could not afford it. At that point in my life, I had not bought a new dress in a year or so. We all had that slightly frayed look about us that comes from not having much money and not getting much sleep.

After a few months, I began to notice that all our social invitations came from other newcomers—none of the old-timers in the congregation. When my husband and I finally did receive an invitation from outside the grad school set, it was for a political fundraiser that cost $100 per person. I did not have $100 in my bank account. It probably never occurred to the sender, a woman who actually liked me, that someone in her parish may have been so financially desperate. I think she was completely oblivious. At the moment, however, it felt like a cruel taunt. I sat home that night and cried while I mended clothes and watched an old movie.

Had it been only personal, such oversights and implied insults might have been easier to bear. But it was not. The anxieties about the newcomers spilled over into congregational life. Whatever their numbers and spiritual passion, the newcomers had little power. The old-timers had the votes and held the purse. Some of the long-time parishioners feared that the newcomers wanted to "get their hands on the money," referring to the St. Stephen's endowment. Nearly everything became a power struggle over finances. The church refused to give Carol money to pay a baby-sitter during her young mother's Bible study—a group that attracted mostly new-comer women. Instead, the young mothers passed the hat and Carol made up the difference from her own purse to pay the weekly baby-sitting costs.

The churchwomen angrily denounced Chip and the tactless newcomers for serving coffee and dessert in the church parlor dur-ing a small group fellowship meeting. They feared someone would spill a drink or drop crumbs on the expensive Persian carpet. For months after, Carol scurried after unwitting newcomers who tried to sit in the parlor with a cup of tea and ushered them instead into the tile-floored parish hall. During an outreach meeting, Buck sug-gested doing a mailing to the Hope Valley Farms subdivision to invite new residents to the church. A long-time parishioner stood up and objected, "You can't be serious! You want us to invite people who live in $70,000 houses to this church?" A number of us sat in shocked silence. We especially did not mention that we lived in $325-a-month graduate student housing. The mailer project never got off the ground.

Chip's new youth minister ran into trouble when he tried to evangelize students at the local high school. A mother complained that such things were inappropriate and that what was needed was better acolyte training. The youth minister was not himself a "cradle Episcopalian" and the parents criticized his enthusiasm for the Bible and personal conversion. Some of their teenagers were taking his views too seriously; a few even said they had been "born again." As Dan says, "This was not something Episcopalians did, in the opinion of most of the congregation." One woman angrily insisted that Episcopalians could not be evangelicals: "We aren't like those Baptists or Methodists." She—and a number of others in the church—accused the youth minister and Chip of being "fundamentalists" and refused to support the youth program. The young man and his new wife could not stand the constant pressure and criticism. They resigned and moved out of state.

One graduate school family had several children and held distinctly countercultural values. Yet they had become deeply involved in the parish and were the backbone of the children's Sunday school program. Early in our time at St. Stephen's, the wife's sister arrived from out West. Having just gone through a messy divorce, the sister was emotionally and spiritually needy. To make matters worse, she was pregnant by a man not her former husband. She was very poor and I guessed she may have been on welfare. She had decided not to have an abortion and, instead, to keep her child. She was the first single mother I ever knew. The evangelicals in the congregation embraced her, supporting her through the emotionally difficult pregnancy, and showered her with gifts to support the infant. When the baby was born, we welcomed her with joy. But not so the rest of the congregation. Other St. Stephen's people clearly looked down on her, actually averting their eyes when she walked into a room. I do not know how she stood it.

When the time came to baptize her daughter, Chip did not do so in the Sunday morning service as was then becoming the norm throughout the denomination. Instead, he baptized her after church, with a few of us gathered around the font. It was one of the most beautiful baptisms I ever attended. As she handed her baby to Chip, the mother radiated joy from her own spiritual rebirth. This was no Mary Magdalene. Rather, she looked like the Virgin Mary presenting her precious infant at the temple. Here was the power of God: repentance, restoration, and resurrection. What had been dead was made alive through the gift of a child. At the time, I wondered why Chip had not baptized the baby during the service. Looking back, I am pretty sure he knew that neither the little one nor her mother would have been welcomed by the larger congregation. A single mom with her illegitimate child baptized at St. Stephen's expensive font? It would have torn the place apart.

Admittedly, we were outsiders to the world of Hope Valley Episcopalianism. Southerners of the type at St. Stephen's hate outsiders—viewing them as agitators. To them, we had bad manners, wore bad clothes, and drove beat-up cars. We talked too much about Jesus and the Bible and prayer. And, of course, as outsiders, we could never "really understand" the way they "did things" there. I guess, from their point of view, we did agitate. We did not intend to cause trouble. We were only trying to be faithful to God. Conflict just sort of happened.

The church became a battleground—a great struggle to control the future of St. Stephen's. Folks picked sides. There was little neutral ground. It was awful.

Even with my allegiance to Chip, however, I remember feeling a certain inner turmoil amidst the conflict. I loved Chip and Carol. We had come from the same world and my husband was enthusiastically committed to their vision. However, I was having doubts. Graduate school was raising serious intellectual questions for me about the validity of evangelical religion—especially its more literalist renderings of the Bible and historic creeds. Friends from that time still remember my vociferous support of evangelical doctrine. I was at least vaguely aware of something they did not know—mine was a theological case of "the lady doth protest too much." If I just argued hard enough, I might convince myself I believed everything I learned at Scottsdale Bible Church, Westmont, and Gordon-Conwell.

From conversations around the seminar table and the graduate student lounge, things were starting to look different as I, for the first time, encountered intellectually credible liberalism. And not just intellectually credible. A good number of my Duke classmates were Episcopalians, pretty serious ones at that, who saw the world from a broader perspective than I did. They did not seem to experience any real conflict between what they were learning in the classroom and what they did in church on Sunday. They moved with relative ease from the worlds of biblical, literary, and historical criticism to the worshipful strains of the *Kyrie* and the *Magnificat* in the Book of Common Prayer. They talked about the Jesus seminar, feminism, and postmodernism and then went to Eucharist. They were on the wrong side of every political issue and were not worried about women priests, homosexuals, or heresy. Yet they gave of their own limited resources to minister to the poor with a spiritual intensity that shamed me. It had never occurred to me that someone could be liberal and a serious Christian at the same time.

In evangelical circles we always talked about "integrating faith and learning," but my Episcopal Duke classmates (and some of the

Methodist, Presbyterian, and Lutheran ones, too) put their intellectual and spiritual lives together with an assurance I envied. I tried to hide inside a protected evangelical world, but they, unwittingly, I think, witnessed to being Christian in a different way. It was getting under my skin. But I was loath to admit it.

I had a lot of questions. I secretly longed to take classes that Buck would have ridiculed as "trendy." Instead I took the safe route and stuck with Aquinas, Calvin, and John Wesley. I was, however, finding myself theologically further and further away from him and people like Chip and Carol. There were intellectual cracks in their system—especially around issues of the history and context of Christian belief.

One day, Gary Brower, a classmate in church history, started talking about the role politics and economics played in the development of the Nicene Creed while we were sitting in the student lounge. If the Emperor Constantine had not enforced the creed with the full power of the state, he speculated, would *orthodoxy* as modern Christians know it ever have become orthodoxy? Wasn't orthodoxy only a social construction of the powerful? Of history's winners? There were, he argued, plenty of other options, things now regarded as heresy, for understanding the nature of God and Christ floating around the ancient church.

I had been taught that God, through the agency of the Holy Spirit, directed the saintly Constantine toward the orthodox definitions of the Divine Being. The creed was orthodox because of its biblical moorings and its supernatural affirmation by the early church. It revealed eternal truth. Politics? Economics? Social construction? These things *created* orthodoxy? I was appalled—especially when Gary confessed that it had become difficult for him to recite the creed.

"But Gary," I protested, "if you start down that road, where do you stop? What is orthodoxy? Is there any theological truth?"

"I don't know," he replied. "I only know that once you ask the questions, it is hard to stop."

I wanted to scream, "Well, then, just stop asking questions. Like me. Just stop asking questions." But at Duke, you could not avoid questions. There were lots of questions. All the time.

Meanwhile, at church there was conflict. And at home, Buck possessed all that theological certainty—a certainty that was beginning to seem oppressive. There was no safe place to think about the questions. The questions—and their implied answers—frightened me. My closest friends were evangelicals—folks who had little toleration for theological innovation or creativity. Evangelicals do not like questions. They prefer answers. But I was in no mood to confess to some of my graduate school classmates that I was beginning to entertain their questions. Emotionally, it felt like theological surrender. I had lived in the evangelical camp too long. I was completely alone.

Unlike Chip and some of his newcomers, I really liked the Episcopal Church and did not want to change much of what they wanted to change. Like them, I considered much of the national leadership less than orthodox and hoped for theological reform in the denomination. But I did not see the institution as a rudderless institution just waiting for our program of evangelical renewal. As much as I liked Chip, his lack of liturgical sensitivity bothered me. I missed Easter Vigil, saints' days, and sung liturgies. I missed the thin places created by the spiritual beauty of those practices. I was taken aback when Chip tried to remove the word *Episcopal* from the church letterhead. He always tried to minimize the distinctiveness of the Episcopal Church, equating it, I think, with an establishment maintenance mentality. He thought it mitigated evangelistic fervor. He wanted the church to be less Episcopal and more Christian.

But I had come to the church because of its distinctiveness. For me, its liturgy—especially the Eucharist—conveyed deep dimensions of discipleship and spirituality. Through it, I found renewed Christian commitment. Faith made sense at the altar; I could go from that altar and try to make it make sense in the world.

I suspect that some of St. Stephen's establishment churchgoers missed these traditions simply because that was the way they had always done things, a sort of liturgical loyalty. I missed them, however, because evangelicalism seemed shallow in comparison with the theological texture of the church's common prayer. There was, for me at least, no real meat on the evangelical bones—something being confirmed by my graduate studies. The Episcopal liturgy provided spiritual depth and gave me intellectual room to move around. From my own experience, I considered its unique identity part of its missionary strength.

Frankly, I worried about some of the newcomers myself. Like the woman who one day stopped me in church with a message from God: "You know, if you just submit to your husband, God will take away your desire for a Ph.D." This was not exactly a typical conversation starter in an Episcopal church. Lots of the newcomers seemed to share Chip's casual disregard for denominational particularity. They were an odd assortment of the spiritually, geographically, and socially disenfranchised. I defended Chip and stood with the new people, but I sensed it was a kind of evangelical last stand. The Hope Valley set said we were like Jim Bakker and Jimmy Swaggert. For upper-class Southern Episcopalians, them was fightin' words. We, Chip's supporters, knew an insult when we heard one.

Years later, I visited with the Rev. Loren Mead, a well-known mainline church leader and the founder of the Alban Institute in Washington, D.C. He had been a priest in Chapel Hill at the time St. Stephen's was founded in 1959. I asked him what St. Stephen's was like back then. "It had the air of being the chaplaincy to Hope Valley," he recalled. "Insular, a kind of Episcopal club, uninvolved and aloof. Run by Old South patriarchs. They mostly kept to themselves." A friend of mine raised in another Durham parish says, "St. Stephen's was a very closed world. Lots of lines. Not race, really. Mostly class." Chip would later refer to it as a "1950s-type church."

Since leaving the Methodist church a dozen years previously, I had not set foot in a 1950s-type church. The decade was the culmination of what sociologist Robert Wuthnow, in his book *After Heaven,* calls "dwelling spirituality," a pattern in which "family, church, and neighborhood were closely integrated" and "provided a sheltered haven in which to dwell." Religion was a matter of family tradition, of locale, of denomination—institutions that carried and transmitted faith over generations. Personal faith was deeply privatized. Public faith was a matter of civil religion, of God and state. The universe was arranged with divine predictability: God, husband, wife, children, servants. Each person had his or her place, duties to be carried out in home and society. "Congregations became," Wuthnow explains, "comfortable, familiar, domestic, offering an image of God that was basically congruent with the domestic tranquility of the ideal home."

Although I did not know it until much later, St. Stephen's had been a neighborhood church, part of the social fabric of Durham's professional elite—a seamless garment of kin, home, business, social life, worship, rites of passage, family tradition, and even, complete with a graveyard, death. Until the 1980s, the church was essentially a chapel in the backyard of the descendents of Southern plantation and mill owners, a place where parishioners unconsciously passed on the values and traditions of the Old South. The parish church both participated in and maintained these patterns—embodying a kind of Anglican tradition practiced in the South since colonial days.

But it was also a way that had been under attack and had been changing since the 1960s—mostly through the Civil Rights movement and economic development. Feeling besieged, some churches enshrined the old patterns as eternal truth. Wuthnow states that "these spiritual sanctuaries were thus fortresses whose walls needed to be protected from exterior threats so that life inside could be kept under control." From what I would later garner of its history, St. Stephen's was essentially founded as a spiritual fortress of an old way of life. By the time I arrived, these patterns had just begun to break down.

Some churches manage change well. All Saints and Christ Church had changed with the times—and were still changing. In both places, the establishment had either been displaced by newcomers or had managed to adapt to newer theological and social realities. Energetic and innovative leaders guided those parishes. And the congregations had thoughtfully reinvented their identities. Their creative renderings of Episcopal tradition appealed to—and welcomed—younger churchgoers, newcomers, and returnees. They welcomed change. In my years as an Episcopalian, I felt encouraged and supported as a person who had switched denominations. I had taught Sunday school and served on parish committees. Those churches were full of new people, and they were very exciting places to be.

St. Stephen's thought it wanted to change. But it was not ready for it. When offered the chance, St. Stephen's refused to adapt and chose, instead, to reinforce the beliefs and practices of the Hope Valley elite. Perhaps it was Chip's particular program of change. But I think not entirely. Establishment churchgoers typically resist change in favor of maintaining familiar religious patterns. At St.

Stephen's, and parishes like it, that meant holding on to the ideals and methods that had shaped 1950s churchgoing.

I was so naïve, however, that I had no idea there existed any kind of establishment that might resist new ways of doing things. I liked—and still like—change. St. Stephen's shocked me out of that innocence.

Buck and I could not afford to visit family in Arizona and California during our first Christmas in Durham in 1987. Chip and Carol invited us to celebrate with them. On Christmas Eve, I pulled out an old burgundy-and-lace bridesmaid's dress to wear to the festivities and we went to Chip and Carol's for supper. Afterward, we walked to church for the midnight service. We arrived earlier than most of the crowd, sat next to Carol, and enjoyed the Christmas hymns being played on the organ.

As people entered the church, I began to notice something quite amazing: the women were wearing furs, expensive jewelry, and elaborate party dresses. Some wore brand new evening gowns—looking as if they had just walked off the set of *Dynasty.* And a number of the men were wearing tuxes! I had the distinct impression that many of them had come from the same party. By comparison, my handmade bridesmaid dress looked as if it had come from the Salvation Army. I would never feel less welcome in a church service than I did that Christmas Eve. Chip wryly commented, "I felt like I was serving communion to the debutante ball." I am not sure he realized it, but he was right. They had come from a Christmas ball at the club. From cotillion to church without even changing clothes.

As a newcomer, I was unfamiliar with the elite reputation of the church, but other people knew all about the Episcopal establishment. In his essay "Episcopal," humorist Garrison Keillor writes of his impression of the Episcopal Church while growing up in

Minnesota: "Our clear picture of Episcopalians was of wealthy people, Yale graduates, worshipping God in extremely good taste. Episcopalian was the church in wingtips, the church of the Scotch and soda." In the class hierarchy of American denominations, Episcopal was always at the very top—especially in the South.

Having grown up in Arizona in the 1970s, *class* was an almost exotic concept to me. After all, I grew up in a rigorously egalitarian world in which on fancy occasions men donned leisure suits. Even in wealthy Scottsdale, local debutantes were chosen on the basis of personal achievement upon, we were told, Thomas Jefferson's vision of the "natural aristocracy" of the "common man." The girls of my year lived in apartments and mansions, were Christian and Jewish, the daughters of doctors and furniture salesmen. It was a society disconnected from kinship, inheritance, and most traditional social structures. Nobody ever told me that people—much less religions—had stations.

Throughout most of American history, however, religion and class have been interconnected. Certain denominations occupied particular rungs of the social ladder. For generations, Episcopalians and New England Congregationalists sat at the top of the religious-class pyramid, with the Presbyterians slightly behind them; Lutherans and Methodists got the middle ranks; Baptists were resolutely lower class; and Pentecostals, evangelicals, "holy rollers," and other sectarian types were at the bottom. Middle-class Methodists like my parents married other middle-class Methodists and raised middle-rank Methodist children. If you wanted to get ahead, you joined the Episcopal Church—or maybe you married into it. Theologian H. Richard Niebuhr writes in *Social Sources of Denominations* that it was the church "of the landed gentry." Or, as Garrison Keillor puts it, "turning Episcopalian was a case of social climbing straight up the hill."

Few things had suffered so greatly in the turmoil of the 1960s than traditional class structure. Well-off baby boomers rejected and rebelled against their birthright. Middle- and lower-class ones rose in power and wealth as the ideals of a new class, the educated meritocracy, took hold. For most of my life, class has been a flexible entity, unboundaried, where the daughters of Methodist shopkeepers like me work and mix with relative ease with children of privilege. I have often lived in the geographic centers of meritocracy—places like southern California and Washington, D.C.—where what matters is where you went to school and what you do. Not who your parents are or what church they attended. The lives we sketch for ourselves—including religion, faith, and spirituality—are choices. And we are often very irreverent—and sometimes unaware—of the boundaries and traditions of those who still live in that older, inherited world.

Chip Nix, born in 1942, was technically not a baby boomer. He was raised in that older world—his father a doctor, a cradle Episcopalian, part of the country club set. By virtue of his background, he could relate to the Durham upper class. He managed to earn the trust, respect, and support of some of the wealthiest members of the congregation. But he was also a Vietnam veteran, the first wave of what would become the protest generation. "After Vietnam," he confesses, "I became a real boomer. All my attitudes toward institutions, especially the church, changed. I guess you could call me anti-establishment." St. Stephen's Old Guard probably thought him a class traitor.

In 1987 St. Stephen's was still mired in inherited class structures and at a point of tension with the ways in which the denomination was being reshaped. A different kind of Episcopal congregation, one priding itself on diversity and inclusion, was just then emerging. In his essay, Garrison Keillor describes his parish in New York: "Black faces in the sanctuary, old people, exiles from the Midwest, the lame and the halt, divorced ladies, gay couples: a real good anthology of the faith." At St. Stephen's it was not so. Before the newcomer invasion, the sanctuary was full of white Southern families who sat with their kin in church. Chip's newcomers changed that.

Not being a Southerner, I was surprised when locals assumed certain things about my "station" when I mentioned my church affiliation. "Episcopal" earned a subtly raised eyebrow from a Methodist or Baptist—a gesture of mildly defiant deference if ever there was one. I would eventually figure out that Episcopal was "big house" religion, the restrained faith of the masters. St. Stephen's old families believed they were protecting their sacred way of life from Northern evangelical carpetbaggers. To the Hope Valley natives, the parish church was a kind of last stand of civility and order, Southern society, and *real* Episcopalianism. Unwittingly, I had stumbled into a world in which a 1950s church, a final vestige of the Old South, was fighting for its life, a place I had assumed was gone with the wind. At St. Stephen's, rife with generational, class, and regional warfare, it was more like a whirlwind.

Chip was doomed.

I wish I could have understood the war at St. Stephen's as a sort of inevitable sociological and historical conflict. Since then, I have come to sympathize with the Old Guard in some ways. It must have been frightening to see the world crumble. No wonder they seemed so desperate, so angry.

We were all caught up in things much bigger than we ourselves were. In 1987 I did not know that I was a member of the baby boom meritocracy, part of that new information class of people who were living at the cutting edge of the multicultural, consumerist, tech-driven New South. Sure, people talked about it, but who could really know? I had only just bought my first Macintosh computer. I thought I was so far ahead of those parochial Hope Valley Episcopalians. But even as a graduate student at Duke University I was only beginning to be aware of concepts like postmodernism, pluralism, new economy, globalism, racism, social displacement, and religious diversity. And who could know that struggles like those at St. Stephen's were playing out in congregations throughout the New South?

I sure did not know. Seeing the world through my theological prejudices at the time, I thought the St. Stephen's fight was between conservatives and liberals—evangelical renewal Episcopalians versus old-time Episcopal liberals. After all, my evangelical education taught me that nearly the whole of history could be understood as good versus evil, God versus the devil, us versus them. Because the old St. Stephen's families opposed Chip, I assumed they were theological liberals, the enemies of God and true religion. Who else could possibly oppose his dream? It was hard to know anything of their world, what impulses of faith and family shaped Chip's opposition. I did not possess any insight into their religion or the society then slipping through their fingers.

Chip would say things like, "They don't want to hear the Bible," or, "They are so closed to Jesus," implying, at the very least, that their hard-heartedness arose from theological liberalism. Some of my newcomer friends prayed earnestly for the Old Guard's conversion, that "they would come to Jesus and know him." Vigorous Bible preaching, orthodox theology, and a vision for evangelism and missions would win the day at St. Stephen's. A spiritual and theological change of heart would bring them around to our—and God's—side.

Some of the St. Stephen's old families might have been theologically liberal, but, looking back now, I doubt it. The men worked. Their wives raised children and volunteered. They lived in an essentially segregated community and were fiscally conservative Southern Democrats—although many had recently become Republicans. In the 1970s they opposed every national church initiative regarding racism, feminism, and social justice.

Much of this they drew from a traditional Southern way of interpreting the Bible—particularly certain passages from St. Paul. "Wives, submit to your husbands." "Children, obey your parents." "Slaves, obey your masters." Christian faith provided order in a fundamentally disordered universe. From this tradition, they shared Chip's opposition to homosexual ordination. They were angry with him only when he contradicted their bishop on the subject on local television. Chip's views did not upset them. Rather, he had embarrassed them when he aired his disagreement with his bishop. Sin was getting out of line, deviating from God's established roles of authority and submission. Chip was spiritually insubordinate, a partisan in denominational warfare—not the genteel parson whom they really wanted as their priest.

St. Stephen's traditionalism put them at odds with other North Carolina Episcopalians, many of whom had learned, mostly through the crises of the Civil Rights movement, to read the Bible in new ways. Thus, St. Stephen's carefully distanced itself from the rest of the diocese. At one diocesan convention, fellow Episcopalians booed their former rector for his opposition to civil rights—a moment he boasted was one of the proudest in his ministry. The current rector elegantly understates the case: "This earned St. Stephen's a reputation as a conservative parish and explains some of the tensions in our life today."

Oddly enough, Chip was more liberal than the parish on a number of issues. Although I am pretty sure he is a Republican, he certainly did not share St. Stephen's perspective on the Civil Rights movement or race. Chip and Carol believe in "traditional family values" and, to this day, they state unequivocal opposition to gay rights and homosexual ordination. However, Chip and Carol were strong supporters of the full inclusion of women in Christian leadership. Carol, in particular, urged me to reexamine the issue biblically. As an evangelical woman with leadership gifts, she rejected both fundamentalist and Roman Catholic arguments against women's ordination. Eventually, her example of public ministry encouraged me to try out my gifts of teaching, leadership, and preaching.

They were liturgically innovative as well. Although they preferred the beauty of traditional church music and hymns, they wanted to experiment with a variety of musical styles in worship to reach out to younger Christians. Chip wanted to "cut and paste" the order of the service to make it more meaningful for spiritual seekers. He was one of the first priests I knew of to argue that the Prayer Book and hymnal were unwieldy for newcomers during Sunday worship. Instead of the two hefty books, he wanted to hand out weekly liturgical leaflets to make the service more user-friendly.

Ultimately, the events at St. Stephen's led me to conclude that *liberal* and *conservative* are almost completely inadequate terms to describe church conflict. Even Chip would later confess that he, too, had gotten it wrong, stating, "It wasn't a theological thing; it was about power." At St. Stephen's, multiple cultures collided, all vying for congregational control: the culture of the New South with that of the Old, baby boomers with their parents, newcomers with old-timers, the emergent new class with the traditional upper class, North with South, American evangelicalism with traditional Episcopalianism. It was not a "theological thing." These multiple clashes could be understood under a larger rubric. They were all, in some measure, clashes between two styles of being a mainline church—the styles of establishment and intentional religion.

The establishment churchgoers—the St. Stephen's Old Guard—took things for granted and organized reality around inherited categories of family, society, and denominational loyalty. You were an Episcopalian because your parents were. You went to church or joined the country club because you were obligated to do so. Church was a place of comforting prayer to bless life's passages and bury you when you died.

The intentional churchgoers, Chip's newcomers, took nothing for granted. Everything—from personal identity to religious commitment to family structure—had to be negotiated, explored, and, perhaps, finally, chosen. For them—for me—you pick a church, a gathering of serious seekers and faithful discipleship, a community that stands, in many ways, at odds with the values of the world. The real issue was that of identity and not theological particularities of evangelicalism or liberalism. What kind of church should St. Stephen's be? A family chapel or a gathered community of disciples?

In the short run, at least, St. Stephen's chose the former. Of course they would. It was their life, what they had built, created, and known all their lives. We had more than a little hubris to try to change it, to take it away, to make it different. Dan Willey notes sadly, "For my own part, I wish I had been more able to see things from the viewpoint of the established people in the church. I was much too quick to take an 'us' versus 'them' stance and made little effort to understand." We were interlopers in that isolated little world, the last bastion of a society disappearing in the sweep of social change. I may disagree with their values and worldview, but I had no real right to try to undermine them. Forces much larger than Chip Nix or I were already doing that.

It may be taking a while, but establishment churchgoing is becoming a thing of the past. It is an ethos of a generation now dying, an ethos rejected by that generation's own children. Time, as the Isaac Watts hymn graciously puts it, "bears all our years away; they fly, forgotten, as a dream dies at the opening day." What one generation enshrines, the next rejects or transforms. And so it goes. That includes the Old South, old Hope Valley, and old St. Stephen's. People tell me it is different today. Probably so. Congregations have to adapt to survive. A friend says that that is the beauty of it. But it is also the agony. For some people, change can be hard.

Chip eventually gave up. His daughters were sick with stress. He grew weary of being questioned at every move. Somebody went through his garbage looking for "evidence" to condemn him of any sort of impropriety. In one horrible meeting, several members of the congregation accused him of lying. The purse strings tightened. A professional consultant failed to help. It came down to, as Chip put it, ecclesiastical "guerilla warfare." The bishop suggested it was time to go. The Vietnam veteran priest knew when the war was lost. He resigned, took his family overseas for several months, and eventually went west to Seattle to serve a parish on a more amiable high-tech frontier.

On his last Sunday at St. Stephen's, in an overly dramatic protest, I wore a black dress and a black hat to church. I mourned my friend's defeat, the failure of his dreams. Even more, perhaps, I mourned the loss of what I hoped could be. Chip and Carol envisioned a spiritual synthesis between evangelicalism and Episcopalianism, a place where I could put the pieces of my theology and spirituality together. Part of me died that day. I did not know, however, what part. I felt terrible.

Locked in my own pain and self-doubt, the larger issues escaped me. I certainly could not ply my own trade as a scholar of American religion and analyze my own situation. I never wanted to set foot in St. Stephen's again. I blamed it on "those liberals in the church." I was angry, hurt, confused, and lost. I felt betrayed and rejected. Could I even remain an Episcopalian? Many of the St. Stephen's newcomers abandoned the denominational ship. Some went back to the churches whence they had come. Some went to places like the fundamentalist Chapel Hill Bible Church. But I could not do that. Deep inside, obscured by the St. Stephen's crisis, all those graduate school questions were taking root. I was further from evangelicalism than anyone—including myself—imagined. On one hand, I found it difficult to stay loyal to the Episcopal Church; on the other, I knew I could not go back to the simple faith of my youth.

So, just where could I go to church now? I had no idea.

CHAPTER FOUR

Practicing Faith

CHURCH OF THE HOLY FAMILY

Chapel Hill, North Carolina, 1989–1991

The Episcopal Church of the Holy Family is ten miles and an entire universe away from St. Stephen's in Durham. It sits at the far edge of the University of North Carolina (UNC) campus in Chapel Hill on the busy 15/501 bypass. As at St. Stephen's, many trees grace the church's property. But, unlike St. Stephen's, they do not hide the church. Rather, the trees serve to frame the building and preserve a modicum of pastoral serenity as SUVs whiz by at sixty miles per hour.

The 1960s vintage building is painted white, a traditional-looking brick church with clear glass windows. There is no sense of protectiveness or isolation here—the church's red doors open directly to the street, and a large sign announces its presence to passing cars and the neighbors. When you sit in the sanctuary, those windows make you feel as if you are worshiping outdoors among the azaleas, holly bushes, and dogwood. The inside is simple, with light oak pews, plain white and blue walls, patched cracks, and serviceable carpet. There is nothing foreboding about it. The place has a much-loved feeling, the handcrafted sensibility of daily faith. Indeed, the sanctuary exudes the warmth of a close friend's living room, a home full of quilts and everyday dishes. Its spirituality is not so much grandeur, mystery, or beauty—unless, of course, one is seeking the grandeur, mystery, and beauty of intimacy with God in community.

I will never forget finding the Church of the Holy Family in the summer of 1989. Wounded by the St. Stephen's experience, I was spiritually and emotionally exhausted. By rejecting Chip, I felt in some way that the church had also rejected me. I wondered if I could remain an Episcopalian and if, indeed, there was any place for me in the church. I had no idea how to retain my evangelical commitments in relationship to either church or graduate school. I was so appalled by the anger and pettiness I had recently witnessed that I did not want to go to church. I remembered what my agnostic grandfather used to say: "I don't go to church, because it is full of hypocrites." For the first time in my life, I wondered if he was right.

In the months before Holy Family, I skipped church many Sundays. On other Sundays, Buck and I visited churches in the area—some Episcopal, some not. We went to a new Presbyterian congregation that met in an elementary school gymnasium, complete with child-size seating. A friend called it "that church with the long sermons and the little chairs." We liked the people but they were the sort of Presbyterians who would not let women read the scriptures in worship or allow them to teach adult Sunday school. My husband, who did not approve of women's ordination, found this an extreme but acceptable position. However, it made me mad.

We almost settled on worshiping at the magnificent Duke Chapel on a regular basis. I loved its English cathedral-style sanctuary, with the dark pews and the hundreds of brilliant stained-glass windows. The university minister, the Rev. Will Willimon, was an inspiring preacher whose sermons were both better and shorter than those at the Presbyterian church. And the chapel's high church Methodism, especially the Wesley hymns, tugged nostalgically at my heart. But the popular Willimon attracted huge crowds and the place was so big that we felt lost. A number of friends mentioned Holy Family as a possibility for us. We were, however, reluctant to visit because the parish was currently involved in a search for a new rector. Given the St. Stephen's debacle, that prospect worried us.

One Sunday, however, I could not face another week of sleeping in, little chairs, ecclesiastical misogyny, Methodist sentimentality, and feeling lost. I craved the Eucharist and, in my heart, had no desire to stop being an Episcopalian. I did not care who was or who would be the minister at Holy Family. In spite of the hurt from St. Stephen's, I wanted to go.

It was a small congregation. Maybe seventy people. Maybe. There were some older folks and a number of student couples. Not many families. Given its simplicity, it was immediately obvious that Holy Family was an unpretentious place where Persian carpets and endowments and organs and debutante balls did not matter. The interim rector, the Rev. Ralph Macy, preached an acceptable sermon. I was not there, however, for the sermon. I was there for the Eucharist. And it was obvious that everyone else was as well. When the liturgy began, the small congregation suddenly seemed larger, as their voices blended in eager anticipation of God's table. My heart soared back to a familiar place, the place grace had carved in my soul for God. I did not care if this little parish called a heretic for its minister. I had come home again.

After the service, nearly everyone attending that morning welcomed us: "We are so happy you are here." "We've got a number of young adults who have started here in the last year. They have recently begun a fellowship group." "Hey, you're a Dukie? What are you doing over here?" David Frauenfelder, a graduate student in classics at UNC, literally grabbed my arm: "Come on. We're going out to brunch." Within a few minutes, we were sitting at Shoney's with David, his wife, Leslie, Brian and Ingrid Towey, Peter and Laura Brown, Todd Granger and Jill Martin, and Lesley Stanley. We talked about St. Stephen's, about graduate school pressure, about theology, about experiencing God in deeper ways, and about our desires for community. By the end of that meal, I knew that these people would be my friends. Although I came to them reluctantly, wounded and embittered from the battles at St. Stephen's, they reached out and brought me in. Indeed, they would become, for the short time I was there, my family. No church ever lived so well into its name.

At the beginning I felt drained and confused. Not quite knowing what path to take, I simply put one foot in front of the other, attending to my spiritual life through the practices of faith. Slowly, by reading the Bible, worshiping every Sunday, and working at homey parish tasks, I began to understand the Christian life in new ways. I think that was true for all of us. By practicing faith together, the good folks of the Church of the Holy Family became brother- and sister-pilgrims, an intentional family of faith on the verge of birthing a new congregation. We were only vaguely aware that this was happening or that we stood so close to the Spirit's tremors of re-creation. But we were profoundly aware that we needed one another in order to get to wherever God was taking us.

The Church of the Holy Family had not always been a small congregation. It had been founded in 1952 in the full flush of postwar church growth as the second Episcopal parish in Chapel Hill. The first church, Chapel of the Cross, had a long history and a distinguished national reputation. By the 1950s, however, Chapel of the Cross could no longer accommodate all the Episcopalians in town. So a mission was established at the edge of the city next to a postwar housing development full of graduate students and young professional families. By 1962, the new church served 270 adult members and 250 children. They christened it the Church of the Holy Family, a name that mirrored the composition of the early congregation.

The parish's second rector, the Rev. Loren Mead, came to Holy Family in December 1957 and would stay for a dozen years. Although he was still a young man when he arrived, Holy Family was his second church. His first congregation had been a small, rural church in South Carolina with "lovely people." But, with a huge Confederate flag hanging over the altar, Mead knew that it was a place that "would never change." And Loren Mead does not like the status quo. Even today, more than forty years later, he is energetic and visionary, a bit edgy and edge-cutting. He almost turned down the call to Holy Family, but he opted to take it because of "the excitement of the university community" and because it "offered the possibility to change."

It seems odd in some ways that anyone would want to change Holy Family. After all, it was the 1950s, a time of unprecedented church growth for mainline Protestants. Why tinker with success? Established religions boomed as war-weary Americans sought emotional comfort in the familiar cadences of church. Protestant congregations offered old-fashioned faith for new nuclear families and prospered accordingly. Historian Robert Ellwood notes in his book *The Fifties Spiritual Marketplace* that mainline religion and mainline clergy "tended to be conventional, well-organized and businesslike." Mainline religion worked.

In the 1950s, time-honored formulas for church and community, of passing down religion from one generation to another, were working better than they ever had in American history. Mainline Protestants were birthing a new generation at a remarkable rate—Sunday schools were nurseries of faith, full of future churchmen and churchwomen. These cradles of mainline piety were supported by the surrounding culture. With Billy Graham and Norman Vincent Peale on the airwaves, *The Ten Commandments* and *Ben Hur* at the movies, and prayer and Bible reading in the schools, what could ever go wrong?

Even at the time of its founding, in the heyday of high Episcopal birthrates, Holy Family was never really a 1950s church. It has always been a little ahead of its time—perhaps because of its university location, perhaps because of all those graduate students, perhaps because it never had any establishment, no Old Guard to protest innovation. In the 1950s and 1960s, under Mead's leadership, Holy Family was already anticipating future cultural trends. Despite its birth rate, the church did not benefit from a stable population. The congregation was a transient group—early citizens of the mobile society. In 1963, for example, they experienced a 63 percent turnover. They developed a missionary mind-set as they constantly needed to attract new people to the congregation.

They were culturally ahead of the curve; some parishioners were at the forefront of breakthroughs in medicine, psychology, and technology. They thought in regional and urban terms as their city embarked on a long-term economic development project known as the Research Triangle. They lived in one of the South's more liberal cities, Chapel Hill, long a refuge for Southerners uncomfortable in less progressive places. They lived and struggled with the end of segregation. They were, in short, a cultural vanguard—social and intellectual pioneers living at the very edge of a new kind of society. "Chapel of the Cross was the established church," Mead recalls. "Church of the Holy Family was the young folks' church." These people were not thinking very much about the past—they were thinking about the future. They were, essentially, the nascent New South.

And Holy Family did many new things. In 1963 Mead spent time in England and experienced firsthand the liturgical experimentation going on in the church there. The Church of England had not significantly altered its Prayer Book since 1662 and its services were woefully out of date. "Everybody was putting together their own liturgies," he recalls, "and I realized I could do that, too. It had never occurred to me before that I could actually change the Prayer Book." When he returned to Chapel Hill, Mead introduced innovative new liturgies, offered the Eucharist weekly, and instructed the parish in liturgical renewal. The congregation approved these and other changes—they even wrote their own folk mass and experimented with liturgical dance.

Mead was also influenced by Church of the Savior, an innovative interdenominational church in Washington, D.C. There, Pastor Gordon Cosby had discovered a dynamic relationship between the inner life of worship and prayer and its outward expression in mission, a balance between "the journey inward, the journey outward." Long before many other mid-century liberal Protestants thought about it, Cosby argued that "if you've got a group that calls itself church, Christian church, and doesn't oppose and confront the culture, I don't think you have a New Testament church."

Mead understood the radical nature of Christian discipleship. He and his congregation mutually challenged one another to live faithfully. Holy Family's people began to see themselves as the church's ministers, their parish as a miniseminary, and their congregation, as Loren remembers, a "community able to 'infect' their city with health." In short, they became, he says, "a new kind of Episcopal Church in the New South, a kind of hothouse for new ideas of what it meant to be church."

While the church embraced the new understanding of the inward journey, the journey outward caused a certain amount of tension and conflict. Mead admits that social issues—his liberal position on the Civil Rights movement—often proved troublesome in the 1960s. "Some people did get angry, some pledges were cut, some just stopped coming." No matter the opposition, the parish liberals persisted and insisted on doing the right thing. They held a Vacation Bible school for black and white children, welcomed the parish's first black members, and supported integration of the diocesan camp. Toward the end of the decade, tempers cooled and, as the Holy Family history states, "people began to return to services and to pay their pledges."

After a dozen years in Chapel Hill, Loren Mead accepted a call to Washington, D.C., where he would eventually found the Alban Institute, an organization dedicated to strengthening congregations. Upon his departure from Holy Family in 1969, he wrote in a letter to the church: "I believe, and this parish has underlined my beliefs, that parishes are terribly important in the ministry of the Church to its people. I also believe that parishes are hung up in structures and organizations and procedures determined by the past and generally not open to the possibilities of the present and the future. But I believe that is not necessarily the way it has to be— and what has happened at the Church of the Holy Family gives me real hope for other parishes. This parish," he concluded, "is a center of life and celebration for the whole Church."

Whatever its successes, however, the church's next two decades would not be entirely happy. The rector who followed Mead did not share his enthusiasm for lay ministry, liturgical renewal, and social justice. Instead, he reasserted clerical authority and Prayer Book traditionalism. Although he was a capable preacher, the Sunday school, youth, justice, and outreach programs began to decline. When he resigned after ten years, another minister came to the parish—a man admittedly struggling with spiritual and emotional burnout. Holy Family's light slowly dimmed. For twenty years following Mead's departure, the once-healthy congregation would languish, only occasionally tweaked by the Spirit toward its initial promise. In 1989, however, Holy Family's founding vision would be reawakened—largely through the idealism of dedicated churchgoers and the arrival of an energetic new clergyman, the Rev. Timothy Kimbrough.

In the years I attended Holy Family, nothing much seemed to happen. No crises, no dramatic conflicts. Instead, life at Holy Family unfolded in small moments through ritual in community—through daily and weekly practices of faith. The church was a gentle and accepting place whose spiritual perspectives would change me. Those changes would come slowly, unexpectedly, and without great turmoil. I am not exactly sure I understood the breadth and depth of these changes at the time, but they would prove real—and would ultimately form the foundation for my own renewal of faith.

Before the new rector arrived, the twenty- and thirty-something churchgoers, mostly newcomers, formed the Fellowship of St. Timothy. The group was named for I Timothy 4:12: "Let no one despise your youth, but set the believers an example in speech and conduct, in love, in faith, in purity." Over the years I have often heard ministers and denominational executives moan over the lack of commitment in this age group. Maybe the graduate students of

Holy Family were exceptional, but we were, long before our children were born, deeply committed churchgoers—most of whom were converts to the Episcopal Church from other denominations and many of whom had spent some time in the institutions of American evangelicalism. We were idealistic reformers who wanted a place to live out our convictions in meaningful ways in community. David Frauenfelder remembers: "We were at a time in our lives that was ideal for the intensity of heart and purity of spirit necessary to the building of a new community. We had no children, we were all far from traditional family, many of us were engaged in deep academic exploration. Holy Family gave us a nearly blank canvas on which to create."

A few people remained in the parish from the Loren Mead years, but there was little generational tension at Holy Family. Instead, the church's founders welcomed and supported us in our enthusiasm to renew the congregation. Indeed, they were happy that a new generation of reinforcements had arrived—a number of them said we were "an answer to prayer," as they fearfully watched the parish shrink in the 1980s. They gave us free reign to design programs and events to meet our needs. But they did not leave us adrift. Senior members of the congregations gently imparted their wisdom and experience to the Fellowship of St. Timothy as we energetically embarked in ministry to revive the once-flagging congregation.

This energy was most obviously concentrated in a single small group that met weekly during those years at Holy Family: the Thursday night Bible study. This group comprised many of the young newcomers. David refers to it as "a significant engine of spiritual growth," which was true for both its members and the congregation. At first, the group was very small—a few people who gathered to study the upcoming Sunday Gospel reading. The format was simple. The group opened with prayer and a different leader each week began with a few insights and questions about the passage. They discussed the text and closed by sharing personal needs and then prayed for one another.

The Thursday night group, to which Buck and I had been invited on our first Sunday, seemed a natural way to enter into the community. We wanted to be part of a small group. But a Bible study? I had been part of innumerable Bible studies throughout the years—almost all of which were tedious. Even before graduate school, I had a hard time with group Bible study. Now, my head spinning with questions regarding the nature of scripture and its historical context, I wondered if any Bible study could reach my soul's troubled places. Although I was not aware of it at the time, I was suffering from depression and feelings of failure and self-doubt. Bible study did not seem particularly relevant. But it was the only small group Holy Family offered. So I went.

Despite my concerns, Bible study is a venerable practice of Christian faith—originating from the practice of early Jewish Christians, who cherished the Torah and other Hebrew holy texts. Those who embraced Christianity have read and memorized their books, seeking from them direction for life and the whispers of God. "Happy are those who do not follow the advice of the wicked," extolled the Psalmist. "But their delight is in the law of the Lord and on his law they meditate day and night." The earliest Christians, given the love of God's books from their Jewish kin, revered their own sacred letters and stories as the tales about Jesus began to be written down in the first and second centuries. Throughout Christian history, the church has supported and promoted scholarly study of the Bible. But it has also engaged in the practice of holy reading—reading while in prayer—in order to hear and understand the deeper meanings of God's word. According to the Book of Common Prayer, Episcopalians "read, mark, and inwardly digest" the scriptures so that "we may embrace and ever hold fast the blessed hope of everlasting life."

Part of my reluctance to join the Thursday night group came from my growing discomfort with evangelical readings of the Bible. Evangelicals usually engage in *inductive* Bible study, a method in which group members read the passage and try to draw the meaning of the passage from the text itself, without any help from scholarship or tradition. Inductive Bible study assumes a commonsense approach and clarity to the scriptures. Whatever the text says is exactly what it means. Because most evangelicals are not familiar with—or reject outright—modern scholarly approaches to the Bible, such church groups tend to read the Bible literally without any sense of the linguistic, historical, or cultural context of a given passage. The words on the page are the actual words of God, written by the Holy Spirit. Thus, evangelical Bible studies tend toward subjectivism and literalism: What does this verse mean to me and how do I apply it to my life?

At that point in my life, I saw the shortcomings of evangelical Bible reading. Without any interpretative guidance, such groups quickly devolved into an opinionated free-for-all. As proved by the conflicts at Christ Church and Gordon-Conwell, evangelicals can make the Bible say anything. They have little to guard against a multitude of conflicting interpretations. My reservations about Bible study grew from my own experience of participating in such inductive groups and seeing how poorly the Bible was treated by those who claimed to revere it.

Yet I had no idea how other, more liberal, Christians read the Bible. Indeed, I suspected that liberals did not read—or even care about—the scriptures at all. I had been taught that liberals dismantled the Bible with the tools of literary criticism and history without any regard for the consequences of their actions. To them, the Bible was just one more book, a product of natural human processes, to be eviscerated by secular scholarship. Evangelical literalism seemed one extreme when it came to reading the Bible; liberal naturalism seemed another. One method was overly simplistic, and the other, overly skeptical. I never suspected that another way existed.

By the time I arrived at Holy Family, I was well aware of the problems associated with both approaches to scripture. I felt caught between the two extremes and I could no longer read the Bible on my own. It bored me. It scared me. It made me mad. I did not know what to trust. But Bible reading, as a practice of faith, was deeply ingrained in my spiritual consciousness. Its way is a way of spiritual formation and, like the liturgy, it is something Christians do even when they do not feel like doing it. Putting my doubts aside, feeling the need to make friends and find community, I joined the Thursday night Bible study.

The group's core consisted of the same people who had greeted us on our first Holy Family visit. In the autumn of 1989 the Thursday night group grew from about six to twenty and began to deepen in both commitment and quality. I was astonished to learn that other members of the group felt the same way about studying the Bible as I did—that it had often been predictable and dreary. We decided to lay aside our prejudices regarding the week's text. Instead, we urged each other to "see the Gospel anew" and place ourselves in the midst of the story.

We brought to it a good deal of technical knowledge about theology and the Bible—several members of the group were seminary graduates, graduate students in religion, or students in closely related disciplines. Discussion was lively and, at times, raucous or controversial. We often argued over interpretations, struggling to come to terms with the differences in the group and the insecurities bred in graduate school classrooms. Thursday nights were the first time I heard serious Christians—people whose faith I knew from praying together—engage in contemporary biblical scholarship in spiritually meaningful ways. On more than one occasion someone would remark, "Of course, scholars believe Jesus did not really say this," "This is a later addition to Isaiah," or "Paul did not write I and II Timothy." Such comments initially surprised or offended me, but I began to see how these insights clarified difficult passages and resolved problematic conflicts in scripture.

In college and seminary, evangelical professors taught us to explain away contradictions through complex attempts to harmonize parallel passages. Reading the Gospels closely, for example, it appears that Peter denies Jesus six times—not the divinely predicted three. I remember one professor presenting to us a tortured explanation to make "sense" of the problem. Although it looks like six separate occasions, it was actually only three—each Gospel writer told only a part of the story. But if you put the stories together, into a sort of cut and edit version, the accounts did not really conflict. From Genesis to Revelation, much of evangelical biblical scholarship is directed at such tasks—proving that the Bible is wholly without error and trustworthy in all that it teaches.

In the Thursday night Bible study, however, most people rested easily with less literal approaches to the text. No, Peter did not deny Jesus six times. Rather, each Gospel writer used poetic license, depicting the denials differently to make particular theological points. Perhaps the episodes did not even historically occur and were, instead, literary devices to encourage early Christians to persist in faith. Through the arguments and insights of the group, I began to understand that the Gospels were not history books—they were theology books and were to be read accordingly. As theology, my friends at Holy Family read the Bible and trusted it. It was possible to read the Bible seriously but not literally. We recognized that God could speak through scripture without having had supernaturally transmitted every specific word. Critical studies did not undermine faith but aided in answering puzzling questions about scripture. And when no answers were forthcoming, when doubt overwhelmed faith, we could still pray and care for one another. Our faith was based in our experience of God in community, whether that be the written experiences of Christians long ago or our own.

Through the months, I found myself wanting to go on Thursday night. No one read the Bible in ways I expected. They took seriously the mandate to read the text with different eyes. Every week, a new leader brought some perspective on chapters and verses that seemed otherwise tiresome or worn. David recalls that "the Bible study felt so important and precious to those who were in it." It did. All of us were experiencing the power of reading the Bible in community and finding healing—spiritually and intellectually—through it.

Eventually the Thursday night Bible study changed me. When I first arrived in 1989, we had studied Luke. In Advent that year, we moved on to Matthew—a book with which I had never felt much spiritual empathy. My favorite Gospel had always been John, long noted for its exalted view of Jesus as the Christ, the divine savior of the world. Indeed, the book held such sway in my theological imagination that I read the other Gospels primarily through its lens, particularly chapter three. There, Jesus tells an eager inquirer that "no one can enter the kingdom of God without being born of water and Spirit. . . . You must be born from above." Evangelicals interpret this as being "born again." All scripture points toward John 3:16—"For God so loved the world that he gave his only begotten Son that all who believe in him might not perish but have everlasting life." I had been taught that this was the most important moment in the life of Jesus; indeed, this verse was the most important in the whole Bible. Everything else was spiritual gravy.

But in October 1990 the Gospel of Matthew undermined these assumptions. The text was Matthew 22:34–46. A lawyer went to Jesus and asked, "Teacher, which commandment in the law is the greatest?" As a Jew, he was asking what to do to be a faithful follower of God—in contemporary parlance, to be "saved." In the parallel passage in Luke 10:25, this emphasis is more obvious when the lawyer asks, "Teacher, what must I do to inherit eternal life?" In both cases, Jesus replied, "You shall love the Lord your God with all your heart, and with all your soul, and with all your mind. . . . You shall love your neighbor as yourself. On these two commandments hang all the law and the prophets." He did not say, "You must be born again."

I had read Matthew's words hundreds of times, and I do not know why they hit me with such force that night. Perhaps it was the disciplined study of reading scripture for a year; perhaps it was the safety I felt with the group. As I sat there and listened to the discussion, I realized that John had been written much later than Matthew, and was, historically, the least reliable of the Gospels. Yet I had pinned my whole understanding of Christian faith on a single chapter from its pages. Now, looking at the words recorded closer to Jesus' own ministry, Jesus said something I had never really heard before: Love God and love your neighbor as yourself.

I remember looking around the room in stunned silence as it occurred to me that, for nearly fifteen years, I had been reading the Bible through a particular interpretation of the text—and had largely been ignoring the words of scripture itself. David was earnestly making some point about "feeling" the passage and these words being the basis for social justice ministries. Lesley Stanley was looking thoughtfully at her translation, ready to jump into the conversation. Jean Wagner was smiling in agreement with Jesus' directive, with her husband, Bob, sitting and nodding at her side. Todd was turning pages, looking at the parallel passages.

I wanted to shout, "No, this cannot be! Jesus told us the point of the whole thing? Love? How do you love God and your neighbor? How can I love myself? Have I gotten it wrong for all these years?" The point was not scaring someone into heaven or saving them from hellfire. The point was not about what you believe about Jesus but what you do in his name? The point was love. Loving God and loving my neighbor. That simple? That complex? The Gospel turned me inside out. I felt sick. I felt like I had been cheated by pastors and teachers and professors my whole Christian life. But at that moment it changed. Indeed, the Bible has never looked the same to me since.

In the weeks following, I spiritually ran to that Bible study. Passage after passage sounded brand new. Bible stories that I had known since youth seemed freshly written—intimate and personal words from God—refreshing and renewing my entire sense of Christian faith. Faith was not about fleeing from something. It was about joyfully running toward something. Or sometimes, as I felt at the time, limping, wounded and helpless, toward it. The open arms of God, a motherly God embracing the world and strengthening us to embrace it as well, reached toward me. I ran. Faster than ever before in my life. I drank in the words of the Word.

I had been so worn down by graduate school, by dawning realizations of the pain of my own childhood, and by the inadequacies of an unsatisfying marriage that I felt God carry me through those weeks and months, aided by the prayers of that group. My inner terrain was changing—sometimes so quickly that I feared sharing who I might be becoming with even those closest to me. The Bible study on Thursday and the Eucharist on Sunday became the frame that supported my life. I—no, we—moved from that Thursday group into the life of the congregation in Sunday worship. Supported and challenged by one another, transformed into an intentional family of prayer and sharing, we were a small community within a larger one—and the Thursday night Bible study began to work as spiritual leaven throughout the whole.

Perhaps the single most significant event in the parish during those years was the much-anticipated arrival of the new rector. Timothy Kimbrough, his wife, Darlene, and their two boys came to Holy Family on December 3, 1989. He was only thirty-one, and he had been ordained for five years. At that time, most Episcopal priests were much older, because the denomination had adopted a policy of seeking only "mature" candidates for the ministry. Despite his youth, Timothy had made it through the process and had already served as both deacon and vicar in a mission congregation in Laurinburg, North Carolina. I had never known a priest my own age before—much less one who would be in charge of an entire parish. I remember his first day. He was extremely personable, very eager, and somewhat nervous. He would later confess, "I had no idea *what* God had done, putting me here." I liked him. And so did the rest of the congregation.

He liked us, too. It was a wonderful moment of confluence—a congregation already moving ahead and finding the right pastor to help focus and empower a growing vision for mutual ministry. He remembers that the church was eager for a new start and that there was "lots of excitement and enthusiasm." He was particularly impressed with the young adults and with the Thursday night groups that had already "formed community among themselves." There was openness and support from the long-time members, too—most of whose spiritual lives had been transformed through involvement with charismatic renewal movements in the 1970s.

And Timothy's predecessors had created a legacy of social justice activism that remained central at Holy Family. As is the case with many mainline churches, the parish liked to serve, to do good things for people in God's name—working with prisoners, protesting the death penalty, teaching disadvantaged children to read, raising money for missionaries, and feeding the poor. Someone always had a new cause to support and the congregation would respond. People at Holy Family liked to get their hands dirty for Jesus. But there were some weaknesses, as well. The church was small with a small budget. And, for a decade, leadership had not deepened the church's worship and spiritual life. As a new rector, Timothy had much to work with and for: "There were many people who had inquiring hearts, a real hunger for God, and a nascent love for the liturgy."

The search committee who recommended Timothy expressed a desire to continue the church's outreach and for "making disciples, forming Christians," but there was no clear sense of how that would happen. Neither he nor the vestry who called him had a particular agenda for the church—especially regarding growth. He says, "I was not thinking how is this going to grow the church, rather I was trying to be faithful to the moment." To him, the priesthood was about "being present," through "doing your job" in providing liturgical leadership and caring for people. As a young priest, he appeared to like being called Father Timothy, a title that reflected the nurturing presence he brought to the community. Years later, when I read Jan Karon's winsome novels about Father Tim, an Episcopal priest in North Carolina, I read her character through the priestly practice of Timothy Kimbrough. Although he had no specific plan for the parish, Timothy possessed powerful convictions about the nature of the church, the life of God's people, and his own vocation as priest. To him, the point of priesthood was bringing God's presence into community through the sacraments. "The life of faithfulness, of Christian discipleship," he states, "begins and ends in the Eucharist."

Thus, Timothy began to focus his early ministry around the table, developing the Eucharist as the center point of Christian nurture and witness. Although the interim rector, the Rev. Ralph Macy, had served Eucharist every Sunday, Timothy remembers that "this was not a settled matter when I arrived." Some people lobbied the young rector for Morning Prayer as the regular service. But Timothy persisted and continued the interim practice of weekly communion.

Both Chip and Timothy came into their respective parishes and immediately changed the liturgy. Where Chip, however, failed, Timothy succeeded. The churches, although founded within a few years of each other, were very different places with different outlooks and congregational histories. And these factors certainly accounted for some of the differences. But Chip had taken away from the liturgy; Timothy added to it. Chip tended to emphasize belief and conservative theology; Timothy emphasized worship and community. Chip assumed certain things about the parish and proceeded on those assumptions; Timothy assumed nothing.

Early in his ministry, Timothy began to teach and preach on the nature of the Eucharist, of Christian life and ministry shaped by the sacraments. He insisted that this vision was at the heart of what it meant to be Anglican. Week after week, he began sermons asserting that "Anglicans believe," or "Anglicanism teaches," as he attempted to inform our identity with a eucharistic vision. He led the congregation in an instructed Eucharist, a service where the minister goes through the Prayer Book step by step, teaching on each aspect of the liturgy's history and theology.

Timothy essentially turned the Sunday morning service into a hands-on seminary class in sacramental theology. Drawing from his own talents as a composer and pianist, he would add new hymns, chants, ancient prayers, or some current ecumenical practice to the service—each time explaining the theological dimensions of the change. And, like the choir, the congregation would actually practice the change in the minutes before the service began so that we would feel comfortable with it in worship. At Holy Family I learned new music and new prayers, and reached into parts of the Prayer Book of which I was previously unaware. Timothy's passion for worship, drawn from the historic practice of the church, helped knit together my spirituality with my studies in church history and theology. For the first time in years I felt very whole at the altar. "I wanted the parish to understand," he recalls, "that the apostolic character of the church's practice was as important as serving in the soup kitchen." I was beginning to understand, the congregation was beginning to understand.

As his vision grew, Timothy began to "seek out people who would help this along." He nurtured their growing excitement, and awareness of faith centered around worship. David recalls that "Holy Family was where I developed my theology of the Eucharist as the meal after a barn raising.

"As I continued the weekly discipline of Word and Sacrament, I began to think of reading the word, listening to the sermon, praying for people, and saying the creed as work, the work of the people—like an Amish barn raising. And then, when we went to take communion, it was as if we were sitting down at the table and refreshing ourselves from the work while at the same time celebrating our togetherness and accomplishments."

The parish was getting it and Timothy began to enlist others to help communicate this vision—including me. For the first time, a parish gave me room to explore gifts of teaching and speaking, of instructing and leading. And as I began to teach, I realized how many questions I had myself. Timothy's eucharistic theology sounded a bit too "catholic." I was worried that he might be sacrificing the Protestant nature of Anglican tradition, with its emphasis on scripture, in favor of Roman Catholic conceptions of worship. I wondered if his take on Anglicanism was only a kind of liturgical romanticism. The kind I had seen at Christ Church. The kind that had led Tom Howard to leave the Episcopal Church and embrace the authority of the Pope.

Oddly enough, Timothy also worried me because I perceived him as being too liberal. He completely supported women's ordination and encouraged us to theologically explore the new inclusive language liturgies produced by the denomination. Holy Family is the first place I took Holy Communion from a female priest. It was the first place I read worship texts that replaced "Him" with "God." Timothy also seemed overly flexible when it came to tradition. Theologically, he preferred adult baptism over that of infant baptism because adult baptism embodied the intentionality of Christian discipleship. He wanted to replace the small baptismal font with a large baptistry where new Christians could be fully immersed. He confided to some of us that he wanted to baptize completely naked babies by dunking them in this baptismal tub! He allowed any baptized person—even tiny babies—to take communion. I liked and respected him, but I was having a great deal of trouble figuring him out. It was difficult to understand how he could be so committed to tradition on one hand and be so intent on reforming it on the other.

I am not sure I consciously understood this dynamic, but I was learning from it. Timothy demonstrated how to appropriate tradition. As was the case for me, he confesses that "the Episcopal Church becomes home for me in being connected with the practices of the early church." Although I never used those exact words, my experience of the Anglican liturgy was essentially the same. Its power was the power of connection through tradition. Through it, I became part of something much larger than myself, part of Christ's body stretching back through time to its earliest communal expression. I had been drawn to it because I sensed I was part of the communion of saints—a doctrine that Timothy insists "can only be taken seriously if you maintain the practices of that early community." We are part of them and they are part of us insofar as we are joined around the practices of prayer, worship, and service. We were the church because, through the mystery of baptism and God's grace, we continued doing the work of the church.

At Christ Church, the problem was that many people interpreted this idea woodenly. For some I knew in South Hamilton, the practices of faith must be *exactly* the same through time in order to be theologically legitimate. For the Catholic-leaning parishioners, contemporary Christians had to do and believe just as had Christians in the Middle Ages or the ancient world. And the evangelical Calvinists in my acquaintance, including Buck, had the same attitude toward the Bible and the Protestant Reformation. Tradition was interpreted as static, an objective reality passed from one generation to another, maintained through adherence to some teaching authority, and, if necessary, its parameters enforced through ecclesiastical discipline.

Timothy, however, taught that ancient practice informs contemporary practice. Tradition was not static; rather, it was dynamic, a living entity passed through time that each generation adds to and enriches by its own experience and understanding of God. He also believed that certain aspects of Christian tradition had been obscured or ignored—such as the ministry of women in the earliest churches. He would later tell me that "there are sources within ancient tradition that point toward a broader, more inclusive direction." For the church to live into its mission, for God's people to be formed in faith, parish and people must reappropriate tradition, honoring it and reforming it at the same time. By virtue of baptism, Christians are bound to tradition but are not bound by it. Or, as my Lutheran friends put it, we are the reformed church always reforming.

Nowhere was Timothy's gift for appropriating tradition more evident than in Easter Vigil. Before he arrived, I had not been to an Easter Vigil in two years. Chip did not offer the service at St. Stephen's. Holy Family did not celebrate Easter Vigil either. But Timothy believed it to be the primary service of the Christian year, the time when the whole story of faith—salvation, baptism, Resurrection, and God's eternal banquet—were presented symbolically to the congregation. Everything else pointed toward that night.

With characteristic liturgical enthusiasm, Timothy scheduled the Great Vigil of Easter for ten in the evening—wanting the first Eucharist of Easter around midnight. He remembers the early vigils as small, liturgically awkward affairs in comparison with the shape they would later take. But I remember them warmly as a tiny band of liturgical pioneers moved forward in Christian practice together. Before celebrating the day, Timothy, who enlisted Todd Granger to help, taught on the nature of the Vigil and its role in early Christianity. I learned more about the Triduum, the three-day sacred drama retelling Jesus' Passion. Timothy instituted an all-night prayer vigil from the end of the evening Maundy Thursday service until noon on Good Friday. Taking seriously Jesus' plea to the disciples to "watch" with him in the garden, parishioners stayed awake through the night and prayed with the preconsecrated bread and wine, so that they might solemnly feast on Christ's body dur-

ing the day on which the elements could not be consecrated. He also had us venerate the cross on Good Friday—to go up and kneel before it or kiss it as the congregation sang haunting chants in the background. As at Christ Church, Holy Family entered into Holy Week with spiritual gusto. But at Holy Family it was more intimate, less a religious production and a bit more like a sacred family reunion.

Through the years, although I would not be at the church to see it, Easter Vigil has molded the character of Holy Family. Timothy linked the service to a parish-created adult education program, Journey in Faith, a year-long preparation of teaching that was required for one to become confirmed in the church, and is, to quote Timothy, "absolutely central to who we are." Journey in Faith reflects the practice of early Christian communities that required long periods of teaching and prayer in order for one to be baptized or confirmed. According to ancient tradition, those who wanted to embrace Christianity, called *catechumens,* submitted to intensive faith formation. After a three-year period, they could be baptized and received into the local Christian community at Easter Vigil.

Holy Family's catechumenal program lasts a year and includes periods of inquiry, exploration, teaching, and commitment. Persons wanting to be baptized—and over the years Timothy has baptized a number of adults and families—and be confirmed in the church—do so during Easter Vigil, at which time the bishop makes his yearly visit. In the last couple years, the service has had "an apostolic feel," with people standing at the windows outside the building because the sanctuary was full. With the people gathered in anticipation of Christ's Resurrection, God's Word read in darkness, candlelight shining on the newly baptized, the bishop's solemn charge to believers, the bells ringing at midnight, and the joyful first Eucharist of Easter, Holy Family makes ancient faith live. Of it,

Timothy says smiling, "It is the closest thing I've ever experienced to being part of the primitive church."

For all the splendor of Easter Vigil, life was not always so exciting at Holy Family. Mostly, we washed dishes. Men, women, married couples, single people, long-term members, and newcomers. We washed dishes after church, after making emergency meals for parishioners, after potlucks and parties, after making muffins for the coffee hour. We washed dishes at church and in each other's homes. Holy Family loved table fellowship. Not only the fellowship of the Lord's table, but also the shared times around parish hall and dining room tables. And it was around suppers and sinks that God's presence came to us in unexpected ways. Thinking back on the days at Holy Family, I realize I spent more time in the kitchen than in the sanctuary. And in the kitchen I learned how to let down my guard, let go of my pretenses, and be myself. There is something completely humbling and profoundly human about baking bread in community.

In the seventeenth century, a French monk named Brother Lawrence wrote a prayer expressing kitchen spirituality: "Lord of all pots and pans. . . . Make me a saint by getting meals and washing up the plates." At Holy Family, kitchen work helped form us into a community of disciples—it was the place where we practiced the priesthood of God's people. As we prepared meals and washed dishes, we shared worries and concerns, listened to struggles and joy, offered pastoral advice, and, more than occasionally, laughed uproariously. Lesley Stanley organized us into a monthly muffin-baking brigade. On a Saturday we would bake hundreds of mini-muffins, to be served during coffee hour. Once every three months we would spend the day filling the freezer with casseroles to be distributed among the congregation as the need arose—sickness or childbirth or strained graduate school budgets. Anyone, anytime, was free to go to the basement and simply take food as needed.

There were potlucks and parties for every occasion—birthdays and holy days, comings and goings, passing exams or missing home, Easter, All Saints' Day, Thanksgiving, and Christmas. The food tended to be either Southern or traditional English specialties— reflecting Todd Granger's passion for Louisiana cooking or helping Lesley Stanley feel less homesick for England. At every event the tables were laden with dozens of dishes. In Holy Family's basement I first tasted grits and okra, black-eyed peas, biscuits and gravy, pecan pie, and several waistline-expanding versions of candied sweet potatoes. We poured our limited resources into preparing food—the table was sometimes graced with extravagances such as Beef Wellington or crawfish étouffée. The potlucks became tangible ways of expressing our gratefulness to God for one another. I worked hard on the dishes I created, wanting them to honor the table and its guests. Often created by a sacrifice of time and money, my casseroles were an offering. I placed those dishes on the rickety church-school tables as reverently as I gave the Sunday collection plates to Timothy on the days I served as an usher. As with the Sunday morning offering, the Saturday night suppers were places on which we presented the work of our hands to God.

There were always dishes to wash. And tables to set and linens to iron. There were vestments to keep clean and orderly. Altar clothes to press. Flowers to be arranged. Bulletins to be folded. Music to be played, and hymns to be practiced. We just pitched in and did it. Throughout my life I had often resisted the "Martha" tasks of housework, thinking them somehow less than the "Mary" task of doing theology and being with Jesus. But at Holy Family I began to see the irony in the sisters' biblical story. The "better part" that Jesus urged could be discovered among the pots and pans if the tasks were done intentionally. We did the work of spiritual house-keeping purposefully—as ways to love God and one another. As we knew God to be in the Eucharist, we discovered God's presence at the sink. As writer Kathleen Norris found to be true elsewhere, and so observed in her book *The Quotidian Mysteries,* "Laundry, liturgy and 'women's work' all serve to ground us in the world, and they need not grind us down." They were all of a piece.

For those of us in graduate school, these simple tasks gave us a way to live outside our heads, away from the ivory tower, to expe-rience the sacredness of the mundane. I learned that God might be known through intellectual endeavor, but that God would always be found in the round of daily mindfulness. As Brother Lawrence discovered, "The time of business does not with me differ from the time of prayer; and in the noise and clatter of my kitchen, while sev-eral persons are at the same time calling for different things, I pos-sess God in as great tranquility as if I were upon my knees at the blessed sacrament." So, I went about doing what I did—Bible study, worship, offering hospitality, making meals, washing dishes, arrang-ing flowers, and singing hymns. Holy Family taught me that some-times the smaller the thing, the greater the spiritual transformation.

By emphasizing the dailiness of faith, Holy Family was antic-ipating a trend in American religion toward spiritual practices. In his book *After Heaven,* Robert Wuthnow suggests that "practice-oriented spirituality" is a quietly growing religious phenomenon. Often, Americans think of spiritual practices—things such as prayer, meditation, discernment, and spiritual direction—as pri-vate. Yet, at Holy Family, practices were corporate. They emerged from our desire to create meaningful community, strengthened in Bible study, fed at the Eucharist, and lived in the kitchen and out in the world. We made churchgoing itself a practice of faith.

It was not simply the fact that Holy Family was a congregation; it was a congregation involved in sacred reflection in worship and community life. We did not assume that faith would always be found in a church building because it had so been for our parents—as did the congregation at St. Stephen's. Rather, we chose to be a holy household and imbued our building with sacredness. Holy Family was not "holy" unless the "family" was there. The vestry would later write, "Holy Family's buildings have never been ends in themselves, but rather tools with which the People of God and the Holy Spirit worked to accomplish the mission of the Church." God could be found there insofar as an intentional spiritual family dwelt within.

One of the favorite hymns at Holy Family in those days was the traditional Shaker song, "Simple Gifts." Its words summed up those two years for me: "'Tis the gift to be simple, 'tis the gift to be free, 'tis the gift to come down where you ought to be." At Holy Family I had been given the gift of being exactly who I was at exactly where I needed to be. When I arrived at the parish, I was a spiritual and emotional wreck. The simplicity of the parish, with its kind people and its practice of faith in daily life, put the pieces back together for me. There I became a true congregant, a member of a parish family, loved and valued for exactly who I was and what I was called to do in the world. At Holy Family I began to sense the contours of a faithful life—one not defined by strict doctrines and moral certainty but one lived in true friendship and daily practice. I was stepping out of a world riddled with fear into one shaped by God's gracious and accepting love.

In August 1991 I left Holy Family for a new job—a teaching post back at Westmont, my undergraduate college, in Santa Barbara.

On my final Sunday in North Carolina I walked into church and was surprised by the lovely flower arrangements gracing the altar: "Given by David and Leslie Frauenfelder in honor and celebration of the ministry of Diana and Buck Butler among us." It was a bittersweet day of tearful hugs and good-byes. Holding an armful of yellow blossoms bestowed on me by Leslie, I lingered on the patio until the very last—enjoying the company of our friends. I wanted that Sunday to go on forever. It was odd, too, knowing that I had helped renew that little church by simply being there and giving of myself. It would go on without me and I would never again be part of it in the same way.

It did go on—in extraordinary ways. In the years since then, they adopted a mission statement that expressed exactly what I had learned there: "Pray and worship, celebrating life together in Jesus Christ, centered in the Eucharist and in the stewardship of our daily lives." By 1999, the congregation had grown to nearly eight hundred baptized members—half of them children.

One autumn Sunday in 2000 I sat in Holy Family's sanctuary for the first time in almost ten years. The space—which once seemed rather empty on Sunday morning—strained to hold the crowds as ushers sat people on folding chairs in every conceivable corner. A building program is under way. Timothy will finally get his permanent baptistry, where he can immerse the congregation's naked babies in the water of God, have a communion table set up in the middle of the sanctuary, and have enough classroom space to accommodate all the children. The little congregation with no plans to grow grew faster—and deeper—than anyone could have imagined a decade earlier. With its emphasis on liturgy and outreach, its openness and willingness to experiment, its ability to translate tradition into new practices, Church of the Holy Family had returned to themselves and their own history. Or, to paraphrase T. S. Eliot, they had arrived where they had started and knew the place for the first time. How did they get there? Timothy muses, "I guess this is what happens when you take church seriously—when you are devoted to what the church teaches and [has] taught, when you put it in[to] practice and work with it."

I had come to Holy Family wondering if I could ever be part of a church again, and they gave me a place to be. Like the parish itself in those years, I came home and "knew the place for the first time." Holy Family was my family, in whose spiritual household I had learned to practice faith. They had become the kind of family I had always sought. I dreaded leaving. There, I had glimpsed healing and a way of being Christian different from any that I had known. I wanted to be with my friends, those good people of Holy Family, who had become my family. Despite all that I had learned, I did not feel strong enough to go it alone.

I sobbed all the way to California. I could not begin to imagine that the next several years of my life would make graduate school look like kindergarten—and that soon I would have to put into practice everything I believed to be true about God and faith.

CHAPTER FIVE

Interim

Santa Barbara, California, 1991–1994

The coastal fog lingered that summer. Typically, it comes in late May and stays through June or early July, thus giving rise to the nickname for Santa Barbara's seasonal weather curse: June gloom. When it eventually abates, the rest of the summer is sunny and warm. But in 1991 the fog persisted. When I returned to Santa Barbara late on an August afternoon, the city was shrouded in fog. California fog is not for the timid. It closes in on you when you least expect it. Dense and dark, it cuts you off from the rest of the world. Funny thing about that fog, though. If you drive into its thick cloudiness and lose your bearings, you cannot simply stop waiting for it to clear. Instead, you slow down and follow whatever bit of visible road lies immediately ahead. If you stop, someone will hit you from behind. You keep moving, slowly and more deliberately, but you keep moving. You must go through it.

It was still foggy on my first Sunday in my new hometown. Buck and I walked to church, the small mission of Christ the King in Goleta, a suburban area north of the city. Despite my happiness at Holy Family, Buck had grown increasingly uncomfortable with the Episcopal Church—especially over the issue of women's ordination. He insisted that when we moved to Santa Barbara we would join a parish with no female clergy. Although this bothered me, I went along with the request. We had grown apart during those years at Duke, and I no longer wanted to be a missionary. We argued over theology—a smokescreen, I suspected, obscuring deeper issues. To preserve the marriage, I learned to keep many of my opinions to myself. Church was the only place where we experienced the semblance of a relationship. I did not want to jeopardize that. Holy Family had helped. Maybe a new church, along with a job and steady income, would help even more.

Buck's requirement eliminated All Saints-by-the-Sea, which, by that time, had a woman associate with a reputation for being very liberal. The other two churches in town appeared unsatisfactory for other reasons. Only Christ the King remained. Assured by the phone book advertisement: "The Rev. Donald Stivers, Vicar," we headed to Christ the King on a gray, nearly silent Sunday morning.

I had not been to Christ the King for years. The church was founded in 1967, at the height of the charismatic movement in the Episcopal Church. Throughout the 1960s some mainline Protestants had indulged in Pentecostal-type enthusiasm and experienced New Testament *charismata,* or supernatural spiritual gifts, such as speaking in tongues and miraculous healing. They believed this to be a divine visitation, a manifestation of God's spirit renewing their church. For a time, the Episcopal Church proved hospitable to this new movement. Christ the King began as a charismatic renewal mission. They prided themselves on having a Catholic altar, evangelical preaching, and charismatic worship, thus combining the "three streams" of historic Christianity—Catholic, Protestant, and Pentecostal.

When I was a college student, some of my friends, including Rich Yale, regularly attended Christ the King. Indeed, Rich, who by 1991 was himself an Episcopal priest, had been mentored by the congregation's first vicar, the Rev. Bob Harvey, a man respected in charismatic Episcopal circles. I had visited Christ the King with Rich a decade earlier for a Lenten healing service. The congregation met in a utilitarian structure that resembled a California ranch house. A multipurpose room served as the sanctuary, with stacking chairs and no decoration. Even then, the church's evangelical message, Pentecostal enthusiasm, and political conservatism seemed narrow—especially when compared with All Saints. I did not like it very much.

Christ the King was walking distance from our small condominium in Goleta, surrounded by a grove of walnut trees in what was once a lush farming community. We entered the church's property, passing a filigree wrought iron cross and memorial garden, and were stunned by an unexpected sight: a fifty-something woman wearing a black suit and collar walked out of the church office. She hurried into the sanctuary. A woman priest? At the church door, my husband grabbed a bulletin and read with a moan, "The Rev. Michelle Woodhouse, interim vicar." The good Rev. Stivers had recently retired. The woman was the church's temporary minister. "I'm so sorry," I mumbled. "I checked. The phone book said they had a man. It is too late to go elsewhere." He replied, "I'll manage. I just won't take the Eucharist. We can go somewhere else next week."

"Maybe she's okay," I suggested. But inwardly I panicked. I was tired of his judgmental attitudes. If Christ the King did not work, there would no Episcopal "somewhere else" in town for him. "After all," I said, "these are conservative Episcopalians. They wouldn't have a liberal priest. Even as an interim."

"Maybe. I doubt it. A conservative woman priest?"

"Perhaps they've already found someone new," I speculated. "Maybe she won't be around for long."

The people seemed friendly. They warmly addressed the priest as Mother Michelle. The service followed the prayer book liturgy—the only charismatic elements being the praise songs that replaced traditional music and a healing service that followed the main Eucharist. The Rev. Michelle Woodhouse read the liturgy with a mature assurance. With an equally capable sense, she stepped behind the pulpit and began to preach. "Please, Lord," I prayed. "Don't let it be heretical."

I do not remember the specifics of that sermon. I do remember thinking that she possessed a strong preaching voice and a scholarly command of the biblical passages. I was startled as she marshaled church history to her cause. And I distinctly remember her correctly quoting St. Augustine. She interpreted the scriptures deftly. If I were ever to preach a sermon, I thought, I would want it to be like this one.

I looked over at Buck. At the beginning of her sermon, he sat with his arms crossed tightly on his chest. By the middle, his grip had loosened. And as she ended, he was leaning forward in rapt attention, with his elbows on his knees and his chin in his hand. He looked both surprised and bewildered. She had passed his orthodoxy test.

When it came time for the Eucharist, he went forward. It was the first time he took communion from a female priest. After church, I waited for his theological verdict. The fog had lifted and we chatted on the sunbathed patio with other parishioners. He questioned them about the search for a new priest. All the candidates were men. "Well, I don't believe women should be priests," he told me later. "But she was so biblical. I just thought I could take communion from her. It is probably okay if she is temporary. After all, they plan to hire a man as their real priest."

But Michelle continued to impress this reluctant churchman. About three weeks later he would say to me, half in jest, "When you grow up, I hope you are just like Mother Michelle." Although I was growing weary of such comments, this felt like implicit approval. So I sought her out and asked if she would be my spiritual director. As Santa Barbara's summer fog dissolved into autumn memory, I knew that my inner life was still shrouded in the gloom. Removed from the comforting practices and community of Holy Family, I was not sure I could find my way. I remembered the words of the fifteenth-century monastic reformer, St. Antonius: "To assist at the love of God and devotion, to possess peace . . . it is useful and necessary to have a spiritual guide to whom you can report at all times your conduct and your failings that he may help and counsel you." I had no peace. I needed what ancient Celtic Christians called *anmchara,* a soul-friend.

An interim time in the life of a congregation is the time between pastors, and it is often associated with feelings of loss, confusion, and uncertainty. Roger Nicholson, an expert on interim ministry, says in his book *Temporary Shepherds,* which I later read, "A congregation facing that time between the end of one pastorate and the beginning of another is entering strange territory. . . . It has been likened to the biblical time of wandering in the wilderness after the flight of the Hebrew people from Egypt." As "temporary shepherds," interim ministers help people through this wilderness—enabling them to deal with grief and anger, helping them to find their identity in God, working with conflict and change, strengthening their own leadership skills, and preparing people for the new ministry. Interim periods are corporate liminal states. The old has passed; the new has not yet come.

I had experienced some liminal times in faith, times of questioning and change—most notably in 1980, when I first became an Episcopalian. And I had experienced a couple interim periods as a church member—empty, worrisome months—after Barry Howe left Christ Church or as we waited at Church of the Holy Family for Timothy to arrive. But rarely had the two—my own internal liminality and a congregational interim—converged. At Christ the King, they did. Inwardly and outwardly, I was in a wilderness of not knowing, not seeing, not understanding. The old was passing; the new had not yet come.

In some ways, mainstream Protestantism has been in a sort of liminal place, a corporate interim period, for the last two or three decades. During that time, most of the old mainline churches either approved or more vigorously supported the ministerial vocations of women—a change of such magnitude that it forced whole denominations into a sort of spiritual wilderness. In some cases, intense controversy over clergywomen drove life-long members away. In most cases, the increasing numbers of women in leadership raised additional theological, practical, and institutional issues—such as feminist theology, inclusive language, sexual harassment, and management styles and systems.

As women entered the pulpits of more local churches, however, women's ordination became less an "issue" and more a matter of personal relationships. This immediate reality forced churchgoers to examine their attitudes toward women in ministry and decide for themselves whether to accept or reject the practice. In churches across the nation, churchgoers have renegotiated traditional gender roles and their expectations of clerical leadership around women's ordination. The impact of women in ministry has been so sweeping in American church life that even *Time* magazine dubbed it "the second Protestant Reformation." Although Protestants recognize the magnitude of the changes, we still have no idea where we are ultimately going with it all. Upon her election, Episcopal Bishop Barbara Harris preached that "although we may not see clearly the full pathway that lies before us . . . we trust our God for the next step of the journey." A journey had begun, but where? Even after three decades, we are still not entirely sure.

Like other Protestants in mainline churches, I could not avoid the issue of women's ordination. But like most evangelicals, I had been indoctrinated into a world defined by more traditional gender roles than those experienced by other Americans my own age. For years I struggled with conflicting ideas about women and faith. Could women be religious leaders, ordained ministers, and bishops? And if so, what were the implications of women's ordination for the church and its practices, worship, and theology? My conservative friends—my conservative husband—said no, they could not. Intellectually, however, I was pretty sure I disagreed with them but could not bring myself to say so. I would lose friends, maybe a marriage. The struggle left me in a sort of intellectual and spiritual cul de sac—a place where I could not see the way ahead.

As a teenager at Scottsdale Bible Church, there were clear roles for men and women. Men were teachers, preachers, and theologians; women taught children and other women, might become missionaries, and served meals. My high school youth minister remarked that it was "too bad" I was a girl, otherwise, with my interest and abilities in theology, I could go to seminary. In the 1970s, however, more liberal views of women's roles even challenged evangelicals. In college, I had rejected much of this as nonsense and, for a short time, toyed with the idea of becoming a Methodist minister. That interest abated, however, when pressed by the antifeminist theological backlash at seminary in the mid-1980s. It became obvious to me that evangelical women could not succeed without men supporting them, and I buckled under the weight of their gender-traditionalism. In the process, I had married someone with deep antipathy toward women in leadership. As an impressionable twenty-something woman, I did much of this unconsciously—seeking, as young women often do, the approval of the authorities around me.

While at Duke Divinity School, however, the once-powerful arguments of my male seminary professors began to lose their force. In graduate seminars I heard new things about the role of women in church history, the influence of women on theology, and what the Bible said about women. Although I sometimes resisted listening, I was hearing at a level much deeper than was obvious to my classmates or friends.

And while a graduate student I taught in the Divinity School. The seminary women, many of whom were pursuing ordination in the Methodist Church, impressed me. They were good students—often better than the men—mature and assured in their sense of call and vocation. They had struggled with women's ordination as well, in deeply personal ways. Many were mothers starting their careers—or older women pursuing a second life path. I liked them. And I liked having them in my classrooms. They enriched discussions by bringing their experience to bear on the subjects we studied. Many possessed levels of insight and wisdom that I did not—they taught me when to be quiet as a teacher and when to let the students teach. It was impossible to deny that most of these women had experienced genuine calls to the ministry.

Teaching female seminarians became deeply problematic for me. How could I help prepare them for ordination if I did not believe that they should be ordained? I began to notice that, despite my regard for some of the women as students, I actually treated my female students with less care and attention than I did my male students. Having experienced the same treatment as a student myself, I was horrified to realize my own sexism. I tried to convince myself that my job was to teach them—and what their denominations did with them after that was not my business. I rationalized the problem away. But I tried to equalize my classroom attention and stop favoring the men.

Much of this would have remained an internal and personal struggle if not for a specific issue facing the Episcopal Church. Although the denomination had ordained female clerics since 1976, few women actually served in churches in those early years. By the end of the 1980s, however, local congregations were calling more women to their pulpits and altars, and the theoretical possibility of women's ordination was becoming a reality in the lives of churchgoers. Many conservative Episcopalians still believed that the Bible and tradition forbade women's ordination. They could theologically bend the rules by citing Paul's injunction, "I allow no woman to hold authority over a man." Female clerics, some argued, only held authority insofar as a male priest or their male bishop delegated it to them. Hence, a woman serving as rector held no real authority. She only served as a sort of vehicle for ultimate male authority. As long as the church ordained women only as priests and refused to consecrate them as bishops, this theological two-step enabled conservatives to grudgingly allow for female priests while insisting on the normative authority of a male priesthood.

Disgruntled Episcopalians drew their theological line at female bishops and threatened schism, should any diocese dare elect a woman to the apostolic office. In 1988 Massachusetts called their theological bluff. They elected Barbara Harris, a liberal African American, to serve as their suffragan (or associate) bishop. She was the first female bishop in the worldwide Anglican Communion and the first woman consecrated into a pastoral line believed to stretch back to the apostles.

In most of my experience as a churchgoer, national church issues rarely intrude into local congregational life in any meaningful way. This, however, was different. In the weeks between the election and Harris's consecration, Episcopalians fretted openly about schism. To make matters worse, Harris's noted liberalism made conservatives feel as if the move were a personal attack on them, a kind of theological slap in the face. Some of my right-wing friends, mostly from Christ Church days, tried to recruit me for the "traditionalist" side, sending me long missives and propaganda warning of "apostasy." During the Harris election, I was still at St. Stephen's. For a short time, the national controversy even muted the furor over Chip's ministry. Chip and Carol tried to stay out of the fray, but some of their supporters vocally opposed her.

Including me. Around that same time, I gave a magazine interview about women's ordination in which I took the opposing side. Some evangelicals held "biblical feminist" views and generally approved of women's ordination. That position had been quite popular in evangelical circles in the 1970s. By the late 1980s, however, most evangelicals had retreated on women's issues. My position could be best described as "soft opposition," arguing that the scriptural passages seemed clear enough that woman were not to hold ecclesiastical authority, but I recognized that the prohibition might take different forms in different denominations. Hence, a woman might under some circumstances serve as an associate pastor or hold authority in the mission field. Such nuanced traditionalism won the approbation of some evangelical colleagues, who seemed to approve of well-educated women who did not bend to the winds of secular feminism. The position won me friends—mostly conservative men.

When the day came for Harris's consecration, February 11, 1989, I stayed at home to watch the historic event on television.

I was angry and I expected to be appalled by the service. Something strange happened to me, however, when Barbara Harris knelt to receive the laying on of hands from the sixty-three bishops there gathered. As the men crowded around her, I felt humbled, indeed, deeply moved. There was one black woman, doubly an outsider in American society, elevated to the historic episcopate, being endowed with Christ's authority, a pastor in the church catholic, serving in a line stretching back to the earliest Christian communities. From the ancient liturgy they prayed words never said over a woman before: "Father, make Barbara a bishop in your Church. Pour out upon her the power of your princely Spirit, whom you bestowed upon your beloved Son Jesus Christ. . . . Fill, we pray, the heart of this your servant whom you have chosen to be a bishop in your Church, with such love of you and of all the people that she may feed and tend the flock of Christ."

She stood among them and they vested her a bishop. As the ecclesiastical garments enfolded her, I saw a woman—friend and apostle of Jesus commissioned to continue his work—being draped with the authority of high priesthood. This was no heresy. It was bringing into the heart of God those whom society had rejected and despised. An earthly icon of God's love to all humanity, signifying that "those who were humble have been lifted up and those who were far off have been brought near." The Episcopal Church had done the right thing. I had been wrong.

Although I was too scared to admit it, the Rt. Rev. Barbara Harris had converted me that day. One white woman in North Carolina, watching the event on television, experienced the power of being included in God's family as another of her sex was made bishop. When quizzed about the event, I offered a noncommittal reply: "It surprised me." It is hard to admit that I had been wrong and even harder to do so with the full expectation of opposition.

It was not until more than a year later, at the Church of the Holy Family, that I would receive communion for the first time from a woman priest. No woman had ever served at Holy Family. Timothy took one summer Sunday off and asked another priest to fill in for him—a female colleague. In keeping with parish policy, no announcement regarding the celebrant was made ahead of time. When we arrived and discerned the situation, Buck swore he would not take communion. I felt confused, torn between personal willingness and family loyalty. I do not know her name. As she stood behind the table with her hands raised in prayer, I had no idea what to expect. The roof did not fall in, lightning did not strike the building, no visions of pagan priestesses appeared before my eyes. Suddenly, the altar, a sometimes forbidding reminder of Jesus' bloody sacrifice, became a family table with a meal laid by God's motherly love. I felt fully part of Christ's body, a member of the priesthood of all believers. As she lifted the bread toward God, I almost heard myself saying, "I am part of her priesthood. Women are priests, priests to God."

When the usher signaled our pew, Buck did not move. But I left my seat, walked up the aisle, knelt at the rail, and held my hand out for another woman to place the bread in my hand. I felt myself truly Christian, an invited guest at God's banquet, redeemed and restored in grace. Taking the Eucharist that morning was the most joyful act of rebellion I have ever performed. When I returned to my seat, my husband turned to me saying, "I can't believe you did that." And he was not the only one to notice that I had gone forward. Others at Holy Family, friends worried about my ambivalence regarding women's ordination, made similar remarks.

On the way home from church, I told him about the day of Barbara Harris's consecration. But he really did not understand. By the time we moved to Santa Barbara, I was a quiet—but firmly committed—convert to women's ordination. We rarely broached the subject. He never expected that I would break familial ranks, and he labeled me a partisan on the wrong side. It had become important to me. I wanted him to change his mind. I had a hard time keeping my opinion to myself. More than anything else, however, I wanted to maintain the unity of this fragile relationship. Faithful Christians work things out. One of our friends said to us a month before our wedding, "You know, divorce is not an option for Christians." My marriage mattered to me. When he insisted that there should be "no church with a woman priest," I outwardly agreed. My mind had changed, but I was reluctant to make an issue of it, knowing what consequences might arise.

Despite my vocation as a teacher, I was effectively silent. A different woman inside from the one who appeared on the outside. What a relief it was to see Michelle Woodhouse at Christ the King on that morning in August 1991. I hoped she might help me through this wilderness.

Spiritual direction is an ancient Christian practice that has taken many forms in its long history. The spiritual director is a friend, guide, mentor, and companion along the journey. A midwife, a mother in faith. At its most basic level, spiritual direction is, as Kathleen Fischer writes in *Women at the Well,* "a conversation in which a person gives expression to her experience of faith and discerns its movement." A director listens, and in that listening she helps birth a story of faith. She plays midwife to words. "Women," Fischer claims, "need someone who will hear their stories *on their own terms* and help them find their own horizons."

Although I had just finished writing a lengthy doctoral dissertation on the history of the Episcopal Church, my truest self was silent. Marriage had something to do with it, but it went back further than that. I do not know how or where I learned it, but I had learned not to say what I really thought or truly believed or most desired. I internalized Tolstoy's *Anna Karenina:* women who express their deepest passions get run over by trains. The way of safety is to say what others want you to say, to repeat the words of those who hold power. And if you do that well enough you might gain a modicum of control over your own life. By age thirty, after a decade of higher education, I knew everyone's words but my own. Holy Family had given me a place to use my hands and, very tentatively, hear the words forming within. When I left, I had only just begun to realize that I might have a voice of my own.

Christianity is a faith of words: "In the beginning was the Word, and the Word was with God, and the Word was God." God speaks creation into being, the Spirit whispers life into the world. Wisdom is God's name and holy words impart the way of holiness and the mystery of being. Saints and martyrs witnessed through their words voices so powerful that torture and death could not silence them, and they sometimes continued to speak when their tongues had been cut from their mouths. Through scripture, theology, prayers, and hymns, the church proclaims God's presence in the world.

Throughout church history, however, the words of women and children, of the poor, the sick, and enslaved, have often been silenced by words of the wealthy, learned, and powerful. And if no one listens, you learn not to speak. When such voices are lost, the Word is diminished. I could express few genuine words. I needed to find my voice. Poet Marge Piercy writes in "Unlearning Not to Speak":

She must learn again to speak
starting with I
starting with We
starting as the infant does
with her own true hunger
and pleasure
and rage.

I went to Michelle Woodhouse because I needed someone to talk to—someone with whom I could have a real conversation. I knew she was wise. I thought she might help me hear my own voice. Michelle is a large woman with a generous smile and intelligent eyes. She had been everything from a Hollywood stand-in for Elizabeth Taylor, junior tennis professional, and Alaskan bush pilot, to teacher, therapist, and priest. As a divorced grandmother, she had begun studying for her doctorate in religious studies at Claremont. She reminded me of the seventh-century saint, Abbess Hilda of Whitby, who commanded respect as she presided over a renaissance of English spirituality and learning. In token of that imagined similarity, I took great pleasure in addressing her as Mother Michelle.

Mother Michelle listened. After a couple months, she pointed me back toward voices that I had once loved and listened to with enthusiasm—the voices of medieval Christian mystics. In college, studying the mystics had given me a great love of church history. But in seminary, most of the professors ridiculed medieval mysticism and extolled the virtues of rational Christianity and systematic theology instead. Students who expressed such interests were shunned and ignored by influential faculty members. Texts by John Calvin replaced those of Francis of Assisi; Charles Hodge displaced Teresa of Avila.

Occasionally, I would fight to hear the church's mystical voice and write papers on Calvin's piety or Jonathan Edwards's spirituality. But for the most part, treatises of devotional theology gathered dust while I pursued the life of the Christian mind through scholastic Protestantism. Evidence, argument, counterargument, revised thesis. Feelings, emotion, and intuition had nothing to do with it. You were graded down for personal opinions, for feeling something about a text. It was like a puzzle. Like math. Learn the formula, plug in the numbers. I found I was pretty good at it. Feelings got reserved for church, but a few professors even found ways to belittle those feelings.

One day, Michelle said, "Diana, your life is like a garden. The front of that garden, your mind, is well tended, watered, orderly, neat. But the back of the garden, your emotional life, is not well tended, it is withering. You need to tend the whole garden." My feelings? No one had asked me about my feelings in years. I had no idea how to cultivate them. I was so numb, so disconnected from my emotions, that her comment terrified me. I think she sensed that fear. She got up out of her chair, walked over to her bookshelves, and pulled down St. Bernard of Clairvaux's book about loving God. "Have you ever read this?"

"Years ago," I replied. Church history, I thought. Good. That does not frighten me. Something I can handle.

"Read it again," she suggested.

I read it again. "You wish to hear from me why and how God ought to be loved," Bernard wrote. "I answer: The cause of loving God is God himself. The way to love him is without measure." Great, I thought. That helps. But Bernard pushed on: "Know yourself, know that you are only through grace, love God because God first loved you," and "Love God with all your heart and with all your soul and with all your strength." He went on to describe four degrees of love. And at the fourth, Bernard declares, "When man loves himself for the sake of God, to love in this way is to become like God. As a drop of water seems to disappear completely in a quantity of wine, taking the wine's flavor and color . . . so, in those who are holy, it is necessary for human affection to dissolve in some ineffable way and be poured into the will of God."

I had lived inside my head for so long that I had forgotten the point: love. I had heard it in the Thursday night group at Church of the Holy Family and recognized its call, but I had no idea how to get there. To love, to become like God, or "Christ-like," as my evangelical friends used to say, was the purpose of it all. Somehow, this ancient wisdom must know the way. I read and I kept reading. From Bernard, I went back to Francis, John of the Cross, and Teresa; from there, I found Clare of Assisi, Hildegard of Bingen, Julian of Norwich, Catherine of Siena, and Mechthild of Magdeburg. I reread some modern writers, too—old favorites like Martin Luther, Dietrich Bonhoeffer, and Henry Nouwen. And back to the Bible. The lyrical parts, like Psalms, the Song of Songs, and Isaiah. Stories about the women in the Bible, too: the Canaanite woman who shouted at Jesus, the widow of Nain, Mary and Martha, Judith, Esther, and Ruth. I planted herbs and vegetables in a small garden. I spent hours sitting on a bench above the ocean in Shoreline Park and prayed. I wrote poetry and kept a journal.

At first it was all on the surface, that journal of mine. And then, about five months into it, in the summer of 1992, I finally blurted out on its pages, "Where is God? Why do I feel so abandoned? Is there only unhappiness?" From that point on, I lived in that journal and, like a devout Puritan trying to discern her salvation, I wrote down every perceptible move of the Spirit. The more I wrote, the more I wanted to write. And the words spilled out onto the pages of cheap school notebooks—words that I was still afraid to speak. Fear and joy, anger and hope, pain and insight. My words interlaced with the words of mystics and theologians, sermons and hymns, friends and mentors. But they were my words—stronger and surer as the months passed. I wrote down the words of the poet Denise Levertov as if they were mine:

An awe so quiet I don't know where it began.
A gratitude had begun to sing in me.
Was there some moment dividing song from no song?
When does dewfall begin?

An emotional garden was growing in the Santa Barbara sun.

And of Michelle Woodhouse I wrote, "She helps me so much. She helps me feel strong." A good spiritual director is part gardener, too.

As the fear abated some, anger took its place. I felt as if I had been a caged animal for years, never able to be myself and always living into the expectations of those around me—husband, teachers, employers, colleagues, clergymen. But now I wanted out. About that time, a monk-friend showed me a quote from Irenaeus of Lyon, an early Christian theologian: "The glory of God is the human being fully alive." I hung it above my desk as hope, prayer, and mantra. I wanted to be fully alive—expressing who I really was. But vocalizing this did not come easily. Fits and starts, awkward and unsure, often spurred by anger and not love. It was neither easy nor pretty. Speaking after silence is hard.

The most awkward voice sounded at church. In the spring of 1992, Christ the King called a new vicar, a theologically conservative man from a well-known charismatic Episcopal congregation back East. Shortly thereafter, Michelle Woodhouse left and joined the staff at All Saints across town. I still saw her for spiritual direction. But at Christ the King, where the new vicar was taking over, I became increasingly isolated.

I argued with people over theology and politics. I can still remember one particularly unpleasant dinner when I expressed the tentative opinion that, in some cases, a Christian might permit abortion. Immediately, four men—including my husband and the vicar—attacked me. Although I tried to defend myself, I eventually backed down. If any of the women in the room thought the same as I did, they did not come to my rescue. I do, however, remember one staring at me, her eyes large with fear. It was so wrenching that I fled to the bathroom and promptly got sick.

On another occasion I expressed my honest discomfort with a verse from Romans 6 in a Bible study: "You have been freed from sin and made slaves to God." I recorded my insights in my journal: "The text from Romans 6 was surprising to me. I've never *felt* so strongly about that slavery metaphor before. 'Slaves to God' is so offensive. Does that mean God is 'Masser,' who must be obeyed without question? Does it mean that in this relationship there is no love, no mutuality, no room for my desires, wishes, or passions? That doesn't seem possible. Other parts of scripture indicate a more mutual relationship: 'Brothers and sisters, bride and groom, friends. . . .' If we are slaves, what does that imply about God?"

My uneasiness with this text was not, of course, outside the Christian tradition. For at least two centuries, women and African Americans have expressed similar discomfort with such oppressive imagery.

Questioning the Bible, however, was not something with which Christ the King felt comfortable. As I explained my anxiety about this verse, my fellow parishioners took it as an attack upon the Holy Scriptures, the Word of God. Unlike the Holy Family Bible study, this group seemed to expect pious submission to evangelical readings of the text. Yes, we were slaves to God. They said I did not understand, that I had a "spirit of rebellion." Well, so did Harriet Tubman and Martin Luther King Jr., I argued. Indeed, I was in no mood to submit. It turned into a row.

At Christ the King I was moody and uncooperative. I did not want to know God as they understood God to be. I began to overhear people pray things like, "Lord, free Diana from the clutches of the evil one." I had been in enough evangelical churches to understand that. When people start praying for you, run for the exit! You have been marked an outsider, spiritually deficient, a target for evangelism. I wrote, "I feel so lonely. . . . I don't think it was a very good idea to go back to a charismatic church." I had terrible altercations with other people there. I felt I was struggling to be born and they wanted to commit infanticide. I fought just to breathe.

Looking back, I realize that we were in a surprisingly similar place during that interim, Christ the King and I. Through his tenure, the Rev. Stivers had worked to bring the charismatic mission toward the denominational mainstream and mitigate some of its Pentecostal excesses. Michelle continued this, trying, against difficult circumstances, to widen the theological perspectives of the congregation. There was a bit of tension in the parish between the "old-timers" and a small coterie of newcomers. At Christ the King, the founders were now graying charismatic Episcopalians, whose faith had been forged in the heyday of healing and renewal movements in the 1970s. They tended to be both insular and inwardly focused.

The newcomers were mostly baby boomers, some of whose attitudes resembled those at Holy Family. They displayed a more traditional sense of liturgy, a relatively more liberal outlook on issues related to women, and tended to be activist in orientation. During the interim, Christ the King had to choose: the church could maintain its more sectarian charismatic stance, or it might open its doors to a broader experience of Christian life and practice. Much depended upon the new rector. They would choose someone who stood in line with their own evangelical and charismatic past. Not someone like Michelle Woodhouse, who might take them in a different direction.

Christ the King knew its identity as a conservative, charismatic parish. It spoke in that voice. I was trying to find mine. My struggle with them was not really their fault. It would be impossible for me to do what I needed to do in that particular congregation. Instead of welcoming me, they were always trying to make me fit. I do not think the parish was necessarily a bad place. They had created a community in their image of what they thought Christianity should be. From my perspective, it was narrow and constraining.

In any case, I did not fit. I did not want to fit. I was tired of fitting. And I was not a charismatic. Charismatics want God to change, fix, or heal people. Questions and doubts are not generally welcome. Happiness, submission, and kindness are of the spirit; anger, fear, and confusion are of the devil. I did not fit and Christ the King could not change. They could not see that I needed to feel anger and fear in order to go deeper, to find the fullness of love and peace. That I needed both acceptance and freedom. And they did not understand that even positive emotions have shadow sides, a kind of wholeness that makes them human. But, in my experience, charismatics do not want to be, as Irenaeus put it, "humanity fully alive." They would rather be spiritual, removed from the mundane, disconnected from the world of suffering, sin, and ambiguity. "Be ye perfect as I am perfect" is a favorite verse. Be "slaves to God" and not to any earthly passion.

I was starting to understand that earthly passion was not so bad—nor was fear or doubt or suffering or sin. All the "stuff" of humanity needed to be brought into the center of God—as God had come to the center of humankind in becoming one of us in Jesus. I was beginning to live into what Christians call the doctrine of the Incarnation—the belief that an embodied God blesses our embodied lives. God and humankind partake of each other's fullness in mutual love. Instead of being freed from the devil, I prayed as I recorded in my journal: "Spirit who hovered over the waters and the water of my own baptism, protect, claim and continue your creative work in me. . . . I need to be myself in the midst of your Eternity. I am part of your All, even as you dwell in me."

Standing on a spiritual cusp, I could no longer remain where I was. Christ the King and all it represented was no longer an option. Great, I thought. I am married to an evangelical and working at an evangelical college. If I chose the path opening before me—if I chose speaking my voice—I would possibly lose my job, my career, and my marriage.

Sometimes you find your way by retracing your steps. It became painfully obvious that I could not remain at Christ the King. In late summer 1992, going forward meant going back to All Saints-by-the-Sea, where I had first become an Episcopalian. All Saints had changed in those years. Many new people had joined the church, and the number of services and ministries had multiplied. The worship and music were still beautiful. They had renovated the sanctuary. The implicit promise of what I had sensed eleven years earlier had become reality—the church had essentially re-created itself as a new kind of parish. But Gethin Hughes had recently left.

A few months earlier he had been elected as Bishop of San Diego. His assistant, the Rev. Anne Sutherland Howard, was serving as All Saints' interim priest.

Anne Howard was the liberal priest my husband wanted to avoid. When I left Christ the King, I went to her and explained why. She affirmed my choice to return to All Saints. Her insight and thoughtfulness impressed me. Although Anne would later become a trusted friend, a woman whose theological savvy and personal integrity I admire, I was wary then. She and her husband, Randy, had been parishioners at All Saints in Pasadena and held degrees from the most liberal seminary in the Episcopal Church. I still had an unnerving evangelical habit of putting the world into orthodox and heterodox camps. I had heard faculty colleagues criticize both her theology and her preaching. I suspected that she and I would come down in different theological places. It appeared, however, that she understood my immediate dilemma. Whatever our differences, she was on my side. And Michelle liked her, I reassured myself. Besides, there was nowhere else to go to church in a small town like Santa Barbara.

After a few weeks, I began to feel more confident about the move to All Saints. I wrote in my journal that I had been "afraid that I wouldn't be able to be happy there again—that I wouldn't find what had drawn me there in the first place." But one Sunday, as recorded in my journal, I gazed at the saints in the stained glass windows and "I felt drawn into the central mystery of the church.

"What is that mystery? The brilliance, the glowing ardor of Christ in, with, and through the church, which binds it together through all the ages. It is the healing power of Cuthbert's bones, it is Hildegard's viridity, it is Luther's grace and faith, Calvin's sovereign God, Jonathan Edwards's almost mystical sense of nature, Harriet Beecher Stowe's compassion over slavery, Dorothy Day crying out for the poor, the voices of Latin America and Africa speaking God's justice. It is the radiance of God's acting, speaking, and revealing—a sharp, clear, and profound voice against the spirit of the world. I feel it pulsating through me, carrying me along, bidding me to be free."

What had been calling me there twelve years earlier called me again, strengthening me and giving me a renewed sense of purpose and confidence.

And it was challenging me. When I had first gone to Christ the King a year earlier, I had never before experienced the regular ministry, the weekly priesthood of a woman. Now, during All Saints' interim, two women presided at the table, preached at the pulpit, and served as pastors. One Sunday that fall, the entire party was female—altar girls, lay readers, lay eucharistic ministers, with Michelle preaching and Anne serving. After so many years of seeing more women sitting in the pews than standing in front of the congregation, it was a startling moment. How church had changed since my childhood! Back then, women baked cookies, poured coffee, made clothing for the poor, and cared for children. When I was little, women only raised their voices in song. Perhaps that was why I loved those Wesley hymns so much. Even as a girl, those hymns gave words to some of my deepest desires. At All Saints, women spoke—they spoke about God, to God, and for God in ministries of word and sacrament. And that Sunday, the voices were all female—only alto and soprano—singing and praying and reading and speaking. To me, it sounded a heavenly choir. But to Buck it was discordant: "That was awful. I never felt so excluded in my life," he told me. I replied without a moment's thought, "How do you think I have felt for the last thirty-three years?" Until that moment, I never knew I felt that way.

Anne spent time in England that summer. Women could not then be ordained to the priesthood in the Church of England, but the church was nearing its point of decision. She preached in some churches and evangelized for the cause. Like me, she loved Celtic Christianity and had made pilgrimages to many holy sites connected to that ancient form of faith. When she returned, she shared her experiences of being a woman priest in a church without ordained women. And she preached a number of memorable sermons on Celtic spirituality. It was clear that Anne Howard, free to be herself as priest-in-charge, was finding her voice, too.

One Sunday, she mounted the pulpit and began by telling the congregation of her visit to Durham Cathedral, the place where the bones of St. Cuthbert rest. Cuthbert, born around 625, was a shepherd who heard God's call and dedicated himself to Christian service. As a saintly and compassionate monk, he eventually became the Bishop of Lindesfarne, a great spiritual center of early English Christianity. When he died in 687, his popularity did not wane. Almost immediately, local believers made pilgrimages to his tomb, seeking miracles in his name. During the Viking invasions of England, Cuthbert's bones were hidden for safekeeping. Eventually the monks of Lindesfarne carried his sacred remains to Durham, where they were interred at the cathedral.

Cuthbert became one of England's most popular saints. Anne went to Durham to pay homage to him, to touch the remnants of his shrine and tomb, as have millions of Anglicans throughout the ages. With great excitement, she told us of seeing this thousand-year-old sacred site for the first time. As she walked around the great building, however, she noticed something odd about the floor: stones formed a thick, black line running the width of the sanctuary. "What's that?" she wondered. "What's the line in the floor?"

She noticed a small sign posted to a pillar. The line, it informed curious tourists, marked the place where medieval women had to stand. The monks would not let women—who were viewed as evil and dirty—get any closer to the bones of St. Cuthbert than the back of the cathedral.

Anne looked down the long aisle to the great high altar where the saint's body rested, imagining the building filled with pilgrims—men at the front near the holy relics, women exiled to the back uttering their prayers far from the saint. This, she said, was the church's sad history—a history of exclusion of those deemed unworthy or unclean. And, after centuries of sin, it is the history of which the church is now repenting. "The gospel," she exclaimed, "is the good news of God's inclusive reach, a love for all humankind—men and women, straight and gay, rich and poor, all races, adults, and children. God's love destroys thick, black lines. Indeed, the gospel proclaims that there are no lines."

A faith with no lines? Anne's assertion, "in the gospel there are no lines," was almost beyond my comprehension. Christianity was about drawing lines—doctrinal lines, behavioral lines, lines between the saved and the damned, lines between us and them. In seminary, one of my professors taught an entire section of his contemporary theology class on the necessity of drawing lines and the weakness of modern Protestantism because of its failure to do so. I remember thinking that this analysis was brilliant. "That's what good theology is about," I argued to friends. "Protecting orthodoxy, drawing lines of faith. The church needs lines."

That sermon was deeply unsettling. Weeks later, I wrote in my journal, "I'm still thinking about Anne's sermon about the line in the floor at Durham cathedral and the inclusive reach of the gospel. Inclusion makes me uncomfortable. I always want to have limits." On the day I wrote those words, I had read Acts 15 as part of the daily office. In that chapter, early Christians held a church council in Jerusalem—the first church council—to resolve an argument between Jewish Christians and Gentile converts to the faith.

The Jewish believers insisted that Gentiles must be circumcised in order to become Christians. I wrote in my meditation: "These Jews insisted that people become like them before they could come into the full embrace of God."

The council of Jerusalem decided that the Judaizers were wrong. The Apostle Peter argued, "God, who knows the human heart, testified to them by giving them the Holy Spirit, just as he did to us; and in cleansing their hearts by faith he has made no distinctions between them and us." What did this mean? I wondered. *No distinctions between them and us?* God let everybody in? "As much as I hate lines drawn to exclude me," I admitted in my journal, "I draw lines. Yet God has torn down the dividing wall of hostility. *All peoples? ALL?* No distinction?" God lets everybody in? There just had to be lines. It could not be that easy.

That same week, I showed a film in class on the Protestant Reformation, titled "Martin Luther: Heretic." One scene portrayed Martin Luther teaching his students the Bible. Having newly awakened to the radical nature of grace, Luther insisted that salvation was available to all through "faith alone." A student protested, "Faith alone? Why, Master Luther, every peasant in Germany has faith. Does that mean heaven will be full of German peasants?" Luther responded, "Maybe." "I can't believe it," said the student. "It can't be that easy." Luther replied, "You think faith is easy?"

Did I think God's inclusive love was easy? Luther's words thundered through history at me. In the darkened classroom, I cried, hoping the students would not see. Faith was not easy. Love was not easy. Line drawing is easy. Walking over thick, black lines is hard. Tearing down walls of exclusion is hard. Living safely inside established boundaries was easy; there is no real faith inside lines. Only on the other side of lines can there be faith, that adventurous journey of embodying God's love in the world.

Instead of lines, I began to see circles. Everywhere I looked, I saw spirals, healing wheels, mandalas, circles of faith. Not people divided, but people joined. One night, I dreamed I was back at Holy Family, singing an old Southern favorite, "Will the circle be unbroken, bye and bye, Lord, bye and bye." Jean Wagner smiled at me and said, "I knew you would understand, Diana, I knew you would understand." Anne Howard was right: Christianity was not about lines. It was about the inclusive reach of God's love. Galatians 3:28 became my watchword: "There is no longer Jew or Greek, there is no longer slave or free, there is no longer male and female; for all of you are one in Christ Jesus." Faith meant standing with the outcast, speaking for the silent, breaking through lines. In my journal I prayed, "This is a hard truth. God, give me the courage to face the revolution in my life and to be revolutionary." All Saints was helping.

I remember first hearing my voice coming from the deepest places within. As I explored my inner terrain in spiritual direction, that voice sounded initially in my classes at Westmont. My students were, for the most part, open and eager, an accepting community who welcomed what I had to say. Perhaps because I had once been a student in those same chairs, I honestly loved my students there and could identify with them more than with any other students I would ever teach. Lectures became excuses for me to learn new things, try out new ideas, and stretch my intellectual and spiritual wings. Although I was teaching at an evangelical college, I began to bend the unspoken rules—portraying medieval Roman Catholicism, modern Protestant liberalism, and contemporary feminism in positive ways while criticizing American fundamentalism and evangelicalism. I felt a little like Luther in that film. I was realizing so many new things—and, as a teacher, they were all coming forth in the classroom. And like Luther, whose new insights challenged his Roman Catholic authorities, I was biting the hand that fed me.

At the time, I was teaching a course called Introduction to Christian Doctrine. There are few more constraining academic tasks than teaching doctrine at a Christian college. It can quickly devolve into a sort of orthodoxy checklist—running through basic theology and making sure everybody is in line. I hated it.

On one particularly tedious morning, my doctrine class was covering "Anthropology: The Doctrine of Man" by examining the first three chapters of Genesis. The students were unusually quiet and uncooperative that day. "What does the book of Genesis teach us about the human condition?" I asked, trying to introduce the doctrine of original sin. No takers. "What does Genesis say about us? Who are we?"

Finally, one young woman sensed my pedagogical desperation and raised her hand to alleviate the tension. "Yes, Elizabeth?"

She responded, "The book of Genesis says that God made me evil through and through."

I stared at her, barely believing what I had heard. She had repeated some mantra learned at her home church about original sin. She was eighteen years old, had long dark hair, clear eyes, delicate skin, was a nice girl, a beautiful young woman really, intelligent, with a polite and gracious demeanor. Evil? Who told her that she was evil? A sinner, separated from God, dirty and wicked in his sight. The disjunction between her words and the reality of her person was appalling. Could she really believe she was evil? A miserable sinner in whom there is no health?

I must have been quiet for one second too long. The whole class was looking at me, waiting for me to respond. Instead of thanking her, however, I blurted out, "Does the Bible say that?

Does the Bible teach that you are evil? Pick it up. All of you. Pick up your Bibles. Pick them up. Turn to Genesis, chapter one."

The startled students obeyed. I actually startled myself. Did the Bible really teach that? Is that what I thought about myself? If I were less theologically sophisticated, might I have said to a professor, "God made me evil through and through"?

"When God creates light, what does God say about it?" I asked.

"It is good," replied some eager male student.

"And water?"

"God saw that it was good."

"And earth and seas?"

"God saw that it was good."

They were all awake. Most of them looked as if they were seeing it all for the first time.

"Vegetation?" "Good." "The seasons, sun and moon?" "Good, good." "And all the creatures?" "God saw that they were good."

"And what does God say when he creates man and woman, humankind?"

Silence again filled the room.

"Why, I never noticed this," answered another young man. "It says, 'God saw everything that he had made and indeed, it was very good.' Very good. God says we are very good."

"Right. Now, turn the page to chapter three," I directed, "to the story of the Fall. Adam and Eve disobey God and sin. What does God say about it?"

They looked. They pointed out the consequences for sin: sorrow, shame, pain, sickness, hard work, and death. "Does God ever take it back?" I asked, "The 'very good'? Does it say that we become, we embody evil? That we are wicked, unacceptable in God's sight?"

Quiet again. One woman slowly said, "No, it doesn't. It says that we *know* good and evil. It doesn't say we stop being good and *become* evil."

"No, it doesn't. It says we will do bad things because we have a choice. Because we know that good and evil exist. But it doesn't say that we are bad. We are still good, very good, just as God created us."

Class ended. I could hardly believe what had happened. At the heart of evangelical Protestantism is the belief that people are bad, completely bad, sinners by nature and, without hope, separated from God, and who must be saved by Jesus' blood. The wicked are exiled from God, we are all wicked, we all will be banished from eternal bliss. Turn or burn. Terrorize 'em into faith. Although Elizabeth had overstated the case—"God made me evil through and through"—she expressed the kind of theological self-loathing that is implied—or taught outright—in many evangelical churches. People are shit.

When those words came out of her mouth, I realized that I thought the same of myself. And I realized that this was a complete misreading of scripture, a reading originating with early Greek converts to Christianity who had little regard for creation and the material world. Much of early Christianity was influenced by religions that taught that created matter was evil and that only spirit was good. To be holy, we must escape the body and achieve a kind of disembodied wisdom, a state disconnected from our corporal selves. Human beings are evil, and some—women—were more evil than others—men, and spirit is the only good.

In spiritual direction, I rejected these views. I was seeing myself connected to and not radically separated from God and creation. Sin was not some essential state to which we are condemned and only a few escape by responding to an altar call. Rather, sin was the refusal to recognize that everything, everyone, was part of God's wholeness, part of the created good, a reflection of the divine image, intended to be one with and in God. Sin obscured our true nature, that image of God, but, according to my church's own liturgy, the stain of sin had been washed away in the waters of baptism. Yes, we would sin. But sin was something we did—not who we were. Sin is in the sinning.

I had crossed over a theological line. I knew I had violated a fundamental tenet of evangelical theology, the basis on which the entire doctrinal house was built. Now what? I rightly guessed that the whole thing would come crashing down. What of salvation? The nature of God? Christian living? The church? Who was I theologically? What was I called to do in the world? I would have to rethink, reread, and rediscover Christianity. I thought about the college's doctrinal statement, the one faculty members had to sign yearly to keep their jobs. I was pretty sure that "sin is in the sinning" fell outside its parameters.

I walked down the hill and went into the religious studies office. I approached the department chair and told him I did not want to teach doctrine any more. I was trained in church history, I insisted. Let me teach that. If I stuck to the safe stuff, they might not figure out that I thought they were wrong. Unbiblical, really. Maybe I could keep my opinions to myself.

By January 1993, part of the road ahead became clearer. Buck and I were on two separate journeys. We had been since St. Stephen's back in Durham. Maybe since we had been married, really. In not being true to myself, I could never be whole in this marriage. We had both wanted soul mates, but we were badly mismatched. No matter how much time and effort we put in, there would be no real oneness—the spiritual ideal of Christian marriage—between us. Despite the pain it had caused me, it was all very sad. After months of counseling, I asked him to move out. As Michelle would say of the situation, "the marriage had died." In recognition of that fact, I filed for divorce.

In May 1994, on what would have been our tenth wedding anniversary, I went to church, to All Saints, where we had been married, one foggy weekday afternoon. Wearing a white dress and carrying a single white rose, I knelt and prayed at the small altar in the side chapel. I opened the Prayer Book to the burial service: "I am Resurrection and I am Life, says the Lord. Whoever has faith in me shall have life, even though he die. And everyone who has life, and has committed himself to me in faith, shall not die forever. . . . Happy from now on are those who die in the Lord!"

On my knees in that chapel, I thought back over the three difficult years since I had returned to Santa Barbara. I knew my interim was over. It was time to get on with things. I was finding my voice and, in the process, seeing myself and the way ahead more clearly. But this did not make me immediately happy. I was alone and divorced. I made personal and professional mistakes as I struggled to figure things out, to make things right. In my pain, I had caused others pain. I had learned that many people do not like to forgive. I had little idea of what it might be like to be independent, to make my own decisions, to be responsible for myself. My closest friends put up with a lot of tears, anger, and confusion. And I was broke. There were days when I felt desperate.

Neither my internal changes nor my external circumstances sat well with some of my colleagues or employers at Westmont. Teaching church history did not help. It kept sneaking through— all my deviant opinions, that newly birthed voice, the stuff about no lines and no original sin. About an inclusive gospel. These things did not mesh with their idea of Christian faith, with their evangelical stance. They wanted me to be someone who I was not turning out to be. Westmont, too, was proving a bad match.

In my quest to understand Christian theology in deeper ways, I turned to liberation theology, feminist theologies, Protestant liberalism, contemporary Anglican theology, the Jesus seminar, and postmodernism. I immersed myself in sociology of religion. I learned about Judaism, Buddhism, Native American spirituality, and New Age religion. It was acceptable to teach about such things, but some people at the college had a sneaking suspicion that I believed them, too. For me, it was like going to graduate school again. Only this time, I resisted the urge to put up boundaries and listened to what each taught. I stopped fearing new ideas. I stopped being afraid of changing my mind. I came to believe some of it; some of it I did not embrace as my own. I learned from all of it.

During the interim, I had made friends with faculty members from the religion department at the University of California across town—well-regarded scholars like Catherine Albanese, Walter Capps, and Wade Clark Roof. Only a few years earlier I had read most of their books and disagreed with them; now I found myself learning from them and seeing issues informed by their perspectives. I started to write a column on religion for the local newspaper—expressing opinions often popular with other Santa Barbarans but controversial on campus. I was beginning to think most of my religious studies colleagues were intellectually and spiritually narrow. We did not get along. Some of my students began to think the same and challenged what they were hearing from other professors in the department. When I tried to live outside the lines, indeed, when I encouraged others to do the same, people took sides. They lined up for and against lines. They lined up for and against me. Things got ugly. Very ugly.

Complicated by a number of other issues, including the virulence of the evangelical religious right in the early 1990s, the campus became bitterly divided. Although I did not entirely realize it at the time, I was trying to find out if there was room for me at that same school that had intellectually birthed me. The answer came quickly.

Some of my coworkers tried to have my employment terminated. We were engaged in a bitter and protracted argument as to whether or not I would remain at the school. It would go on for another year, but I knew it would not work. I knew I did not fit in there any more than I had at Christ the King. I no longer lived in their world. When the president of the college later told me the same, I did not know whether to cry or laugh in relief. I am pretty sure I did the latter.

On my knees at All Saints that May afternoon, I realized that more than my marriage had died. My old life had died, too. I glanced at my Prayer Book. "O God, who by the glorious Resurrection of your Son Jesus Christ destroyed death, and brought life and immortality to light: Grant that your servant Diana, being raised with him, may know the strength of his presence, and rejoice in his eternal glory." I laid the white rose on the altar, stood up, and made the sign of the cross. "Happy are those who die in the Lord!" I walked out praying that Christianity was true, that the Resurrection was not a lie, and holding out hope that new life could come from death. As I left the sanctuary, I noticed that the fog had moved offshore and that misty sunlight was falling on the flowers. "The Sun of Righteousness is gloriously risen," ends the burial service, "giving light to those who sat in darkness and in the shadow of death."

I fingered the Celtic cross hanging around my neck and silently thanked God for Michelle and Anne. I had followed them through the fog and was nearly to the other side.

CHAPTER SIX

The Open Door

TRINITY CHURCH

Santa Barbara, California, 1995–1997

One Sunday in March 1996, Bishop Fred Borsch of Los Angeles rededicated Trinity Church. As the service began, he banged his pastoral staff on the church doors and commanded, "LET THE DOOR BE OPENED!" The massive oak doors swung wide. A few weeks previously, and after a year of exile, the congregation had moved back into the sanctuary. We gladly opened those doors.

The church had been restored. Founded in 1866, Trinity Church is one of the first Protestant churches in Santa Barbara and one of the oldest Episcopal parishes in California. It also has one of the state's most beautiful church buildings. The present church was built in 1912 to replace an older structure lost in a fire. The architect was Philip Hubert Frohman, who later became the chief architect for the National Cathedral in Washington, D.C. Trinity is English Perpendicular Gothic—in the style of King's Chapel in Cambridge, England—rendered in golden-tinged sandstone, with splendid stained-glass windows, a luminous California version of

Anglican establishment. Although the building seems to embody the once-privileged religious world of the city's Anglo-Protestant elite, Trinity's grandeur tells another, less obvious, story. Its stones radiate God's presence in some mysterious way that fires the spiritual imagination of even the most casual visitor. A secular acquaintance, a photographer, once commented to me, "I love to shoot weddings there because that church glows. The stones actually seem alive."

Living stones? Her words echoed an ancient image found in the New Testament: "Come to him, a living stone . . . and like living stones, let yourselves be built into a spiritual house, to be a holy priesthood" (I Peter 2:4–5). Jesus is the "cornerstone chosen and precious," and his people, the church, are not to be a stumbling block but a temple of living stones. Trinity sees itself that way—not as an institution or a building to be preserved, but as an organic community, an intentional gathering of God's people. Its beauty does not lull spiritual sensibilities; it awakens them to this invisible reality. There is nothing establishment about it.

Through its history, however, Trinity had not always been so conspicuously alive. When I first returned to Santa Barbara, I stopped by and checked out the church. Since reaching its membership high in the 1960s, Trinity's fortunes had fallen precipitously. Paint peeling and dusty, the faded neo-Gothic building housed a sparse congregation. Sad, I thought. Trinity is dying. By 1990, attendance for two services hovered just below a hundred. Only six or seven children remained in the church school. The once packed Christian education building had been leased out as a secular school. Financial distress—a $25,000-a-year deficit—plagued the church as it dipped into reserves to pay the bills. The endowment was going fast. To make matters worse, the state of California demanded that Trinity retrofit its eighty-three-year-old sanctuary for earthquake safety by July 1, 1996. The cost: $1.5 million. Professional fundraisers estimated that, with luck, the parish might be able to raise $350,000. A friend confidently predicted, "Well, that will finally kill the old place."

But Trinity didn't die.

On March 17, 1996, I witnessed its resurrection. In eighteen short months, the congregation raised the money and retrofitted the sanctuary. But it was not about the money. People were coming. New people. Lots of them. Including me. The church's membership doubled in those few months. And it would double again in the next couple years. No program or evangelistic strategy prompted this growth. Rather, Trinity did something few churches think of doing—it just opened its doors. It opened spiritual and theological doors, doors of gender and class, actual doors and symbolic ones. And people started walking in. Sometimes right in the middle of a service. And they would stay. Straight and gay, rich and poor, able-bodied and ill, healthy and wounded, the respectable and the outcast. Mostly liberal churchgoers. Baby boomers who had not been to church since college. Some people who had never even been in a church or seen a Bible. Doubters, skeptics, and questioners. Families with lots of children. People bruised and battered by more narrow forms of religion—former Roman Catholics and evangelicals, mostly.

On that Sunday, the once empty sanctuary was packed with hundreds of people celebrating the rededication of a church recently threatened with the wrecking ball. The cobwebs were gone, the walls had been painted fresh, the stained-glass windows were sparkling clean. "LET THE DOOR BE OPENED!" shouted Bishop Borsch as the liturgy to rededicate the church commenced. The command struck me as ironic. No one needed to tell us to open the door. We wanted it open. Opening doors was our mission. We practically threw them off the hinges.

The choir led the congregation in an African anthem, "Freedom Come," which gave voice to Trinity's emerging theological identity:

Inside these walls, Inside these come,
One and all, come one and all
Freedom come, freedom come. Hallelujah!

Tears and applause poured forth in enthusiastic praise. People were swaying, singing, and sobbing. It may not have been a Pentecostal revival meeting, but it sure felt like one. In restoring the building, the congregation was renewed. Everybody called it a miracle. Ann Jaqua, one of Trinity's lay leaders, would say of these events, "I don't really know what happened here. It is all very mysterious. The power of the Spirit, I think." We had found something all too rare even in church: the freedom to be exactly who God made us to be. A community to which we could bring everything. A church with an open door.

"This is my commandment," proclaimed the Gospel lesson that day, "that you love one another as I have loved you. . . . I do not call you servants any longer, because the servant does not know what the master is doing; but I have called you friends." The mystery of Resurrection was revealed. Love draws all into the circle of God's eternal friendship. Through Jesus we find an open door to God. The message was powerful and its spirit palpable. Jesus had predicted that "even if these were silent, the stones themselves would shout." We rescued the building and found that it did not matter. We were its living stones.

In January 1995, I moved from All Saints to Trinity. As is often the case with Christians who go through a divorce, I found it difficult to remain part of the church where I had been married. To make matters worse, a number of people with whom I worked attended the church. Tensions around my tenure at the college spilled over into worship. Sundays, once a refuge from weekday hassles, were fraught with difficulty. In other circumstances, I might have managed the personal conflicts and remained at the parish. But an additional factor prompted the move: I was spiritually bored. Spiritual boredom is, I think, relatively common with long-term churchgoers. Year in, year out. The Christian calendar goes through its paces. The lectionary readings—and the resulting sermons—begin to sound the same. Even in churches with breathtaking worship, liturgical repetition can get tedious.

For most of the fifteen years previous, I had found the cycles of liturgy grounding. But by 1995 I experienced them mostly as weights. At that point, my spiritual life was primarily internal, all the restless seeking awakened through the mystics and my widening theological vision. Although it had shaped me, All Saints had become dull. In comparison with the inner transformation, the Episcopal Church seemed dull, too. Its spiritual luster dimmed; its ability to draw me into wonder diminished. Perhaps because Anne Howard had left and Michelle Woodhouse spent most of her time developing a ministry to seniors. Whatever the case, my inner life and its outward expression in worship were out of sync. I needed a place where the two could be brought back together.

My friends Clark and Terry Roof, also lifetime churchgoers, had changed from All Saints to Trinity and encouraged me to do the same. Clark, a professor at the University of California in Santa Barbara, had taught a class on baby boomer spirituality for the church's vestry retreat and found the lay leaders engaging and innovative.

"Isn't that church dead?" I asked somewhat skeptically.

"They have had a difficult time," he admitted, "but I think things are changing there. They are really going somewhere. You'd like them."

Despite my restlessness, I remained reluctant.

That reluctance was a kind of theological gut reaction. Since I was a teenager at Scottsdale Bible Church, I had been taught that the world was divided into two camps—orthodox and liberal; for God and against. I knew about Trinity from college days. Then it was known as the gay church, and a few brave homosexual students attended its services. It had the reputation of being one of the most liberal churches in town. From my college student perspective, it seemed they were more interested in politics than preaching and in social action than spirituality. During the 1980s, when I lived back East, Trinity supported the sanctuary movement to provide refuge for illegal immigrants fleeing from repressive Latin American regimes. They held a prayer vigil for El Salvador, protesting Ronald Reagan's policies in that country. They started a homeless shelter and soup kitchen. With all the empty space they had, the church turned the parish hall into temporary sleeping space for the poor. In the theological world of evangelicalism, these folks were on the wrong side of almost every issue. Although by 1995 I was intellectually in a different place, a kind of knee-jerk fundamentalism kicked in. It was hard to imagine being happy with a bunch of liberals.

Besides, they were, as I said to Clark, dying. Although social activism gave them a big political presence in Santa Barbara, that did not translate into big numbers. By the early 1990s, Trinity comprised a small group of gay men, a few stalwarts from the "old families," and a few social radicals. In short, they were a dying urban parish.

But I did not have much choice. Santa Barbara had four Episcopal churches. I had already gone through two. The third was a tiny university mission at the far edge of town. That left Trinity—the downtown church and the closest to my apartment.

Ultimately, a man I did not know, the Rt. Rev. George Barrett, would convince me to attend Trinity. Then in his eighties, George had retired from active service as a bishop and assisted in the parish as "bishop in residence." A champion for social justice and civil rights, George was the second bishop to ordain women as priests before it was approved by the church. Unbeknownst to me, the opinions expressed in the column I wrote for the local newspaper resonated with the theological views of a number of Trinity parishioners—including George Barrett. When my difficulties at work became gossip fodder through town, George wrote an authoritative letter to the college president, demanding that I be treated justly. At that moment in my life, the support of a stranger was a welcome gift. It seemed appropriate to visit Trinity and thank him.

Once there, I stayed. And I learned. Trinity would prove to be one of the most remarkable churches of which I have been a part. I found there a palpable sense of God's spirit, a warm, accepting, and honest community. Similar in some ways to Holy Family, but wrapped in a California package.

Even at its lowest ebb, Trinity possessed a remarkable spiritual energy—often restless, undirected, and disempowered. For many years, a small group of committed laypersons had struggled to express the power of the Christian message—in essence, to be the church in the world. There were serious Christians, deeply spiritual and passionate people of prayer. But their desires had been inhibited by an equally long history of patriarchal clergy, especially under the lengthy postwar tenure of the Rev. Richard Flagg Ayers. Father Ayers, as he was called, oversaw both Trinity's dramatic religious boom in the 1940s and 1950s and its equally dramatic bust in the 1960s and early 1970s. In 1973, an overly optimistic parish booklet hinted that hard times had fallen on the congregation, with this enigmatic statement about its history: "It merely comes to a convenient stop, until the next appropriate time for a reworking, reappraisal and rewriting arrives." Ann Jaqua, who joined Trinity in 1959, is more direct: "Trinity had a long history of 'mainline attitudes,' and in the 1960s people left over Civil Rights, Vietnam, and the World Council of Churches. Most of them never came back."

At that juncture, Trinity's story resembled those of thousands of other mainline churches. In the 1960s, Ann's peers, members of the "silent generation," abandoned Protestant churches in droves. My parents—and most of their friends—had done the same back in Maryland. Although I have never been able to find research to prove it, I suspect that many others, feeling institutionally disenfranchised or following the tug of sunbelt migration, did the same. Scholars have not often commented on this phenomenon, citing instead the tendency of baby boomers to leave mainstream religion. But in many cases it appears to be the Elvis generation, the young parents of those later boomers, who began the break with mainline churchgoing.

Some, like my parents, would eventually return to their childhood churches. But, as Ann rightly noted, many would not. In California, particular cultural trends—ones not yet present in the rest of the United States—encouraged this exodus. When Trinity lost members in the 1960s and 1970s, it lost Santa Barbara's old Anglo-elite, a class structured around old money, Eastern education, and family ties—a community of privileged Protestant immigrants from the East who brought their religious practices with them. Until the 1950s, this group possessed a sense of noblesse oblige, of the social obligation of churchgoing. For the upper classes, that often meant the Episcopal Church. Trinity benefited from its status of being the Episcopal "mother church" in the county, the "old family" church.

Late in Father Ayer's tenure, however, many of the old families left and never returned. People abandoned downtown. And, with the exception of Trinity and the Roman Catholics, so did the churches. When Santa Barbara's new-class moneyed elite—mostly Hollywood people and technology barons—came to power, they were not necessarily Episcopalians, Protestants, or even Christians. Unlike small Midwestern or Southern communities, where traditional church-going was still a social obligation, Santa Barbara had a multitude of religious options—including not being religious at all. To the new guard, Buddhism and the beach were more attractive than the Episcopal Church.

In this pluralistic, post-Christian climate, Trinity had to find its identity—and a new constituency—or close. Oddly enough, it didn't close. However, old Trinity, the elite Episcopal club, did disappear. With only one or two exceptions, no one remained in the church whose family name appeared on the stained-glass windows or memorials. A few, like Ann Jaqua and Margaret Vang, would make it through the lean years until the new Trinity was born, in the 1990s. But they were lean. Attendance dropped. After Father Ayer's protracted ministry, the church would run through a quick series of clergymen who struggled with immediate problems and failed to provide the kind of visionary leadership needed to reinvent the church. A committed core of laypersons envisioned Trinity as a center for intentional spiritual practice and a powerful witness for social justice, but internal problems kept this from happening. The church turned inward and was riddled with conflict. Parish minutes even record a fistfight breaking out during a vestry meeting.

The final rector during this dismal period would occasionally make comments like, "We are a dying urban church. This is the way it is. Churches like ours are dying all over the country. Demographics are against us." He would send young couples with children away, telling them, "We don't have a Sunday school. You should go else-where." People told me that he was a kind man. But he understood Trinity's ministry differently from how they understood it. Evidently he wanted to maintain a sacramental presence as long as possible in a world changing rapidly around him. Ministry meant serving the Holy Eucharist until the very last person left or died, to help the church gracefully close shop. Long-term church members go out of their way to speak well of him. But to me he sounded like the chaplain on the Titanic. Bread and wine while sinking. The last rites.

Ann Jaqua remembers looking out over a small congregation one Sunday morning in the early 1990s and worrying: "It can't get any lower than this. There is a breaking point, a point at which we can't recover." Others felt the same way and knew that they must employ desperate measures. The congregation entered its darkest, most conflicted struggle. A number of laypersons, particularly those on the vestry, wanted to "sever the congregation's relationship with its pastor." Those are genteel Episcopal words for "fire the minister." In the summer of 1992, after three years of consulting and attempts at conflict resolution, the vestry and Trinity's priest "reached an impasse" and they asked the Bishop to "adjudicate a request for the dissolution of the pastoral relationship." Within a few months, the request was granted and the priest was removed. Trinity went without regular clergy for many months—while Michelle Woodhouse filled in—until the Rev. Mark Asman arrived in January 1994 as "priest in charge under special circumstances"—polite Episcopal words for "that place is hopeless."

Mark's arrival at Trinity was a turning point, a rare moment of complete congruence between congregation and clergy and the beginning of a genuine partnership in ministry. Mark Benson, who graduated from Westmont, as did I, went to Trinity for the first time on Mark Asman's first Sunday as priest in charge.

"What was striking," Benson recalls, "was how Mark's coming manifested the spirit of who the people were trying to be. I would sit in the pew and get a real sense of the ministry of the clergy and laity together."

Although they faced the monumental task of raising money for the retrofit, an unusual synergy began to develop in the congregation, and a kind of spiritual excitement started to build. A few new people came. Dodie Little remembers that "there was room for everybody. Everyone, even newcomers like me, had to do stuff. I don't know if it was openness, but it was certainly necessity. All of [a] sudden, there was room. Not only for people, but for fresh air to blow there. And it was blowing everywhere." Dodie would later refer to that time as one of "formation"—when a new congregation was taking shape and beginning to grow in faith. "The community itself was rebuilding," she says. The door was wide open.

I arrived one year after Mark began, in January 1995, as the new congregation was taking shape. I found myself drawn in by that spirit of change, a restless energy that mirrored my own. There was nothing tedious or boring about it. Like me, Trinity had just gone through a divorce and was recreating itself, finding its own identity—one that had been obscured by decades of external expectations. Those external expectations had now completely disappeared. The old guard had left, the building itself was in jeopardy, the cultural supports of the Protestant establishment and Christian hegemony were all gone. We were completely free, Trinity and I, to find ourselves anew, find ourselves in God. Despite my theological reservations and without knowing it, Trinity and I were reaching out for each other. George Barrett's warm support demonstrated that I was a member of that community before I seriously considered joining it. We were—and still are—part of each other. We would be reborn together, Trinity and I.

And whatever seemed discordant with my past, I stayed initially because of a childhood memory. Every Sunday, while driving to our Methodist church in Baltimore, we passed a storefront church with a simple sign hanging outside: "The Church of the Open Door." I asked my mother, "What kind of church is that?" "Not our kind," she replied. "They are holy rollers." She sounded disdainful, but I liked the name. I was entranced by the idea of religious ecstasy, the possibility of expressing the emotions described in the Methodist hymns I loved. Even at age seven, I felt a certain disconnection with the restrained middle-class Methodism of my parents. In my imagination, that ugly little building held out the possibility of a different kind of church, a church with an open door. And I thought of my grandmother Elsie, a Pentecostal, who died when my father was a boy. Had she been seeking the same thing when she abandoned her familial Methodism for the early Pentecostal movement? Did she, a woman of expansive faith, hemmed in by the Germanic authoritarianism of husband and father-in-law, seek the open door of the spirit? A place to be free? Did the same spirit that had inspired her prompt me? Did I inherit her faith?

I remembered this thirty years later at Trinity when I heard Mark say immediately before he administered the Eucharist, "Wherever you are in your journey of faith, know that you are welcome at God's table." Trinity was the church of the open door.

One of the most difficult problems when Mark first arrived at Trinity was a surprising one: the people did not know each other. For years, a small number of people occupied a worship space five times the size of their congregation. They could sit far apart from each other, never shake one another's hands during the peace, and look only at the back of each other's heads. On some Sundays, a single person or couple would take an entire pew. Mark remembers that "it was a politely balkanized parish," with people isolated "in little polite groups." Years of conflict over the former rector translated into a comfortably divided parish, willing to worship in the same building but not willing to sit together in the same pew. Mark saw healing as a priority. Working together on the fundraising project needed to flow from that.

That first year, Mark spent much of his time building relationships, preaching on God's love, and focusing on the church's mission statement. In the process, he realized that he was working from a nearly blank slate. All of the parish's old structures and interest groups were gone. There was no men's Bible study, Episcopal Church Women, or altar guild with which to contend. The church, although more than a century old, was essentially a mission congregation, an entirely new entity. Necessity, as Dodie Little mentioned, became the wellspring of healing. To save the church, people had to pull together. Everyone had to help. There could be no spiritual slackers. The tiny parish began an ambitious capital campaign—"With Strength Renewed"—to provide for the future they could not fully envision. With the assistance of a professional fundraiser, donations were coming in to restore the building.

By the time I arrived, in early 1995, the fundraising campaign was going so well that the retrofit could begin. Just as the congregation's spirits were lifting, however, one more traditional structure disappeared. We were forced to move out of our beautiful sanctuary and into the parish hall for worship. The restoration work would banish us for at least a year. Folding chairs and a portable communion table? No pipe organ? No kneelers? Everyone was apprehensive; some people dreaded the prospect. As we moved into the parish hall, attendance, which had gone up, dropped again.

As it turned out, however, the parish hall may have saved Trinity. Dodie refers to the year in the parish hall as "the miracle." Mark calls it "the gift." It was both of those things, and it was a revelation. The parish hall has clear glass windows and is a much smaller space. We set the chairs up in semicircular rows facing the table. The hall was brighter than the sanctuary, and for the first time we could all see each other during worship. No one could quietly hide in a pew. Worship was no longer a private affair between the individual and God. We began to experience the power of the community gathered for worship and to realize that we, God's people, provided the color and the music of the service. We began to understand the liturgy as something we did, not something the priest performed for us at a distance up at the high altar. The table was so close we could touch it. It became ours as we circled it in blessing.

Unlike the cavernous space of the sanctuary, there were no empty places in the parish hall. "We were forced to look at each other," says Dodie, "and we really *saw* one another for the first time." Indeed, it was impossible to hide. We were sitting on top of one another. You knew if someone was distressed or ill. You had to deal with grumpy parishioners, elbows in your side, talking toddlers, purses and sweaters underfoot, bad manners, and coffee breath. People you were not entirely sure you liked would sit down next to you and spill out their life story. You could not escape being asked how you were or being hugged during the peace. You would be touched, jostled, and poked. You would be observed at deeply personal moments, noticed if you were new, and invited out to brunch. You witnessed joy or bliss on other faces while singing hymns. People smiled with empathy or held your hand if you cried during the Eucharist. It was honest, transparent, irritating, and utterly wonderful. Mark Benson says we found "numinous awe" in one another.

There were people I never formally met whom I came to know. I loved watching Nora Gallagher serve the chalice. She did it with focused compassion, as if she were nursing souls. At first, elderly Elizabeth Corrigan would walk to communion assisted by her friend; eventually, she would sit patiently in her seat, waiting to be served. She was a frail spiritual giant, a woman of great prayer, whose holiness awed me. And every Sunday I watched Alex Velto, a man dying from AIDS, who took the communion bread as if it were given by angels. Each week, Alex witnessed to us that death itself was an open door, a vista of grace, a much-anticipated union with God. I never once spoke with him. I simply watched him and learned from him. Then, he did not come any more. A few months later, Mark announced that Alex had died. I cried.

The parish hall was like that. I had always envied priests because they got to see each person's face when taking communion. I suspected that it would be beautiful. I never knew that it could be instructive, a ministry that we give each other of God's presence in the sacraments. But in the parish hall we all became priests. We served each other the bread and wine. We experienced spiritual intimacy, true fellowship, the kind of church we only dreamed existed. "You are no longer strangers and aliens," proclaims the writer of Ephesians, "but you are citizens with the saints and members of the household of God built upon the foundation of apostles and prophets, with Christ Jesus himself as the conrnerstone. In him the whole structure is joined together and grows into a holy temple in the Lord; in whom you also are built together spiritually into a dwelling place for God." We became church.

Amid this holy mystery, life went on rather as usual that year. People bickered over what kind of cookies to serve during coffee hour and complained about the music. Relationships formed; others fell apart. Nora's brother developed cancer. The mother of a young daughter was diagnosed with a terminal brain tumor. Parents and friends died. One couple lost a baby. I finally left the college and found myself both divorced and unemployed. In that difficult year, we brought every raw emotion and every struggle to that table. In sadness, pain, anger, and fear, we were not alone. In community, we experienced healing—the healing that comes from being known and being loved for exactly who one is. I needed that. Others did, too. The parish that once needed healing became a healing parish. Of that transformation, Nora commented to me, "It was not a simple healing. Rather, we enlarged our capacity to suffer together." In the years since, I have come to think that her words define church—a community with hearts large enough to suffer together.

Something strange started to happen while we worshiped in that small space. We kept adding chairs. Week after week, more and more chairs. Trinity had always considered its elegant sanctuary one of its greatest evangelistic assets ("people join because they love our building"), but almost a hundred new people started coming the year we spent crowded in the decidedly inelegant parish hall. By December, so many new families had arrived that the church school was able to put on the best Christmas pageant in twenty years. Two-year-old angels, four-year-old shepherds, and a couple five-year-old wise women added to the now-normal bedlam. We needed more chairs. And we needed room for those little people. It was noisy.

Although we were raising money to fix our building, polish its pews, and clean its stained glass, we discovered that the church is not its building. If an earthquake had leveled it, we would have gotten along just fine. But against every grim prediction, we raised that $1.5 million to strengthen the historic Gothic building and save it from destruction. It was a much greater miracle, however, that

God had strengthened and saved us. We experienced a Gospel paradox: "He who loses his life for my sake, finds it." When construction finished in February 1996, many of us did not want to go back to the sanctuary. But we no longer fit in the parish hall. We needed the space. Some people suggested that we replace the pews with chairs. We liked looking at each other. In our own faces we had seen God.

One of the most difficult problems I faced at Trinity was the issue of what I thought about being part of a congregation that had a homosexual priest. Although not technically "out" to the congregation the first two years, it was pretty much public knowledge that Mark was gay. The vestry had always been aware of Mark's sexual orientation and supported him and his ministry. In his early months at Trinity, he expressed his approval of Integrity—a national fellowship for gay, lesbian, and bisexual Episcopalians—and a few people left the church. For many years, however, there had been a contingent of homosexual Christians in the parish and no one minded much. People tended to be polite about sexuality and not activist. Mark recalls that "nobody actually used the words *gay* and *lesbian*." Part of Trinity's mission statement read: "Demonstrating God's love for the world, we will serve a diverse population and accept one another without reservation." This mannered Episcopal sentence means "homosexual persons welcome here."

The issue of homosexuality had troubled me since high school, where I had a number of gay friends. In the 1970s, churchgoers were just beginning to discuss homosexuality. My evangelical friends believed homosexuality was a moral choice—not a product of genetics or biology. Basing its argument on the scriptures,

Scottsdale Bible Church viewed "the shame of Sodom" as unnatural passion, a grave sin and evil. Christians must resist homosexual urges in the same way they resist any sin. Homosexuals needed to be born again and freed from sin. My church recognized that those who converted to evangelical faith might have residual same-sex affections, but resisting such temptations was simply a part of heroic Christian living. As an alternative to sin, converted homosexuals should remain forever celibate or enter into heterosexual marriage. In effect, however, it was impossible to be a Christian and remain a "practicing" homosexual.

In college, emboldened by the nascent gay rights movement, a few of my evangelical friends confessed their homosexuality. This shocked me. I simply assumed, as my church had taught, that all good Christians were either celibate or safely married heterosexuals. Yet here were gay students at an evangelical college who went to chapel, majored in religion, prayed with sincerity, participated in missionary work, and regularly attended church. Whatever their virtues, however, I thought these classmates hypocritical and did not hesitate to express my views. After all, the Bible referred to homosexuality as an "abomination." One such friend, Jeffrey Michael, and I held a running argument on the subject. He had grown up Southern Baptist but now wanted to become an Episcopal priest. I thought that was appalling. We had a difficult and often strained relationship.

During Christmas break in our senior year, Linnae Himsl invited a number of us to her family vacation home in Lake Tahoe. Jeffrey Michael went. One evening, he and I drove to the grocery store alone together. On the return trip, the stars reflecting off the snow and icy water caught our attention. We took the long way around the lake to enjoy the wintry vistas while listening to "mellow" seventies rock on my car radio.

Over the strains of "Hotel California," he broached the subject: "You're in favor of women's ordination, aren't you?"

"Yes. Why do you ask?"

"Well, if you believe in women's ordination, I can't see why you don't believe gays and lesbians can be ordained. After all, the Bible says women shouldn't teach or hold authority over a man. Will you submit to your husband?"

He knew I would not.

He went on: "You think that is cultural. A particular prohibition for a certain time and place. Not a universal truth. You don't really *believe* what Paul teaches about women. Aren't the passages about homosexuality the same? Cultural prohibitions. Ancient Jewish sexual practices and beliefs. It is different now. The same argument holds true for women and gay people."

"No. It is completely different," I blurted out. "Women can't pick being female. And Paul's culture taught that we were inferior. But homosexuals can choose not to engage in homosexual behavior. It is two different things—biology versus morality."

"What if they can't?" Jeffrey Michael insisted. "What if God intends for some people to love others of the same gender? What if God made me gay? The church does not exclude anyone on the basis of who they are—women, blacks, or other minorities. It is wrong. What if it isn't a choice?"

What if it isn't a choice? I had never considered that possibility before. "Well, it just is. God does not make sin," I shot back illogically. Case closed. We drove on in silence. We had a hard time talking for years to come.

Although he never knew it, Jeffrey Michael helped change my mind. Not about homosexuality, but about women's ordination. Maybe I had been wrong to dismiss Paul's prohibition as simply "cultural." Maybe I had been too loose in my interpretation of scripture and tradition. Maybe the case for women's ordination was wrong. A little more than a year later, I would be at Gordon-Conwell, hearing the arguments against women's ordination from all those well-educated conservatives. Given Jeffrey Michael's logic, their views provided welcome relief for my homophobic fears. I was willing to change my mind about women's ordination rather than believe that homosexual persons could serve as priests.

By the time I arrived at Trinity, however, I firmly supported women's ordination. I had read a great deal of feminist theology— some of which dealt with lesbian concerns. Jeffrey Michael had been right. The two issues were connected. I went back to the biblical texts, theology, and church history to try to understand the scriptures and Christian attitudes toward sexuality. Prompted by a friend in San Francisco, I read a number of books that evangelicals eschew: John Boswell's *Christianity, Social Tolerance, and Homosexuality,* Virginia Ramey Mollenkott's *Sensuous Spirituality: Out from Fundamentalism,* William Countryman's *Dirt, Greed, and Sex: Sexual Ethics in the New Testament,* Mel White's *Stranger at the Gate: To Be Gay and Christian in America,* and John McNeill's *The Church and the Homosexual.* Indeed, in one feminist theology tutorial, my students challenged me on my attitudes toward homosexuality— attitudes they thought were narrow.

Several of my college friends had died of AIDS. Their suffering had given me greater compassion for and understanding of my gay friends. In the early 1990s, I had seen the damage that denial or "healing" ministries could do. It was better for a person to be him- or herself in God—even if that meant homosexual—than to hide from one's true self. Thus, I believed it was possible to be a Christian, maybe even a good one, and be a gay or lesbian person. I no longer had a problem with being part of a congregation with gay and lesbian parishioners. I still thought that homosexual ordination and same-sex blessings were outside the boundaries of biblical theology.

I continued to read and explore the issue. The biblical and theological case for the full inclusion of gay and lesbian persons in the church was beginning to make sense. I was surprised to learn that Sodom's sin was not homosexuality; rather, God condemned the Sodomites for being inhospitable, unjust, and sexually violent. It was equally surprising to see that the "abomination" passage occurred in the Jewish purity code—a part of scripture long rejected by Christians as having any theological authority. Indeed, the early Church Fathers rarely appealed to those passages as relevant regarding homosexuality. It stunned me to discover that the Bible never used the word *homosexuality* in the same sense that our English word conveys. Over lunch one day, I confessed to Anne Howard both my theological reticence about gay ordination and my growing discomfort with the evangelical view. She laughed gently saying, "You're on your way. You'll get there." I still was not sure I wanted to, however.

Although I felt oddly ambivalent about his priesthood in theory, Mark Asman and I became friends. I liked him. And I honestly respected what he was doing at Trinity. We had both started out as theological conservatives and sojourned through the evangelical world in high school and college. As a young priest, he had assisted at an evangelical Episcopal parish, which he always insists was "a formative part" of his "spiritual journey," for which he is "still grateful." We understood the same language, the same religious code words. And we both found ourselves in a different place from where we had started. Mark and I found friendship through our stories, as well as a common love for theology and a passion for God.

For all the similarity in our stories, there were differences, too. Since adolescence, Mark knew he was called to be a priest and was ordained as a young man. At the same time, however, he felt fairly certain he was gay. The two identities—priestly and personal—were at odds with each other. For a number of years, Mark struggled to resolve the tension. Although he would not completely leave the priesthood, he went into business for a decade as part of this struggle. In 1993 he came to the conclusion that he was, indeed, both. A priest who was gay. And the two needed to be brought together in a healthy, spiritual way. He left his job and wanted to resume his priestly vocation in a parish.

At the same time, Trinity was searching for a priest. Anne Howard, who was working in the bishop's office, remembers some diocesan anxiety about the parish: What are we going to do with Trinity? Close it down? Sell the property? Raise the funds and fix the building? What priest would choose to go to a dying congregation needing a major capital campaign?

Mark Asman, Anne thought. With Trinity's history, a gay priest would probably be acceptable to the congregation. And with Mark's business experience, he would bring them expertise in management and fundraising.

Mark Benson would later say of the choice, "Having a gay priest was not just a project the church undertook, it was part of our healing. Having a gay priest struggling honestly with those issues on many levels gave us freedom to be ourselves. Mark became a metaphor for the congregation; he personifies our notion of inclusiveness." He proved himself a good pastor and liturgist, an able administrator, and an excellent fundraiser. His honest preaching and spirituality became a quietly charismatic presence in the congregation, an empowering focal point for others' faith and ministries. Mark's priesthood served as a doorway on what theologian William Countryman calls "the threshold of the holy." The parish began its extraordinary turnaround. Indeed, an uncommon bond grew between Mark and Trinity. Although it would take some time to admit it, parish and priest fell in love with one another and achieved an unusual level of trust and openness with each other. Eventually, "priest in charge under special circumstances" was changed to "rector." Mark's position was regularized and he fully became Trinity's priest. He was installed the same day we rededicated the church. It was a little like a wedding.

Before I knew Mark and watched him exercise his vocation at Trinity, I knew most of the arguments—pro and con—about homosexuality and the church. Prejudices swayed me one way; intellect, the other. But friendship would clinch the argument. The same had happened with women's ordination: I did not really believe in it until I experienced it and became friends with women who were priests. It is easy to demonize opponents over an issue when they have no human face, when they are problems and not people. At Trinity, we strove to live our baptismal vows. Of those, the final one, to "strive for justice and peace among all people and respect the dignity of every human being," became a kind of congregational rallying cry. Respect demanded understanding and honoring other points of view. My friendship with Mark became a bridge of compassion.

Because the congregation was so diverse, we had to learn how to respect each other if we were to live together. We did not all agree—even about having a gay priest. Trinity was not a lockstep liberal parish; nor did it become a "gay church." Many different people with an extraordinary number of different perspectives walked through that open door. People who were gay, straight, single, married, divorced, middle-aged, elderly, rich, poor, white, brown, black, churched, unchurched, formerly churched, postmodern, post-Christian, Christian, Jewish, Buddhist, and Muslim, as well as families, children, students, the homeless, and drug abusers. It became a safe place to explore faith, to think about God, to bring one's heart and mind together. According to one Trinity parishioner, it is "maddeningly inclusive."

Back in evangelicalism there was an implicit expectation of spiritual uniformity, for fear that diversity would lead to deviation, chaos, and sin. Trinity's diversity, however, was a kind of prism, a stained-glass window of grace. Mark's priesthood, because he was gay, served as an icon of safety and acceptance in God. It held out the possibility that paradoxes might be the way to faith, that mercy was beyond comprehension, and that our suffering opened to healing. At Trinity we experienced unity in this vision—a mosaic of hope created by our diversity. I always thought the church's multifaceted beauty reflected our name—Trinity—and the triune nature of God: three persons, one nature. Diversity and unity. Thomas Jefferson once referred to the Trinity as "that incomprehensible arithmetic." It was not incomprehensible at Trinity; it was the maddening inclusivity of God.

One warm spring day in 1999, Mark and I sat on a park bench in the Alice Keck Park Gardens, talking about the church, about the future, about vocation, and about love, relationships, marriage, and family. We laughed and talked for a long time—two hours at least. As I listened and enjoyed his company, I silently prayed, "Thank you, God, for Mark. Thank you that he has taught me about acceptance, compassion, forbearance, and love. And forgive me for all the stupid things I've said and done to my gay friends." It was my own internal Twelve Step meeting as I repented of all the hurt I had caused others because of my narrow mindedness. I looked at Mark. The sunlight reflected off his bald spot and formed a momentary halo, an unlikely angelic visitation. It was one of Mark Benson's moments of numinous awe. Mark Asman was no project. Nor was he an issue. Somehow we had found what Jewish theologian Martin Buber calls the I-thou. He is a person, my friend. A gay priest. A good priest. And a very human one. A fellow citizen and coworker in God's kingdom.

In the late 1960s, my mother, increasingly disenchanted with the Methodist Church, used to complain that the sermons were not "religious enough." Preaching had become an exercise in political protest; biblical interpretation seemed to disappear from the pulpit. "Why go to church?" she would mumble. "It's just not the same as when I was a girl. There's no purpose to it anymore."

As early as 1964, sociologist Jeffrey Hadden identified a disturbing trend in mainline churches—a growing gap between an activist liberal clergy and their traditional laity. Laypeople expected their ministers to be pastors, gentle shepherds who helped families through their life passages. They attended church seeking comfort through worshiping God, hearing the Word, and working for charity.

By the mid-1960s, however, many preachers abandoned these old-fashioned priestly tasks in favor of a prophetic ministry that challenged middle-class American values. Although this prophetic style initially grew out of mid-century theology, churches appeared to lose their distinctly religious voices. Theological fads like "religionless Christianity" and the "death of God" failed to communicate meaningful faith to millions of American churchgoers. Recognizable religion disappeared. If God was dead and theology only politics, what good was church anyway? Fashionable theology's implicit secularity undermined the churchgoing loyalty of a generation.

For thirty years, scholars have been discussing the "decline" of mainline churches. In 1972, sociologist Dean Kelly proposed that theological liberalism had caused the decline, enervating church discipline and draining mainstream Protestantism of spiritual purpose. Although I disagree with Kelly's argument and its implications, I believe that he may have been right *at the time*. The liberalism of the 1960s often functioned as he described—and most likely initiated the drop in mainline membership.

What Kelly—and most people in the 1970s—could not imagine was mainline churches ever regaining a sense of the sacred—a spiritual center that would displace the secularity that had taken hold. In recent years, however, and in selective places, mainline churches have been rediscovering awe, finding that social activism is not the heartbeat of Christian faith. As a study conducted by sociologist Nancy Ammerman found, people go to church for worship and preaching, to be connected with God and to deepen their spiritual lives. Many congregations have responded to this longing and many have—and are—providing more meaningful worship and resources for spiritual formation.

However, with increased attention focused on the spiritual, the mainline has not lost its historic commitment to public ministry. From what anecdotal evidence exists, it appears that some mainline churches are now more purposeful, linking their spiritual lives with their call into the public arena. Prayer and prophetic ministry. A new sense is emerging in these congregations—the church's mandate for justice springs from its encounter with God, grounded in its worship.

At the center of Trinity's rebirth was what Mark Benson called the numinous awe, the holy mystery of God's presence in a place and a people. Before Mark Asman arrived, the church had begun a quiet turnaround as they began to put back together that which had been torn asunder: spirituality and social justice.

Although I know she would deny it, Ann Jaqua was key in Trinity's ability to integrate prayer and social action. In many ways, her story is a microcosm of that of the parish. As 1960s mainline ennui settled in, Ann left Trinity. She wanted more meaningful worship and spiritual connection and transferred her membership to Christ the King. "The lively energy," she says, "moved there."

But neither the unworldly spirituality of the charismatic movement nor mainline "do-good" social activism would completely satisfy her. After a few years at Christ the King, Ann's family moved to Washington, D.C. Experiencing the isolation of suburban, upper-middle-class motherhood, Ann was dissatisfied with the direction of her life. One day, in search of greater meaning, Ann drove her Mercedes from her ritzy Virginia home into one of the District's roughest neighborhoods and volunteered at the Sojourners Community. In 1971, progressive evangelicals founded Sojourners as a biblical ministry for social justice. As evangelicals, they maintained a traditional theological stance and a commitment to personal piety. But they believed that faithful Christianity should challenge the prevailing materialism and individualism of middle-class culture. Faith demanded radical action on behalf of the poor, the outcast, and the oppressed. In contrast to the liberal mainline, Sojourners kept spirituality and social justice together. It proved that there could be an alternative to both uninvolved piety and spiritually vacuous activism.

At Sojourners, the streams of Ann's spirituality flowed together—intense devotion to God and passionate service to others. In 1979, after she and her husband divorced, Ann returned to Santa Barbara with her children. Her experiences in Washington, however, would prove instrumental in reshaping the congregation. She brought with her a vision of what Trinity could be and a mix of qualities and gifts that would serve as spiritual leaven in the congregation. A longing for meaningful worship. Spiritual discernment. A passion for social justice and serving the poor. Commitment to the practices of faith. Prayer, Bible study, spiritual direction. An intense zeal for God's kingdom. And she possessed a strong ability to buck the system and take risks for God. In whatever mysterious way it happens, many of these traits would come to describe Trinity as well. I think she helped nurture them. I know she held out hope that Trinity could become a place for both prayer and justice.

Although those who remained at Trinity were small in number, they maintained an evident spiritual intensity. Through the 1980s, as the small congregation struggled to redefine itself and find empowering leadership, a quiet spiritual energy began to work itself through the parish. Some people regularly prayed the daily office in the Book of Common Prayer, some sought spiritual direction, and some became directors themselves. Since Sunday worship was less than satisfying, a few parishioners also attended a Friday morning Eucharist at Mount Calvary, an Episcopal monastery and retreat house in the hills above Santa Barbara. There, a couple adopted a lay version of the brothers' Benedictine rule and began to practice its spiritual vision. This commitment further led them to explore Celtic spirituality and centering prayer.

On a trip to San Francisco, some parishioners discovered Grace Cathedral's new labyrinth, a tool for walking meditation borrowed from medieval Christianity, and duplicated it back at Trinity. They learned the contemplative music of Taize, an ecumenical community in France. They read Elizabeth O'Connor's *Journey Inward, Journey Outward, Sojourners* magazine, and books by Henri Nouwen and Thomas Merton. They started base communities—essentially lay-led Bible studies—modeled on communities they had visited in Latin America. Some of the practices were ancient, some were distinctly Anglican, some were recent spiritual innovations.

While they were deepening their spiritual lives, the congregation was also reaching out. They started a soup kitchen and homeless shelter. They protested Reagan's policies in Latin America. They opened their parish as part of the sanctuary movement and provided advice, aid, and shelter to immigrants. Unlike 1960s activists, however, Trinity's people did not eschew mystery, the sacraments, healing, and religious experience. And unlike their forebears, these mainline Protestants were not spiritual introverts; they hugged at the peace, talked about their spiritual lives, and cried together at the Eucharist. They asked for the Holy Spirit's blessing and power. They studied the Bible and took it seriously. They prayed for wisdom and guidance when making decisions. They knew Jesus—with their heads and with their hearts—and they knew themselves to be his hands in the world.

It was all this overt piety, the serious practices of faith, that attracted me to Trinity. Other liberal evangelicals—and the congregation comprises a large number of them—also claim that these Christian practices made Trinity attractive. When the congregation moved to the parish hall, the spirituality practiced in the isolated corners of the sanctuary moved into the center of community. The intimacy and immediacy of that year nurtured and matured the congregation's commitment to practicing faith. Vestry and committee meetings became small groups—places of support and intercessory prayer. Prayer, Bible study, and sacraments both fed and guided what we did. Even now, newcomers still remark that Trinity's seriousness in both spirituality and social justice drew them to the congregation.

Mark Asman nurtured both spirituality and social justice through his preaching. He and Anne Howard—who often assisted—fed the congregation biblically literate and theologically textured sermons. During 1996 they guided the congregation into one of the central theological paradoxes of Christian faith—the God who is known as both love and justice. This insistence that

God is both a loving God and a just God had always troubled me. Was God a stern Father who demonstrated love by punishing his children and sending wayward ones to hell? Evangelical religion argues this. One of my seminary professors even insisted that sending sinners to hell actually glorified God. I hated this idea and suspected that much of my own spiritual uneasiness flowed from this flawed image of God. I know this was true for others at Trinity; I suspect it was true for Mark as well.

A more biblical vision of God—not as a vengeful and distant Father—richly plumbed for its paradoxes, began to heal our wounds. We called it the love and justice year. As Mark explored these twin characteristics of God, we discovered that God's love justified us, it made us right. And doing justice was God's love. We had all been, in the theology of Martin Luther, justified by love and made right by mercy, and we were to be God's people in the world. Broken, sinful, and welcomed. Healed, redeemed, and sent on mission. Gathered around the table, dispersed into the world. Two sides of the same thing. Journey inward, journey outward. God's love and justice.

In the spring of 1999, Dodie Little and I stood in the sunshine outside the church. Trinity was still growing—it had more people all the time. "It is hard to keep up with them all," she sighed.

We reminisced about the events of the previous five years— about the capital campaign, the parish hall, Easter Vigils and parish suppers, busy times and quiet days, about taking back the church school building to accommodate all the new children, about Charles and Phillip's wedding, the inclusive language liturgy, and reconfiguring the worship space. "You know, Diana," she said a bit wistfully, "we did it. We've created the kind of church we only dreamed existed back in the 1960s. And here it is."

As she spoke, I thought about Clark Roof's *A Generation of Seekers,* a book published shortly before he and Terry joined Trinity. Before Trinity became Trinity, really. In that study he argues, "Clearly, major restructuring of religion is under way, particularly the reshaping of religious communities." The values, experiences, and worldview of the baby boom generation, he argues, were just beginning to have an impact on traditional religious structures. As he speculates about the future of American congregations, Clark seems mildly pessimistic. Yes, some boomers would continue in traditional religion; some would switch to new-style evangelical megachurches. But mainline religion? Clark hints suggestively as to how mainstream churches might be revitalized: "The vision is that of a new vital balance of spirituality and social action, of the sort many boomers are looking for. Where congregations are open to new spiritual vision, or in places where boomers 'invade' in large numbers, they will play a crucial role in reshaping their future. They will provide leadership moving in new directions, or at the very least, bring to them a change of sensibilities that in time promises to create 'new wine in old wineskins.'"

Whether or not Clark proved that sociologists also can be prophets, I sometimes quip that Trinity is a "baby boom church." The parish's turnaround was largely (but not exclusively) the vision of baby boom churchgoers. Much of the original leadership came from baby boomers like me, who had remained in church during the lean decades of the 1960s, 1970s, and 1980s. Those who stuck around, sometimes called loyalists, were children of the 1950s mainline hegemony, schooled in the measured tones of Protestant theology, the Bible, prayer, hymnody, and service.

But we were also baby boomers, religious seekers. Seeker-loyalists, I think—bricolage Christians not particularly satisfied with business as usual. We had been around the denominational block, remaining mostly loyal while imbibing new spiritualities on the side. We stayed in church, but not always our birthright denominations. We also got born again, spoke in tongues, sang praise choruses, attended Catholic Mass, learned yoga, went on short-term missions, and practiced Buddhist meditation—things old-time loyalists never would have done. As we grew into congregational leadership, especially at Trinity, where there was a generational vacuum, we were able to experiment with religious styles that resonated with our experience of the gospel. Most of Trinity's core leaders were seeker-loyalists. The church served as a kind of laboratory for what seeker-loyalists always hoped would be.

As the seeker-loyalists created a new congregational culture, the kind of church of which we had dreamed, new people came. Some of the newcomers were also long-time churchgoers of the seeker-loyalist type. Many were disenfranchised liberal evangelicals like myself. But others came, too. Lots of folks arrived who had not attended church since childhood—the returnee baby boomers. There were ex-Roman Catholics, too. And some people who had never been in church. It was exciting to share the Bible with those who had never seen one before. A little like having the mission field come into the building.

In January 1996 I was at an academic conference in Louisville, Kentucky. One of the other participants turned to me over dinner and asked, "Diana, do you know a good church in Santa Barbara?"

Know one?! It was all I could do to maintain an appropriate appearance of academic detachment. Trinity was so exciting that it was hard not to sound like a street corner evangelist extolling its virtues. "I'm familiar with several," I replied. "But Dorothy, why would you want to know about a good church in Santa Barbara?"

She told me that her forty-year-old brother, Richard, lived in Santa Barbara. He had grown up Presbyterian but stopped attending church in high school. Now he wanted to "reconnect" with church, to delve more deeply into his spiritual life. "Does he like liturgy?" I asked.

Before I knew it, I had his phone number. And she called him and gave him mine. A sort of blind church date. A couple weeks later, I took Richard Bass to Trinity. In the months to come, he fell in love—with both the church and me. Trinity and I returned those feelings. As Richard and I grew closer, he became deeply involved in the church. He served on the newsletter committee, joined the Thursday night base community, went to the newcomer class, and became confirmed. He asked questions, read books, studied theology, and participated with enthusiasm. He never missed a holy day or Sunday. He went with me to the monastery. In only a short time, he found friendship, community, and a place to be a thoughtful Christian. "I always wanted to go back to church," he would later say, "but I just couldn't find a good one. It is hard to find a good church."

On January 18, 1997, two years after I arrived at Trinity, Richard and I were married at its altar. Mark officiated, Anne Howard preached the sermon, and George Barrett blessed our marriage. Ann Jaqua and my father arranged the flowers. Nearly Richard's whole family—including his sister Dorothy—came to celebrate. Clark and Terry hosted the wedding reception at their home.

Richard and I remained at Trinity for another six months before we moved to Memphis for me to take a new academic post at Rhodes College. Our lives were so woven into the fabric of Trinity that even four years after our departure the "old timers" (people who have been there since 1994) still consider us part of the congregation. We still consider them part of us. We have never quite gotten over our love for Trinity or the powerful spiritual growth we experienced through the events that transpired there.

But, as is common among our peers, we followed our jobs to a place where we had no connections, no history, and no community. We faced the daunting task of finding a new church in a new city in the Old South. We headed to Memphis, Tennessee.

CHAPTER SEVEN

The Household of God

GRACE–ST. LUKE'S EPISCOPAL CHURCH

Memphis, Tennessee, 1997–2000

The Mississippi River is deceptive at Memphis. Very wide, and wearing delta heat like a shroud, it seems to move lethargically southward to New Orleans. Just beneath the surface, however, a quick, treacherous current sweeps everything downstream to New Orleans faster than you can say "Elvis Presley." Every year, some fool tourist or adventuresome child drowns in its waters. As a city, Memphis is much like the river that gives it life. Although it appears to be much like other American cities, subterranean currents of class, race, and "the Southern way of life" threaten to shipwreck those unfamiliar with its shoals. This hidden story—a "Christ-haunted" history, to borrow a phrase from Flannery O'Connor—violently acts upon everything, threatening to bear it all away.

The good people of Grace–St. Luke's Episcopal Church in Memphis, Tennessee, do not like to fight. As is the case with all Southerners, being nice is an ultimate value, and Grace–St. Luke's is a particularly nice congregation. Parishioners do not generally argue in public, nor will they admit that they have ever fought. But they have. Through the years, Grace–St. Luke's has experienced plenty of conflict about the church's fundamental identity. That unspoken history shapes them—and silently continues to do so.

In many ways, Grace–St. Luke's sits squarely within the American Protestant mainstream. The same issues, questions, problems, and changes that have shaped it have also shaped its mainline kin. Currently, Grace–St. Luke's parishioners are theologically and socially moderate, middle- and upper-middle-class, and mostly college educated. The majority are baby boomers who converted from other traditions. Many have lived in other parts of the country. But lots of old timers—many of them cradle Episcopalians and native Memphians—are still around, too. One member commented that "Grace–St. Luke's is the quintessential Episcopal Church."

In August 1997, my husband Richard and I first visited Grace–St. Luke's. We had moved to Memphis so that I could accept a teaching position at Rhodes College. Although the change seemed right, leaving Trinity was difficult—a little like cutting off a limb. We doubted that any church could approach the kind of community we had found in Santa Barbara.

Unlike Memphis natives, who know not to do such things, Richard and I followed our family practice and walked to church that August Sunday. By 10 A.M., it was brutally hot. I was nearly seven months pregnant; we were both soaked with sweat. The sanctuary's cool, wooden interior provided welcome relief. Grace–St. Luke's is a Victorian neo-Gothic-style building with a long nave and center aisle, choir stalls, pipe organ, and high altar. Built in 1912, the same year as Trinity, Grace–St. Luke's is located in Midtown, once an "old money" enclave and now a changing urban neighborhood. This jewel box of a church bespoke continuity, history, and tradition. Of its red carpets, carved pews, aged oak paneling, and stained-glass windows, my mother would later remark, "It looks just like a church should."

Although our fellow parishioners that morning did not know us, we knew a little of them. Brother Timothy, one of the brothers at Mount Calvary in Santa Barbara, had grown up in Memphis and was raised in Grace–St. Luke's. He mentioned that we might go there and referred to it as a "funny" congregation with surprising spiritual depth. The odd name, Grace–St. Luke's, was the result of a merger of two nineteenth-century congregations, Grace and St. Luke's, in 1940. "For years after that," he reported, "the Grace people sat on one side of the church, the St. Luke's people, the other. Sort of like two churches in one building." Two churches? That sounded troublesome. I was not optimistic about it becoming home.

The look of Grace–St. Luke's meticulously cared-for sanctuary, complete with Tiffany windows installed by Louis Comfort Tiffany himself, did little to placate my concerns. Even on that oppressive summer day, most of the men in the all-white congregation wore suits and ties; the women wore dresses, stockings, and pumps. The opening procession was extremely formal, with participants dressed to the ecclesiastical nines. Even the choir—summer choirs are usually casual affairs—sounded practiced and professional. Everything looked too rich and too perfect. Being neither, I figured this was no place for me. It reminded me a bit of St. Stephen's in Durham. I sensed shadows—unwelcome congregational ghosts—just beyond the places where the glittering Tiffany sunlight fell. Before the service started, I was in near despair.

Something odd, however, happened that morning—a foretaste of what was to come. The Rev. Virginia Brown, a diminutive fifty-something woman who could even be described as mousy, mounted the pulpit and began to preach. At first I had trouble following her—she has one of the most unusual accents I've ever heard—but, listening carefully, I became utterly transfixed. As I sat in the pew, feeling lost in this new place and isolated on my journey toward childbirth, she preached on our hunger for God's generous motherhood:

> The Bread of Heaven is real food, strength for the journey, food that sustains and nourishes the hidden Christ-life within us. It is comfort in sadness, celebration in joy, healing in sickness, reconciliation in brokenness. It is welcome for the lonely, belonging for the isolated, consolation in all our afflictions. It is hope beyond the boundaries of this world, the pledge of eternal life. It is the very substance of love. . . . Tenderly and dependably as a mother feeding her baby with her own milk, Christ feeds us with his own life, his own Body and Blood.

Consumed by this eucharistic vision, Virginia Brown was anything but mousy. She crafted the mystery of God, weaving together biblical insights, feminist experience, and eucharistic theology with a passion rare in any pulpit. The congregation absorbed every word, clearly listening to and respectful of her insights. Genuine warmth and respect bound together preacher and pews.

After the service, many parishioners stopped with comments or prayer requests or to hug and kiss her. Richard and I stopped as well, and I told her how much I appreciated the feminist aspects of the sermon. Years later, when I was sure she had forgotten our first meeting, she gently told me that I was wrong: "Just how many heavily pregnant women newly arrived from California introduce themselves and thank the priest for her 'subtle feminist insights'?" David Fikes, the rector with whom she served, later told us, "Virginia holds the heart of this parish in her hands." Eventually I would come to think of her as the Mother of Grace–St. Luke's.

I commented to Richard that her sermon cheered me. Perhaps Memphis Episcopalians would not be as stuffy as I feared. "There must be more to that place than meets the eye," I speculated, "if they'd hire someone like her." Who would have guessed that two years hence, parish gossips would accuse this petite, saintly woman of moral indiscretion and demand her resignation?

For all the brilliance of Virginia's sermon, Richard and I did not initially settle at Grace–St. Luke's. Perhaps I took Brother Timothy's comments too seriously, but the sense of shadows haunted me. It reminded me a little of St. Stephen's. For several months, we worshiped at a different parish. But finding that church too large and impersonal, we returned to Grace–St. Luke's in June 1998, with our new baby daughter, Emma. Maybe we were oddly predestined to do so. Months later, we would discover that our ninety-year-old house had been previously owned by a man who was once the chair of the outreach committee at Grace–St. Luke's. We thought the clergy were theologically sharp and personable. Perhaps the ghosts were more imaginary than real. We decided to make it our home. When we did, we thought we were only joining a new church. Little did we realize that we were stepping into a river of history.

1998 was a peak in the congregational life of Grace–St. Luke's. Patti Newsom, a long-time Grace–St. Luke's parishioner recalls, "We were in a great place. I never wanted it to change. It was a kind of Camelot." Seven years earlier, in the fall of 1991, the congregation had called the Rev. David Fikes to be their rector. Only thirty-eight, Fikes had never been the minister in charge of a church. He was born in Pine Bluff, Arkansas, and raised Southern Baptist. A college student with a gift for preaching, he was ordained to the ministry by a local Baptist pastor. Even then, however, David was discouraged by the fundamentalist direction of his denomination. He enrolled at Candler Divinity School in Atlanta to pursue a theological degree. He took a class offered by the Rt. Rev. Bennett Sims, the Episcopal bishop of Atlanta. Sensing David's growing discontent with the Baptists, Sims suggested he try the Episcopal Church. David remembers that when he finally went, "it felt like coming home." He was confirmed as an Episcopalian shortly thereafter, and was ordained to the priesthood in November 1986.

Half-jokingly, David occasionally refers to himself as a "hick." He is a country boy who, by providential accident, wound up rector of tony Grace–St. Luke's. He thought his age would disqualify him from consideration as their senior rector. The search committee, however, issued him a unanimous call, pending the bishop's approval. In a theological "grilling," the diocese's reactionary bishop asked David if he was conservative or liberal. David intended to answer, "I am fundamentally conservative until the gospel compels me to be otherwise." The bishop, however, never heard the full testimony. Immediately upon the words, "I am fundamentally conservative," he welcomed the young priest to the diocese, supposing him to be a theological ally. David Fikes headed to Memphis.

In the decades prior to David's arrival, Grace–St. Luke's had experienced a tumultuous series of shifts in clerical leadership and congregational identity. Unlike many urban mainline churches, it had actually grown throughout the 1960s, 1970s, and early 1980s as the neighborhood changed but remained a desirable place to live. Although many old families moved out, the inexpensive fixer-uppers and Midtown's quirky urban energy attracted upscale newcomers, college and graduate students, single professionals, young families, artists and actors, and a number of gay and lesbian residents. By 1991, Midtown comprised a host of extremes: black and white, rich and poor, native and newcomer, Southerner and Northerner, straight and gay. Aided by urban redevelopment, Grace–St. Luke's maintained a relatively stable neighborhood-oriented congregational base.

In the 1960s and 1970s, however, Grace–St. Luke's often grew by resisting change. From 1962 to 1974, the Rev. Brinkley Morton, later the Bishop of San Diego, "ruled the church with an iron hand." Personable, pastoral, and a dynamic preacher, Morton took the congregation through one of its greatest growth periods. But he was "really Old School," as some long-time members say—a kind of Episcopal Boss Crump, who handpicked his own vestry and taught the only adult education class, The Rector's Bible Study, to ensure his complete authority in the congregation.

In 1968, at the height of Morton's tenure, a sanitation workers' strike—the event resulting in the assassination of Martin Luther King Jr.—tore Memphis apart. Influenced by King's message and death, a few brave white ministers in the city—including some of the Episcopal clergy—joined the cause. But not Brinkley Morton. Whatever his gifts, he failed to rise above his place and time. One Sunday during the strike, Morton proclaimed from his pulpit, "This is none of the church's business." Declaring civil rights "a legal thing," he promised that Grace–St. Luke's would remain uninvolved. Every person in Memphis knew exactly what that meant: support for the white status quo. One parishioner remembers her "heart breaking" during that sermon. "He was a fabulous person who could have made a real difference. But he didn't."

Other prominent Memphis churches chose controversy and lost clergy and members because of it. Grace–St. Luke's, however, attracted new members—mostly wealthy Memphians opposed to integration, variously referred to by some forthright members as "malcontents" and "the most conservative sorts of Episcopalians." In particular, disgruntled white parishioners from St. Mary's Cathedral and Christ Church in Whitehaven, both centers of pro–Civil Rights activism, left their congregations and joined Grace–St. Luke's. Morton's silence paid off. Throughout 1968, weekly attendance hovered around 800; a record 1,426 came on the Easter Sunday following the King assassination. Under Morton's watch, the parish roll grew to 1,800.

Morton eventually regretted the arrival of these stalwarts of the Old Order. From 1967 to 1970, the Episcopal Church introduced a number of national programs designed to end segregation, support affirmative action, and promote the economic advancement of African Americans. According to the parish history, such initiatives "were opposed strongly by the Grace–St. Luke's Vestry." Like other intransigent Southern parishes, the church threatened to withdraw financial support from the national church. Southern dioceses talked about seceding from the denomination. Having previously refused to address these issues, Morton now insisted that his congregation must remain loyal to the national church and follow a more moderate course of action. Years later, perhaps tempered by the wisdom of age and distance, the Rt. Rev. Morton, Bishop of San Diego, returned to Grace–St. Luke's and confessed that he had been wrong in 1968.

The church may have been successful in the short run, but these events created a sort of spiritual intransigence, an ineffable sense of Southern Gothic, that would continue to bedevil the congregation. In the late 1960s, while parishes like St. Mary's and Christ Church worked for justice and withered, Grace–St. Luke's maintained its establishment posture and prospered. Morton saved the church by appealing to Memphis's traditional patriarchs and the darkest side of Southern history.

The congregation gained a reputation as a bastion of white elitism. By the end of Morton's tenure in 1974, Grace–St. Luke's made its stand with the Old South. They embodied the same sort of seamless society as St. Stephen's: the traditional family was its locus, private clubs served as social centers, and the church was its chapel.

And it was a vision for society long present in the South—its roots reach back to the eighteenth century, when these institutions first formed. It was also one founded on racial exclusion. The parish history dryly notes that upon his departure, "Brinkley Morton had left the parish in a strong but conservative posture."

These choices did not sit well with the whole congregation, however—some of whom were progressive Southerners who had been grieved by the attitudes of the late 1960s at Grace–St. Luke's. Most Americans do not realize that there is a long history of white liberalism in the South—a tradition that stretches back to the earliest days of Southern history. A number of Grace–St. Luke's parishioners wanted to move in a different direction. When Morton retired, this group somehow gained control of the rector search process. They called the Rev. Burt Thomas. In his first sermon to the congregation, Thomas joked, "I want you all to know that I cannot fill Brinkley Morton's shoes—in fact, we don't even wear the same size." Beyond the levity, parishioners knew that Thomas had put them on notice: Grace–St. Luke's was about to change.

According to the Rev. Anne Carriere, who served on Thomas's staff, no two men could have been more different. Only thirty-five when he began, Thomas implemented a "whole different style of church," based on shared team and lay ministries. Described as innovative and "with it," Thomas introduced the church to the new 1979 prayer book and subsequent new hymnal and oversaw the 1982 ordination of Anne Carriere, the first female parish priest in Tennessee. For the first five years of his ministry, Thomas fought with the Morton Old Guard while struggling to strengthen his own constituency. Some intractable members stopped coming; some stayed around knowing that for the time being, at least, they had lost power. One woman recalls, however, that Thomas "always hung around with the money people," and in spite of whatever changes he made, the church retained "a worrisome establishment edge." He was probably trying to keep his enemies in check.

Thomas, assisted by a young, creative staff, "modernized" the church by pushing the congregation to deal with controversial social issues. The congregation became less insular and protective, more responsive and open to changes in the world around it. It attracted new members who shared Thomas's approach, and a few long-time members, although reluctant at first, eventually embraced the new style. The church sponsored Cursillo and Faith Alive weekends that sparked a genuine sense of spiritual renewal in the congregation. In a few short years, Thomas had seemingly reversed the parish's direction. Of that time, he would later comment, "Out of the seventies, we . . . emerged as the bellwether parish in the diocese. . . . We [became] a leader in liturgical renewal, and the first of the large parishes to have become eucharistically centered." In language echoing Patti Newsom's assessment of David Fikes's years, Anne Carriere characterizes that time "as a Golden Age; it was Camelot."

The analogy is also painfully accurate. For like its mythological predecessor, Thomas's Camelot was doomed to fail. The talented Burt Thomas might have been remembered as Grace–St. Luke's greatest leader, but, instead, the church remembers him only ruefully. Sometime during his tenure, the popular rector started an extramarital affair. Over a period of months, talk of this affair circulated among Thomas's enemies. When confronted by parish leaders about his behavior, he denied that any such liaison existed. Many people, including his loyal staff, felt certain he was lying and were hoping "he would just get over it." "It was hell," Carriere recalls. "People felt so betrayed. If he'd just told the truth, we would have forgiven him. The congregation really loved him." The deception continued—until the offending parties were caught in a tryst.

Thomas's wife filed for divorce. On July 30, 1985, he resigned as Grace–St. Luke's rector.

The incident initiated a series of protracted conflicts around the clergy. The next rector lasted three and a half years before he, too, was forced out under unhappy circumstances. By the late 1980s, Grace–St. Luke's was losing an average of seventy members per year. In 1992 the young David Fikes inherited a still wealthy and historic—but wounded and diminished—congregation with an unhappy reputation as "clergy-killers." Disheartened, one woman remembers the church at the time as being "kind of dead." Another parishioner recalled, "We'd come to church on Sunday to see who wasn't there rather than who was." The Morton-Thomas years left another legacy as well: a church divided between old school and new style, between the establishment and the innovators.

Initially, David sought to restore congregational unity and confidence. But he hoped to do more. He envisioned Grace–St. Luke's as a "Midtown church," a spiritual family reflecting the full diversity of its neighborhood, a "church with an open door." In November 1999, seven years after coming to the parish, he articulated that vision in an address to the congregation:

> I want us to have a Midtown mentality if by "Midtown" you mean actively engaged in addressing the problems of our city and refusing to run from them by hiding in the shadows of the suburbs. I do not want us to be "Midtown" if by that you mean us being identified, as someone once characterized us, as "the University Club at prayer." There was a time when the Episcopal Church could afford to be snobby, exclusive, and for the elite. That time is past. . . . I want us attracting people from all over Memphis because this is the place where anyone and everyone is not just tolerated, but welcomed to pray and worship and serve the world in God's name together.

Part of his strategy included transcending Memphis's traditional barriers of class and kin—hoping eventually to overcome racial ones as well. Most parishioners believe that he succeeded in breaking down many of the class issues at Grace–St. Luke's through his honesty and leadership abilities.

His personality helped, too. Although he downplayed his country roots, David's small-town manner probably reminded the Memphis elite of the farms and rural communities whence so many of their grandparents had originally come. Patti Newsom recalled a retreat where "David took off his collar, dressed like Elvis, and acted crazy. He wasn't a high and mighty priest. He could be with the rest of us." His sermons were carefully crafted Southern-style stories—liberally punctuated with quotes from Will Campbell, Flannery O'Connor, William Faulkner, and Tennessee Williams. Each August during "Elvis Week" David took a busload of Grace–St. Luke's matrons on a pilgrimage to the graveside vigil at Graceland. But he was equally at home with Canterbury Cathedral; next to a hip-swaying Elvis clock on his office wall hung icons of the saints. In his sermons, Flannery O'Connor led seamlessly to the seventeenth-century Anglican theologian Richard Hooker; William Faulkner to Archbishop Desmond Tutu. David's Anglicanism combines Southern quirkiness with Church of England reason; faith echoes through the Blues and the Book of Common Prayer.

After his arrival at Grace–St. Luke's, Fikes suggested that the parish hold an Anglican Festival, a medieval street fair to raise money to fund outreach. He hoped that the event, later christened the Canterbury Festival, would help create the more inclusive community he had envisioned. Every year, splendidly costumed parishioners—and their priests—recreated an English country village on the streets outside the church. From sewing costumes to performing Shakespeare, attending classes on Anglican history, watching films about the English Reformation, selling tickets, and pouring libations at the ale-tasting tent, nearly every parishioner got involved. One woman notes how Canterbury broke down the church's traditional boundaries: "All of a sudden people weren't in their Sunday role, they were in these costumes and had to be someone else." And most of the congregation loved it.

Most, but not all. Before Canterbury, the largest parish event had been the Grand Old Bazaar, a crafts fair dating back to the 1940s, run by the ladies of the parish. The bazaar began initially as a way to unite the women's groups of the two churches, Grace and St. Luke's, into a single organization, with the hope of uniting the divided congregation. It worked. By the 1950s, the bazaar had become an elaborate affair covered in the society pages of the local newspaper. The women's event provided much of the stability upon which Brinkley Morton would later build.

By the 1990s, however, the bazaar existed only as a shadow of its former glory. With the new Canterbury Festival scheduled for October and the traditional bazaar for November, the ladies felt the sting of being upstaged by this young interloper. Some referred to the Canterbury Festival as "that dog and pony show" and simply refused to cooperate. After an attempt to combine the events failed, the ladies shunned Canterbury in favor of the bazaar. Ironically, the Canterbury Festival, David's unifying event for the new generation, relegated the bazaar, the unifying tradition of the original Grace–St. Luke's, to a generational ghetto. Most people my age ignored it.

The tension between the Canterbury Festival and the Grand Old Bazaar runs to the heart of Grace–St. Luke's history. True to Brother Timothy's assessment, Grace–St. Luke's remained two churches. Early on, the competition was between Grace and St. Luke's. By 1990, however, they had transmuted into the "Morton" and "Thomas" congregations. The Morton churchgoers maintained the ethos of the

1950s, a time when churchgoing was a social obligation. In their world, blood kin remained the primary loyalty, and the home, the locus of identity. They ran their fathers' businesses and joined their parents' clubs. They named their children after their ancestors, often using the mother's maiden name as their child's first name. And, above all, they worshiped in the same pews as did their parents and grandparents. Their world was orderly and hierarchical— a society of old-time patriarchs, steel magnolia wives, dutiful offspring, and loyal house servants. The Morton congregation understood itself as maintaining the Southern way of life, the genteel establishment faith handed down through their families for generations. Grace–St. Luke's was their church. They owned it.

In contrast, the Thomas congregation was a seventies church— birthed just as traditional churchgoing fell out of fashion and people began to choose their religion rather than simply inheriting it. Newcomers—both men and women—served on the vestry and as committee chairs. The Thomas churchwomen devoted themselves to making careers rather than tomato aspic and chicken salad. The new gender roles were personified when they accepted Anne Carriere as a priest. Folk masses, Faith Alive, and Carriere's feminism seemed oddly discordant with the traditional harmonies of upper-class Southern life.

Although change comes slowly in Memphis, the times did change and the church was changing with them. One of the biggest changes was in the definition of *family*. Even in the South, divorce, feminism, and mobility were whittling away at traditional family structures. Under Thomas, the congregation was transformed. Church no longer served primarily as a chapel for prominent families. Rather, in a time of social upheaval, the church became a substitute family—a spiritual one instead of a biological one. But Thomas's indiscretion nearly destroyed the work he had done. The old order suspected that when kinship loyalty broke down, immorality would take its place. *Spiritual family* meant license for doing whatever one wanted. Without the steadying influence of familial pressure, what would happen to society?

Whether he realized it or not, David revitalized the old Thomas congregation. But much of the Morton congregation, the Grace–St. Luke's Old Guard, remained aloof and suspicious. The possibility of conflict also seemed to exist at the edges of the church—a conflict between loyalties of blood-kin and the spiritual family. The Old South and the New lived under the same roof, reluctantly sharing the same table.

Despite occasional opposition, David Fikes persisted. To aid him in Grace–St. Luke's rebirth, he enlisted the Rev. Virginia Brown, who arrived as associate rector in 1993, and the Rev. John Baker, who joined them in 1995.

When Emma was an infant, Richard and I took her to worship with us in the sanctuary. I enjoyed holding her in the pew, sometimes feeding her, rocking her, and singing hymns to her during the service. I loved it so much that I would only grudgingly surrender her when Richard asked to cradle her.

On July 5, 1998, only a few weeks after we jointed Grace–St. Luke's, Emma was snuggled in my arms when John Baker began his sermon with Isaiah 66: "For thus says the Lord: I will extend prosperity to her like a river, and the wealth of the nations like an overflowing stream; and you shall nurse and be carried on her arm, and dandled on her knees. As a mother comforts her child, so I will comfort you."

"I find some of my deepest longings are captured in this image," John confessed. "But here in the middle of life, at an age far removed from that simple union, the image Isaiah offers as hope and promise brings with it sadness." He went on: "If we allow ourselves, even for a moment, to imagine such a scene, mother and child delighting in each other, smiling, laughing, lying still in the safe embrace, if we allow such thoughts to break into our busy, goal-oriented world, we risk losing our edge."

Edge. For years, I mused, I had worried about being a mother and losing the edge of career. Unlike John, at middle age I had been forced by the unexpected arrival of the baby in my arms to slow down, refocus, and rethink my life and priorities. I loved Emma, and loved being her mother, but having this little one brought up fears—fears of lost opportunity, of missed adventure.

Once she came into my world, those particular fears were rescinded. Career edge just did not seem quite so important any more. But new fears, unexpected ones, rose up to replace them. Fear of losing Emma. And, most surprisingly, fear of dying myself. Fear of death accompanied new life. Women today speak of these fears in hushed tones, but for our grandmothers and their grandmothers, birth and death went together. In *Women and American Religion,* historian Ann Braude writes of colonial women: "As the day of her delivery approached, a pregnant woman made two types of preparations. She prepared fresh linens for herself and her child. . . . She also prepared herself spiritually to die."

Perhaps I have an overactive ancestral memory, but since Emma's birth, I had become terrified of death. It did not help that my father was dying from cancer. Or, as I would come to realize, that his mother had died when he was a little boy. In many ways, my father never stopped being the six-year-old whose mother never came home from the hospital. He was terrified that he would die young and leave his children behind—a fear he had bequeathed to me. I was haunted by my own family history of loss and abandonment. Fears hidden in some deep place until my daughter's birth. Sitting in that pew, I felt torn between motherhood's joys and its agonies, contemplating the beginning of life and its inevitable end. God the Mother? Was God as terrified as I at the thought of the death of a child? Could God mother me, lost in my own fears of death and abandoning the world of Richard and Emma that I so loved? Does a mothering God embrace mothers as her children? Mothers riddled with silent fear?

John's picture of God was reassuring: "The sustaining, loving embrace of God who adores us as a mother adores her child." Looking down at Emma, I could understand that. "Being dandled on the knee of our mother," he continued, "is not only our beginning, but also our final goal." Was death the same as birth? A complete circle back into the arms of a loving Mother?

I needed to talk. I sought out the motherly comfort of Virginia. She helped. But the questions, and sadly enough, the rawness, of those fears remained. I struggled against this primal inner terrain, these fears nursed so deeply in my soul that previous theological doubts seemed trivial. My father died a few months later. My mother suffered a heart attack. I was learning about motherhood—birth and death, holding the hands of a little one learning to walk and others walking toward the face of God. I loved one and hated the other. Why God, why? I had learned to love life so much that death and suffering seemed to disprove the existence of a loving God. I was finding theological rage.

Isolated by these existential questions, it was hard for me to appreciate Grace–St. Luke's, which I often saw as overly stodgy and traditional. My main connection to the church, surprisingly, came through motherhood. It came through Emma. As she grew from infant to toddler, I watched as she began to respond to God through Grace–St. Luke's. On Easter Sunday when she was sixteen months old, she escaped our pew and ran down the aisle waving and shouting, "Hi Jesus!" to every stained-glass window in the building. At two, she would run to the altar with hands outstretched for the bread and wine. She sang simple choruses and knew bits of the liturgy—her favorite being the Easter "Alleluias," which she would repeat while dancing and her arms raised in joy. She waved and smiled at mommy on the day I preached at the pulpit.

Whatever its flaws, Grace–St. Luke's was a profoundly child-sensitive congregation. The people there loved Emma, nurtured her, took care of her, and helped her grow in faith. Through that love, I grew to love them. They knew, as John Baker would always insist to me, how to be family. I could appreciate that. Indeed, I needed it.

The recent vogue of traditional family values in some Christian circles has often baffled me. After all, in the Gospels, Jesus is tough on traditional families. "Do you think that I have come to bring peace to the earth?" he asked. "No, I tell you, but rather division! From now on, five in one household will be divided, three against two and two against three; they will be divided: father against son and son against father, mother against daughter and daughter against mother" (Luke 12:51–53a).

At the beginning of his ministry, Jesus called his disciples away from kin to follow him and give their complete loyalty to God's reign. "Whoever comes to me," he warned, "and does not hate father and mother, wife and children, brothers and sisters, yes, and even life itself, cannot be my disciple" (Luke 14:26). Jesus proclaims that God's kingdom work, not biological family, is a believer's highest priority. He himself posed a troubling question: "Who are my mother and brothers?"

Indeed, St. Paul rejected the Roman *pater familias,* the Empire's kinship system, in favor of God's egalitarian household: "There is no longer Jew or Greek, there is no longer slave or free, there is no longer male and female; for all of you are one in Christ Jesus" (Galatians 3:28). Roman women and slaves, obligated by law to obey their pagan overlords, heard the gospel message of freedom in such passages and responded by converting to the new faith in droves. By undermining the Roman family, Christianity undermined the Roman Empire. Ancient critics frequently noted that the new religion caused insubordination. They accused converts of licentiousness and other kinds of sexual immorality. Such charges jeopardized what little legal protection Christians had and threatened the safety of the entire early church. Worried followers reversed Paul's message of liberation— later urging wives to submit to their husbands and slaves to obey their masters. But they did so because the Christian inclination was to reject the traditional family in favor of God's household.

The conflict between kin and kingdom runs throughout Christian history. In the eighteenth-century American South, women and slaves reenacted the ancient tension. When summoned by Baptist and Methodist preachers, female and black members of genteel Anglican households embraced evangelical faith. Early evangelicals elevated women's status and denounced slavery. But their new religious enthusiasm undermined their masters' authority. To whose household did they belong? The plantation patriarch or the family of Jesus? Caesar or God? For early Southern evangelicals, the answer was surprisingly easy. They shifted their spiritual loyalty from the big house to the "family" gathered at the local Baptist congregation or the Methodist class meeting.

Their women and slaves influenced by this rabble, the male establishment felt threatened. With the help of the educated clergy, who convinced the devout that staying in one's divinely ordained place was the calling for true believers, these men eventually regained a modicum of control over their inferiors' spiritual lives. For more than a century, the power of this patriarchy would hold sway and become the South's elite establishment. But the worry remained—overly earnest piety endangered the family and thus the whole Southern way of life.

Grace–St. Luke's was haunted by its immediate history of race and elitism, but those stories were only the most recent act in an ancestral Southern drama—the fear of freedom and disorder and the need for restraint and control. As a Southerner and a former Baptist, David Fikes understood this history. Yet he insisted upon intentional faith, taking it seriously, and wanted his parishioners to have life-changing encounters with God. He knew that vital spirituality would shift the congregation's self-understanding away from its residual establishment mentality—thus leading, he hoped, to the kind of inclusiveness he envisioned as God's family.

Shortly before Richard and I arrived, Grace–St. Luke's had weathered a painful crisis when their beloved organist was diagnosed with AIDS. The organist was gay and not "out" to the congregation. As his condition worsened, he sought support from the clergy and the church. Fearing that old-timers would reject him on account of his sexual orientation, David went to the vestry meeting steeled "to do the right thing" in the face of whatever opposition arose. After he informed the vestry as to the organist's condition, silence fell. Finally, one influential parishioner proclaimed, "He is family." The vestryman insisted the church do everything it could to help him. At that moment, David knew that God had broken through in a new way at Grace–St. Luke's. Of this significant event, David said, "Family no longer meant biological family, but a larger sense of communal, intentional spiritual bonds through worship."

David's ministry was clearly changing the parish. Although Grace–St. Luke's maintained a traditional appearance, the church developed a kooky antiestablishment edge—evident in everything from the Elvis impersonators, who occasionally performed at congregational gatherings, to a running joke about bananas, which would appear in the oddest liturgical settings.

Although still not racially diverse, Grace–St. Luke's had become more diverse theologically, economically, socially, and politically. Virginia notes that the most significant change from the time of her arrival "was a substantial increase in fairly open diversity. Not racial, but in kinds of people . . . lots of new people who weren't fifth-generation Memphians, and so on." From both the pulpit and pews, Grace–St. Luke's was turning away from its elite, establishment history and empowering a new, younger generation in vision and leadership. A new parish family gathered around the table.

And the family was growing. Sunday attendance was higher than it had been in years, baptisms and confirmations increased, and the annual budget neared $1 million. A host of activities embodied the changes at Grace–St. Luke's: a sizable Cursillio fellowship, myriad offerings in adult education, a course on daily spirituality entitled Practical Wisdom, a large ministry of spiritual direction, an innovative children's program, an informal Wednesday night potluck and liturgy, and a nontraditional Sunday night Eucharist. David Fikes instilled the old Thomas congregation with a sense of confidence and healing. A luminous spirituality grew in intensity—a sense of God's presence as resplendent as the Tiffany sunlight. With a talented staff and an active laity, Grace–St. Luke's had become, as Patti commented, "a radiant family."

In the midst of this busy, radiant family, when one more ministry, the Rivendell community, began, few people expected that it would become a source of controversy in the parish. Guided by Virginia, Rivendell was a prayer house across the street from the church, envisioned as a parish-based intentional community. Although formalized as part of Grace–St. Luke's in 1998, Rivendell's history began a decade earlier in New Mexico, where Virginia had previously served as a priest. There, she became a spiritual mentor for Cathy Cox, a nurse, seminary-educated layperson, former missionary, and single mother of five adopted daughters.

Cathy was raised Methodist, but spent five years exploring a religious call at a Franciscan convent. In 1982 she moved to New Mexico, and shortly thereafter, because she was seeking spiritual integration between her Catholic spirituality and her Protestant passion for the Bible, a friend urged her to attend a local Episcopal church. "From the beginning," she states, "I was captivated." She met Virginia, who was serving the Eucharist, at a home group for women. The two women felt drawn to each other. They became friends and Virginia became Cathy's spiritual director.

The two women share a deep passion for the contemplative life, and are bonded by a fifteen-year friendship, the struggles of motherhood and vocation, and a common quest for mystical union with God. Virginia exudes holiness, a profound ability to trust God, a powerful assurance of the truth of scripture and the gospel, and an overwhelming sense of God's love. She is kind and gentle, introverted among strangers, quiet, eerily insightful, a careful listener, and deeply prayerful. Cathy is an extrovert, strongly opinionated, and quick with an ironic comment or incisive judgement. For all her embrace of monastic tradition and devotional prayer, Cathy is a sort of edgy mystic. Their friendship developed into spiritual sisterhood.

Cathy recalls that by the early 1990s, the two women "discovered a growing companionship which led us to begin to dream together about a retreat house, or a parish house really available as a place of prayer and community. We found others who seemed to share the same longings. . . . We thought about individuals and families able to come together to celebrate the church year with all the homely richness our Anglican tradition provides."

In person and eventually by e-mail, the women created a community of mutual support and spiritual direction that grew to involve more pilgrims—all praying that the dream would one day become a reality.

In 1993, however, Virginia and her family left New Mexico to accept the call to Grace–St. Luke's. Each year, Cathy visited Virginia during Holy Week and befriended a number of Grace–St. Luke's parishioners. Some members of Virginia's Practical Wisdom class expressed interest in forming community. During Holy Week in 1997, Cathy and another New Mexican, Donna McNiel, experienced a profound connection with a group of Grace–St. Luke's parishioners, who, according to Donna, "shared a desire for a more provocative and costly way to God." On June 2, 1997, this group adopted a spiritual rule written by Virginia and began practicing a way of life together even though they lived far apart. A kind of virtual lay monasticism.

A year later, in June 1998, at the same time Richard and I joined Grace–St. Luke's, Cathy Cox moved to Memphis and purchased a house across the street. Cathy and Virginia christened it Rivendell, having borrowed the name from J.R.R. Tolkien's *The Lord of the Rings:* "The Last Homely House east of the Sea . . . a perfect house, whether you like food or sleep or story-telling or singing, or just sitting and thinking best, or a pleasant mixture of them all." Rivendell would serve as a resting place, a spiritual safe house for travelers on a journey to God.

Grace–St. Luke's vestry supported Rivendell without, perhaps, understanding the full implications of Virginia's plan. In

March 1998, they approved a proposal for a house located close to the church. The house would support the life of the parish through the constant offering of prayer and worship, serve as a focus for the spiritual life in the Episcopal tradition lived with intentionality in community, and be available as a center of quiet conversation, hospitality, prayer, and the simple presence to God. The community house (not yet known as Rivendell) would nourish the entire Grace–St. Luke's community from its spiritual roots and model Christian virtues of charity and hospitality as an alternative to secular culture.

When Cathy arrived, a dozen or so enthusiastic parishioners transformed the bungalow into the Rivendell Community. Part of the living room became a chapel with a handmade altar, a large table was donated for the dining room, a guest room was decorated, and the attic became a bedroom. Cathy resided there (eventually joined by Donna), but the door was open as a "gift for the parish." Community members read the Daily Office and kept the rule. They entertained anywhere from five to fifty for dinner and celebrated the church year, Holy Days, and birthdays. They served the parish in a multitude of ways—providing food for special occasions and baking the bread for the Eucharist.

More than anyplace else, Rivendell embodied household spirituality. Ever since seminary, Virginia had wanted to live in intentional Christian community. A respected professor kindled this desire with a comment in one of his lectures: "Anglican spirituality is essentially a household spirituality." Virginia became captivated by the seventeenth-century Anglican communal experiment of Little Gidding, in which Nicholas Ferrer and a group of laypersons lived together under a common rule. Rivendell borrowed from other Christian communal visions as well—from St. Benedict to

John Wesley and Dietrich Bonhoeffer. From a variety of ancient and modern sources, the women drew inspiration to realize their dream: "The Anglican tradition's special gift of 'homely' spirituality, of ordinary life in the world of work and family lived deeply and joyously, celebrating the daily, weekly, and yearly rhythms of sacred time with intentionality and intensity."

Rivendell was a "holy family" committed to practicing intentional faith. Although Cathy lived at the house and Virginia lived with her family elsewhere, Cathy readily confesses that "Rivendell was Virginia's house," the spiritual community of which her friend had dreamed for nearly twenty-five years. Virginia may have resided in a different house, but Rivendell was her heart's home.

Rivendell attracted mostly—but not exclusively—women. Those who embraced the full rule were called companions. Others, like myself, only stopped by for occasional services, conversation, a shoulder to cry on, or a cup of tea. Many were working mothers, like Cathy and Virginia. Perhaps that is why I liked it. The Rivendell house suggested a thoughtful, theological, and rigorously unsentimental way of integrating my various roles as a wife, homemaker, mother, congregant, and professional. It offered a spiritual vision profoundly different from that of the world: family, worship, service, vocation, and community are all interlaced; their fundamental connectedness is the crux of our truest selves. Women need not be torn apart by seemingly conflicting demands. Instead, by repositioning those demands in the economy of God's household, weary seekers could find the way to holiness. Whatever the appeal, the little community within the parish grew. Within a few months, it became an increasingly obvious part of Grace–St. Luke's as it attracted newcomers to the church through its ministry of hospitality and prayer.

Across the street, meanwhile, was a congregation of nearly 1,400 other people—most of whom had no idea about Cathy and Virginia's friendship or the Christian tradition of monastic discipline. To some, Rivendell looked "weird." All this serious piety and prayer? It was "abnormal." But Rivendell had only taken David's vision of intentional spiritual family and extended it to an actual house, a piece of real estate. There, family and table were no longer theological metaphors, but they were daily realities. Although only a small number of parishioners participated in it, the community became a kind of icon, a geographic embodiment, of the household of God gathering at the new Grace–St. Luke's.

Although not entirely clear to the Rivendellers—some of whom were newcomers and felt welcomed by the church—or most people in the larger congregation, the stage was set for conflict.

There was sometimes an uncomfortable feeling of not being quite welcome at Grace–St. Luke's. As newcomers during David Fikes's watch, Richard and I were mostly unaware of the congregation's history, but we felt the past's persistent sway: the rigidity of roles and stations, the impenetrable networks of gossip and division, some mysterious wounds still festering.

However invisible the past, Richard and I noticed something odd about the present. Parish rolls boasted nearly 1,400 souls in the congregation. Rarely, however, did more than 350 people show up on a given Sunday, out of roughly 700 "communicants in good standing." Those same 350 people thronged to most of the activities. They were, in effect, a congregation within a congregation—largely theologically moderate and socially liberal, serious in their faith commitments, and willing to explore both Anglican tradition and other spiritual practices. And busy. Lots of busy people all the time doing things at church. The same people over and over.

On holidays, however, it would all change. Suddenly, the church was full of people we rarely saw—people whose last names matched the names of streets, businesses, and public buildings throughout Memphis. They simply showed up for some holy day or a baptism, wearing fur coats and expensive suits, and would bestow huge sums of money for improvements on the building. They acted as if the place belonged to them and grumbled about "strangers" sitting in "their" seats. They were, if not biologically, the spiritual descendents of Grace–St. Luke's founders. The Memphis Old Guard in their Sunday best.

True to its history, Grace–St. Luke's remained two congregations. Not now Grace and St. Luke's, but the religion of Old Memphis and the spirituality of the New South. One group thought the church was their chapel, a beautiful building staffed with religious professionals who blessed life passages. The other understood the church as community, the living body of Christ doing God's work in the world. Both understood themselves as members of God's household. But for the Old Guard, that household remained the divinely ordered family domain, an elegant home in Central Gardens. For the others at Grace–St. Luke's, God's household was a community called together through the spirit, an inclusive and egalitarian lot, seeking the kingdom. One was neat, orderly, and patriarchal; the other, unpredictable and untidy. We embodied opposite impulses of Southern character, impulses acted on and reacted against for three centuries. We were all Christ-haunted but just did not know it.

The worst of it was Easter Vigil. As many Episcopalians have begun to do in recent years, David baptized new members during the Easter Eve service. At Christ Church, Holy Family, and Trinity,

I loved Easter Vigil. Entering the dark church in silence, sitting and waiting and listening to Bible passages of God dealing with his people, the service is the height of ecclesiastical drama. In the liturgy, baptisms are done in the candlelight, before Easter's first Eucharist. Typically, I saw adults or whole families baptized at a vigil. Only occasionally would parents present an infant during those late hours. At those other parishes, baptism marked a profoundly serious moment in one's spiritual journey. To be baptized on Easter Eve meant joining the ranks of the persecuted and the martyrs—setting oneself apart from the world.

Not so at Grace–St. Luke's. Baptism in the South is not like joining the ranks of early Christian martyrs. It is a social event, a "christening," in which a family celebrates its inherited faith. Many people who baptize their children rarely go to church themselves; it is something one does simply because it is the thing to do. Although many priests give instruction and use it as an opportunity for parents to grow in faith, in places like Memphis, baptism of the children of nominal Christians remains the norm in most mainline churches. Baptism marks a child's entrance into good society more than into the gathered community of Christian discipleship.

On Easter Eve 1999, our first at Grace–St. Luke's, Richard and I eagerly anticipated the service. When we walked into the church, we thought we were in the wrong place. The lights were lower than usual but still on. Instead of a congregation of hard-core churchgoers huddled in darkness, the pews were full of extremely well-dressed, noisy people taking photographs! It bore no resemblance to the Easter Vigils that had lifted my heart to heaven; indeed, this was exactly the opposite. I felt as if I had stumbled into a private party, a baptism crasher at some family's home.

I never told David, Virginia, or John how horrible that Easter Vigil was at Grace–St. Luke's for me. Richard and I simply left, carrying Emma home on that rainy night. We told everyone we left because there was no baby-sitting. In my heart, however, I did not want Emma's first Easter Vigil to be such a spiritual travesty. I remember holding her close and rocking her to sleep that night promising, "I want a different kind of church for you." Since I never shared this with my clergy friends, I do not know if they had any inkling as to how much of that Easter Vigil congregation appeared utterly ignorant of the theological gravity of the service.

From the pew that night, I witnessed Grace–St. Luke's two churches farthest apart. Out in the church entry, a small band of devoted Lenten travelers stood around David as he lit the Pascal fire, praying, their eyes still moist from Good Friday tears. In front of me, Midtown's light-hearted upper crust—well-coifed mothers posed with their infants, each family out-doing the next with expensive christening gowns. As David entered the only partially darkened sanctuary carrying the Pascal candle, one group followed him chanting the solemn liturgy from memory; the other thumbed helplessly through the Prayer Book's unfamiliar pages. And the baptisms performed that night symbolized entry into one of two different households—depending upon which church you considered yourself a part.

That Easter Vigil exists as a snapshot in my mind of mainline religion at war with itself. Half of the congregation maintained an inherited sense of religious and social privilege; the other half understood that the church lived in a radically different relationship to the culture than it had for previous generations. Things were not often so clearly defined at Grace–St. Luke's. Indeed, a good number of several-generation Memphians became our friends there. And of them, quite a few understood church as much more than social obligation. Richard referred to them as the "new traditionalists," those cradle Episcopalians who experienced faith as intentional spirituality. But there were plenty of old traditionalists around, too. That night, I knew trouble was coming. Just how long would the Old Guard support the clergy if they really understood that two households of faith existed under their roof? As it happened, not much longer at all.

In early December 1999, the parish was busy preparing for Christmas when the weekly newsletter, *The Messenger,* arrived in the mail, carrying an announcement that Virginia Brown had "a change of address." She wrote, "For me, this Advent marks a new chapter, and finds me in a new place, not only in the interior journey of faith but in externals as well. . . . I'm beginning Advent in residence at the Rivendell Community House." Within a matter of days, a group of parishioners confronted David, calling for her resignation and reporting the circulation of a petition that did the same.

It had been a difficult year for Virginia Brown. During Lent, she and her husband of twenty-five years separated. On May 30, 1999, she wrote to the congregation: "I've come to the conclusion that it is now better that my husband Bruce and I live separately. . . . I believe that God, who has asked and made it possible for us to live together in this marriage, and has given us all a great deal of good in and through it, now invites living apart." She continued apologizing for any failure on her part to be a "wholesome example" as a priest to the congregation and requested prayers for herself, her estranged spouse, and their children.

For some Southerners, even relatively liberal ones, divorce is often still regarded as a sin. It represents women getting out of line, rebelling against their God-given role as wife and mother, and being insubordinate to their husbands. In the South, few things are considered worse than rejecting one's place in the divine economy. No matter the pain or sacrifice, Southern women are taught to "stand by their men," a secular version of St. Paul's "Wives, submit to your husbands." And for generations, they have. Hearing reports of comments from some church matrons such as, "So, she had a bad marriage. Who cares? So did I and we stayed married until he died," I knew Virginia was in trouble. By moving toward the possibility of divorce, Virginia had violated the ethics of Southern womanhood.

When she moved from her family household into the Rivendell community, however, she made a difficult situation much worse. Not only was she leaving her husband, but she appeared to reject one family in favor of another. Women in the parish started to ask, "What about her children? She's abandoning her children!" Her accusers said she had turned her back on her marriage vows and kin for monastic ones and spiritual family. Although no one alluded to it at the time, Virginia was like those enthusiastic female converts of the Southern past: she traded her husband's household for God's. Or, in their view, perhaps, that of the devil. She placed herself outside of recognized structures of order and authority. She was a free woman—someone with no place in the Southern household. That threatened the whole fabric of tradition.

The rumor that circulated for months became grist for the public conversation mill: Virginia had abandoned her family for Cathy Cox.

It was, of course, all untrue gossip. Virginia did not abandon her children; nor did she and Cathy have the kind of relationship whispered about by Grace–St. Luke's matrons. After her marriage died, Virginia wanted to move into Rivendell because it was her true home. She wanted to live in a Christian household, one marked by intentional spiritual practices of hospitality and prayer—a reality that had eluded her in marriage. She wanted to put together the pieces of her life. As Virginia herself would say, "The Rivendell House and Community straddle the usual boundaries of household and parish, ministry and private life. Figuring out how best to do this is not always easy, but it is gracious and worthwhile."

But Virginia was running ahead of much of the congregation. To the rumor-mill, talk of transcendence of the boundaries between "sacred" and "ordinary" life sounded like theological mumbo-jumbo. According to her critics, Virginia was a bad wife, a bad mother, and a bad priest. They wanted her gone. On Sunday, December 12, David Fikes attempted to quell the rumors by calling the congregation to account during the announcements. But mentioning the gossip only fueled it, and the whole congregation began to speculate about Virginia's future and what really went on at Rivendell.

One week later, on December 19, David mounted the pulpit saying, "Let me warn you from the outset that my comments this morning have little to do directly with the reading assigned for today, but have everything to do with the gospel and the way the Grace–St. Luke's community lives together." He explained that he had raised the issue the previous week because opposing camps were developing in the church, likening it to a "stench [smelled] before around this place." After chastising the guilty parties for gossiping, Fikes said, "I'll put it to you bluntly. Grace–St. Luke's can ill afford to serve up the head of yet another clergy." He was mad and we were going to the woodshed for an ecclesiastical lickin'.

He listed the facts: one, Virginia and her husband were separated; two, Virginia had not abandoned her children but was working out a joint custody arrangement; and three, Virginia had moved into Rivendell. As to the gossip about clerical impropriety, David stated, "There have been rumors, malicious lies, and sensational accusations spread about Rivendell that I do not even wish to dignify with a response. But I will by simply saying that the sinfulness of Rivendell does not exceed that of what I would expect to find in any other Grace–St. Luke's home, and I suspect that its sanctity exceeds that of what I would find in most Grace–St. Luke's homes. I don't know many of you that have a chapel adjoining your living room."

Never did David more clearly depict Grace–St. Luke's two households.

He went on to explain the crisis as he understood it—generational warfare in the family: "If you spend any amount of time in the Episcopal Church you will soon discover that there is a tension running through most everything we do." He called it the "Teyve tension," after the character in the musical *Fiddler on the Roof.* "Remember Teyve," he asked, "who struggles with tradition on one hand and dealing with progress and changes and growth on the other?" Finding solace in the past, Teyve struggled with the changes in the world around him. "It is the struggle between preferring the past [and] facing the future," he said. He maintained that "most of the fights in the Episcopal Church" were between hanging on to the past and leaning into the future "by adapting, changing, and growing."

The divides, he stated, were often between the "over sixty-five" segment of the congregation and the younger segment—the baby boomers. He also pointed out that many long-time Grace–St. Luke's members had benefited from Rivendell's ministry and that "new and innovative ministries are stretching and leading us into the future." For those upset by the changes, he urged, "Don't let your frustration with the Teyve tension make you snap in inappropriate, misguided ways. . . . Help me ease this tension in a healthy, creative way and help me bring something good out of all the hurt feelings of the past weeks." Always the peacemaker, he ended with a scripture-like exhortation: "As a community gathered in the name of Christ, we are called to love one another, not just love and care for those like us, but love each other."

The majority of the congregation broke into wild applause. A few stalwarts looked stern-faced forward—afraid, I thought, to catch the eye of their fellow congregants. I did not applaud, fearing it would add to the division and pain. Despite David's injunction, Christmas did not pass without incident. A child from the school broke a valuable shepherd from the church's antique crèche and some treasured ornaments from the church chrismon tree turned up smashed—leaving the altar guild women weeping over the loss. Perhaps the tears were for that old way of life—a way discredited by the honesty of David's Advent sermon. Light had pierced the darkness. And from my seat in the pew, Christmas came and went for the first time with no ghosts.

A few weeks later, David Fikes announced he was leaving Grace–St. Luke's. Earlier in the autumn, he had been interviewed by another congregation and they called him as their rector. After eight fruitful years at Grace–St. Luke's, David decided to move on and accept the call from Good Shepherd in Austin, Texas.

In the early months of 2000, Virginia Brown was left as the sole priest in charge of Grace–St. Luke's. The vestry issued a strong statement supporting and affirming her ministry at their annual retreat. The year's stewardship campaign proved the most successful in Grace–St. Luke's history. Although taxed by her personal trials, Virginia led the congregation skillfully and spiritually into Lent. On Sunday, March 26, she preached a sermon that seemed to sum up all the changes of the past year:

Take a look behind you! Isn't the restored Ascension window astonishing? Look at the light around Jesus' head, and the depths in the clouds—and the colors! The blues! The cleaning and the restoration were costly . . . but it was needed in order to preserve and protect this magnificent work of art. It was beautiful before, but now it's restored to us with a beauty none of us have ever seen before because the wonderful Tiffany stained glass was so begrimed by its long years of exposure to pollutants.

I was not sure if she was speaking of the windows or the congregation. But I knew she intended the ambiguity. Certainly, the events of the last year had had a purging effect. I had never felt so spiritually alive in that building. It was as if the congregation was itself cleansed of the ghosts of the past.

We traversed Lent into Holy Week as never before, aware of what gorgeous colors and subtleties and depths Jesus had for us. The Good Friday service, enriched by lay preaching, left those attending in tears. By Easter Vigil, the congregation was nearly spiritually breathless. The traditional baptism visitors, of whom there was a smaller number, must have thought us insane as we stomped our feet, yelling at the top of our lungs the Eastern Orthodox responses to Virginia as she preached the ancient "Easter Homily" of St. John Chrysostom:

Hell was embittered because Death was done away with.
EMBITTERED!
It was embittered because it is mocked.
EMBITTERED!
It was embittered because it is destroyed.
EMBITTERED!
It was embittered because it is annihilated.
EMBITTERED!
It was embittered for it is now made captive.
EMBITTERED!

We laughed, applauded, and cried. Christ was risen. We were free. Dozens of us went to Patti and James Newsom's house for the first feast of Easter, until late in the evening.

And a few weeks later, we wept. Virginia Brown left Memphis and moved to Springfield, Missouri, where she became an associate at Christ Church. The vestry commended her:

> For the imagination and initiative she displayed in forming, col-
> laborating in, and directing new programs and opportunities for
> spiritual growth for young and old alike; for her teaching and
> preaching with great intellect and wit; for the service provided to
> the city as a whole; for listening to our needs and trying to salve
> our wounds, even though she at many times was laboring under
> such personal stress in her own life that others of less courage
> would have given up; and for her glorious smile.

A group of parishioners secretly commissioned a portrait of her and had it hung in the church's parlor—the only Grace–St. Luke's associate so honored. Much of the parish truly loved her, and they finally realized just how much she had loved them. Indeed, she had been mother to Grace–St. Luke's. She helped birth a new kind of household of God, one built with disciplined prayer and suffering love.

I learned a great deal at Grace–St. Luke's about family. With the birth of my daughter, I felt the love and fear of motherhood, the mystical tie between generations, the pull of my own family past. But I also learned that whereas the blood of kinship is thick, the blood of Christ is thicker still. The members of God's household are bound together through the practice of faith, the sacrament of grace, and the experience of the Spirit. And it is a big household.

As with biological family, there are those you like and those you do not. You fight. But families stick it out, arguing, winning, and losing, and reshaping the stories that will be passed down to their children. New generations inherit the legacy, they live with it, they change it, and they pass it on. My household, the home I make with Richard and Emma, lives and breathes and has its being in relation to the larger cosmic household of which it is one small part. My biological family is my closest neighbor; my husband and daughter are also my brother and sister. We share the same blood, and we share the chalice of Christ's blood. It makes a difference—about choices and the way we treat one another. And, ultimately, I think, that makes me less fearful. These days, family teaches me about both courage and compassion.

I will never forget the weeks between Christmas and Easter when Grace–St. Luke's ghosts, embittered by their defeat, fled. Virginia opened the window of heaven for us and we saw both ourselves and Christ anew. Virginia helped connect us with something much larger than ourselves—the God who, as the Bible says, "like a mother hen gathers her chicks under her wings." Those brief months were as loving and spiritually enriching as any I have ever experienced in a church. Knowing she was soon to leave herself, she fed us, nurtured and cared for us, as her own brood.

The ghosts' departure, however, was only temporary. True to its heritage, Grace–St. Luke's is two churches in one building: all those shadowy phantoms and the piercing light of God. No sooner did David and Virginia leave than some malevolent spirits, the handful of people who most opposed Virginia, attempted to wrest control of the rector search process. It is a spiritually schizophrenic place.

The Didache, an early Christian ethical text, begins by saying, "There are two ways, one of life and one of death; and between the two ways there is a great difference." I often wondered which kind of household Grace–St.Luke's would finally choose to be. A household defined by its order and stations, as envisioned by the Old South? Or the household of God, that organic and sometimes even chaotic community, as preached by Jesus? Kin or Kingdom? Or some new way of living faithfully to both?

The vestry, I think, made a choice—filling the search committee with people who understood the nature of the changes at Grace–St. Luke's. They have recently chosen a new priest. He previously served as prior of a spiritual retreat center in Louisiana, where he lived in intentional Christian community with his family. A household within a household. From what I can gather, he is a kind of male version of Virginia Brown. It sounds like he understands kin and kingdom. Maybe the long fight is over. Maybe Grace–St. Luke's luminous spirituality, the glimmer of which has been passed down through generations, will finally emerge as the congregation's dominant identity. Maybe they will finally understand that earthly families—no matter their joys—are ultimately second to the larger loyalty to Christ's family.

Change comes slowly on the banks of the Mississippi. But even in the Deep South, it comes.

My household changed as well. Although we came to love Grace–St. Luke's and our wonderful neighborhood in Memphis, neither of us felt particularly happy with our jobs. Something was missing vocationally. Richard worked at home as a consultant and felt lonely. I came to the conclusion that I wanted to work for the church rather than the academy. After a short job search, Richard was offered a position at the Alban Institute in Bethesda, Maryland. In June 2000, we moved east to the Washington metro area. His new employer is a nonprofit organization specializing in congregational change and renewal. I guess they figured he had plenty of experience.

CONCLUSION

Pentecost

CHRIST CHURCH

Alexandria, Virginia, 2001

A mid the hustle of urban Old Town Alexandria, across the Potomac River from Washington, D.C., Christ Church stands in witness to the whole of U.S. history. Founded in 1773, three years before the Republic itself, the parish served as spiritual home to Founding Fathers and Mothers, the social and intellectual elite who forged the vision for a democratic nation and a long succession of their offspring. Christ Church was one of only a few colonial Anglican churches to remain open and vital during the Revolutionary War. Inside, small silver plaques mark the pews where George Washington prayed for victory against the British, and where, several decades later, Robert E. Lee learned his catechism and was confirmed as a soldier in Christ's army.

Designed by James Wren, reportedly a cousin of Sir Christopher Wren, the red brick building, with its graceful steeple, clear glass windows, white interior, and box pews, epitomizes Virginia Episcopalianism. Elegant and understated, the building itself embodies the genteel faith of the Southern aristocracy. In keeping with the restrained spirituality of Virginia tradition, Christ Church is nearly as plain as a New England meeting house. One powerful symbol dominates its sanctuary: the pulpit, accessible only by a winding staircase, in the center of the east wall, high above the table. On either side of that pulpit are large tablets inscribed with the Lord's Prayer, the Apostles' Creed, and the Ten Commandments. Christ Church is a church of the Word—the Word of a reasonable faith framed by the harmonious architecture of the Enlightenment.

I now serve as the parish's resident theological educator. I am a teacher of the Word in a congregation that has been listening to the Word for more than two centuries. Each morning, I walk through a graveyard that holds the remains of dead slaveholders and confederate officers, of patriots and politicians, all waiting patiently for the promised Resurrection. Once, they sat in pews where my family now sits. They listened to the Word read and the Word proclaimed. Some, I suspect, listened better than others did. Some, I am quite sure, *heard* better.

Theologically, they were an adaptable lot. Early on, most Christ Church parishioners embraced moralism and deism, both reasonable faiths that fit Republican sensibilities. A generation later, after the Revolutionary War, evangelical Episcopalians thought deism biblically untenable, and they transformed Christ Church into a stronghold for the religion of the heart. For nearly a century, an evangelical vision of Anglican preaching, piety, and missions held sway in Alexandria.

Whether deist or evangelical, however, these Southerners succumbed to prevailing cultural norms about slavery. I do not pretend to understand them—those who could fight for liberty and pray for salvation while amassing fortunes off the local trade in human flesh. I just know that they were here listening to the Word and eating God's bread at our table. And that somehow, no matter what I think, they considered themselves good Christians. It perplexes and pains me that these were my forebears.

To Christ Church's credit, at least one of the church's early rectors freed his slaves, thinking it unseemly for a minister of the gospel to keep people in bondage. Despite our moral shortcomings regarding slavery, the Yankees who occupied the city during the Civil War deemed us worthy enough to keep the church open throughout the hostilities. Unlike many Virginia parishes, we never served as a stable or hospital. But, as one friend reminds me, Christ Church remains a Southern church. We have a difficult time—still—with race. And class.

Twentieth-century Christ Church helped shape a venerable tradition in the Episcopal Church—that of "liberal evangelicalism." In the 1920s, influenced by a similar movement in the Church of England, early-century evangelical Episcopalians embraced higher criticism and historical scholarship regarding the Bible. Unlike many of their evangelical Protestant kin, they rejected biblical literalism, choosing instead to meld their traditional commitments to religious experience, scripture, missions, and preaching with newer cultural trends. The Rev. Carl Grammer, professor at Virginia Theological Seminary, and a proponent of the movement, wrote in 1938, "In truth, Evangelicalism and Liberalism are mutual allies, and each has much to teach the other. Evangelicals must learn from Liberals to speak the new language and meet the new problems. The new wine must be poured into new bottles. The water of life must be conveyed in new pitchers. We need a new synthesis."

Grammer's claim that "evangelicalism and liberalism are mutual allies" might sound strange to modern ears, but in Alexandria at the time, they were greeted with enthusiasm at Christ Church and across town at the closely related Virginia Theological

Seminary. Christ Church remade itself in what I call soft modernism. Like many of their mainline kin, the parish embraced liberal optimism and progress, privatized Christian piety, public service, and unquestioning patriotism. This vision was wildly successful and it matched the temper of times shaped by Protestant establishment mores and two world wars.

The church grew—especially as Alexandria grew from a sleepy Southern town to a busy military community in the 1940s. Their vision of church worked for their generation, but we now struggle with it. Some of the congregation's elders, however, have no idea why. They do not realize that optimism, progress, privatized faith, and patriotism are old wine. Christ Church's soft modernism, tied culturally to white Anglo-Saxon Protestant elitism, is irrevocably dated, a dying theological tradition of an earlier American day.

Beginning with the 1960s, this WASP tradition came under intense criticism, and failure to see the problems and change surely contributed to the decline of the Protestant mainline—Christ Church included. Few people believe in the old elite version of American Protestantism anymore. Certainly not churchgoers like myself. The younger baby boom leadership is trying to create a "new synthesis" out of the newer wine of our life experience and the gospel. It is a new generation's turn to add to the Christian story.

We are what sociologists call a "thick culture" here at Christ Church. We have inherited two centuries of stories, along with many puzzling ironies, of living our faith in the world. The parish historian assures me that there is too much to ever write it all down. David Holmes, professor of religion at the College of William and Mary, once remarked of the parish, "This church is a survivor." Indeed, it has survived. But not by accident. From what I can glean of its history, and as a deceptive counterpoint to its pristine colonial appearance, Christ Church has survived because it has been willing to change. At several critical junctures of its history, Christ Church survived—and prospered—because visionary leadership was able to adapt to cultural change, push the congregation toward the future, draw off the resources of tradition, and form new ways of being church. Christ Church does not survive because it preserves the past. Rather, it survives because, generation after generation, it has preached and interpreted the Word for a new day.

Christ Church is a kind of archeological site, a holy tel, with layers of faith and tradition, decline and renewal, new congregations built upon old ones. Past and present, sacred and profane, the sublime and the insane—the jumbled artifacts of a thick spiritual history lie just beneath our feet.

And, as it has done for decades, Christ Church is struggling to adapt once more—building yet another congregation as a new generation fashions its faith in the fertile topsoil of this sacred site. Change is our tradition.

As I neared my fortieth birthday, in 1999, during my second year at Rhodes, an incredible longing engulfed me. After years of roaming the country, following school and work, I wanted to go home. Home to Baltimore, or thereabouts, where I could teach my daughter to catch crabs, watch Orioles baseball, smell the ocean breeze, and go boating on the Chesapeake Bay. Being a mother made me want to give Emma all that was good about my Maryland childhood—especially the textured way we lived with history. I began to think of where I wanted to grow old, one day to die, to be buried. I wanted to go home. I was tired of moving.

Spiritually, I wanted to settle in. My journey, however, does not conclude with a neat conversion from youthful seeking to grown-up dwelling. Just as I had never been a true seeker, nor could I be an old-fashioned dweller. I wanted to have a home and find a parish where faith would be real, an embodied and intentional practice of Christian maturity. And I wanted to teach, to be a good steward of my life by giving life to others. Richard and I wanted to practice our faith in our home, vocations, and public lives. We wanted a sense of wholeness, of personal integration with the past, the present, and the future. The longing for faithfulness led Richard, Emma, and me to northern Virginia, not far from where I was born, and, eventually, to Christ Church.

In many ways, Christ Church and I make an odd pair. It retains some traditions that I find limiting and, frankly, offensive. I remain the restless theological spirit that I have been my whole life, a Christian pilgrim unsettled when faith seems too settled, with the uneasy grace of a prophetic voice. Or, to use biblical imagery, I am a pourer of new wine and a sewer of new wineskins. Some days, I look around Christ Church and sigh: Wineskins just don't get any older than this!

I cannot pretend to truly understand Christ Church. There is too much history, and there are too many stories for even the most venerable parishioner to ever really understand it. I can only bring to the community the insight of a trained academic observer, the angular vision of a newcomer, someone who has been around the denominational block. What I have seen is that even here, in the heart of one of the oldest continuing congregations in the United States, an establishment parish in an establishment city, there is a palpable longing for both new wine and new wineskins. Although parish leaders contend with the weight of the past—along with typical comments like "that's not the way we do things here" and "people do not like change"—many parishioners seem to intuit that it is time for Christ Church to be made anew once again. And that this must happen so that the church will reach its tricentennial as a living congregation rather than a museum.

We are reaching for an ideal—being a historic church that lives God's Word in the daily round of cosmopolitan, pluralistic, tech-driven, media-savvy, politically divided Washington. Although Washington is the ultimate establishment town, it has changed greatly in recent years with the growth of high technology and the new economy and with the arrival of massive numbers of immigrants from nearly every nation on earth. Alexandria, Virginia, is almost as pluralistic as Los Angeles, California. More than sixty languages are spoken by students at the local high school.

The world in which Christ Church exists has changed, and the parish must change, too. Toward that, we are experimenting—with leadership and vision, education programs, and outreach. We are trying to honor the past while building a new congregation. It is both a high calling and an extraordinarily difficult task. Change may be part of Christ Church's history, but it is still hard when you are dealing with 228 years of history.

Sometimes people forget to tell the stories of change. Not very long ago, Christ Church was different. It was a small church where you could gather all the parishioners at a single event at the church. Like its denomination, the parish suffered a late-century loss, declining in numbers and influence from its once unassailable social and political perch. Only the stalwarts of the Alexandria establishment stuck around.

In the last fifteen years or so, however, there has been a turnaround. Lots of newcomers have permanently altered the nature of the church, the same sort of baby boom returnees and spiritual seekers who can now be found in thousands of mainline congregations. Nearly three thousand people now consider Christ Church their spiritual home and every Sunday almost nine hundred attend worship. They do not—nor could they—gather as the entire parish. There is simply no place to put everyone. Christ Church's membership is now larger than the population of the whole city when the church was founded. Most of the newcomers are not native to Alexandria, Washington, or Virginia. They hail from other parts of the country and have moved to follow education, work, government service, or the military to the nation's capital. Most did not grow up in the Episcopal Church. The vast majority of them are baby boomers. They are well educated, part of the new cultural elite, the citizens of the meritocracy, presently inhabiting northern Virginia's toniest neighborhoods.

So many new people have come that despite its quaint pastoral appearance, Christ Church is not a small parish. It is what congregational development experts call a *corporate church*. Alice Mann, a senior consultant for the Alban Institute, describes this size church as "something for everybody—a variety of different kinds of worship, education, spiritual nurture, and social interaction." In other words, Christ Church is a small city, a collection of spiritual neighborhoods, each with its own theological architecture, differing needs, tastes, styles, and, above all, opinions. Although a common table and pulpit draw us together, it is not a self-contained universe—it is a theological multiverse. It is a busy place, both exhilarating and exhausting in its reach and demands.

In becoming a corporate congregation, Christ Church outgrew its twentieth-century dweller orientation. Although some parishioners have trouble perceiving the enormity of the shift, the church can no longer depend on its neighborhood for a steady supply of members—nor can it depend on "old families" to produce new generations for its pews. Even in this ancient place, social obligation and family religious tradition do not a congregation make. In recent years, whether consciously or not, Christ Church has had to appeal to seekers—people looking for a church home—by adjusting to the realities of living in a new spiritual economy. By adding personnel and programs, especially those appealing to newcomers and young families, Christ Church has changed incrementally through the last two decades.

During that same time, I have been part of a number of congregations transformed by newcomers like those at Christ Church and the same shifting cultural trends—most obviously at Trinity in Santa Barbara. Christ Church and Trinity newcomers share a generational ethos—they are more flexible and are unrestrained by tradition, they value creativity, innovation, and personal achievement, and they are more oriented toward religious negotiation than their parents and grandparents. For all their similarities, however, newcomers in the two churches do differ. Unlike the unconventional religious seekers in Santa Barbara, Christ Church's newcomers remained at least loosely connected to the Christian tradition. And instead of seeking mystical experiences of the divine, Christ Church parishioners seem to be seeking practical ways to connect their lives to God and to their work, and to deepen their knowledge of faith.

At Trinity in Santa Barbara, the beautiful Gothic building with its jeweled windows draws worshipers into a kind of eucharistic nirvana, an ecstatic experience of union with God. Christ Church is less expressive and more oriented toward the rational. Sunlight shines through the church's clear windows—symbolizing the powerful light of God's Word to the congregation and reminding us that the world on the other side of those windows needs God's light. Whereas Trinity served as a sacramental mediator of the in-breaking of God's transcendent reign, Christ Church functions as a sacred connecting point between the worlds of human power and the power of God's Word, a sort of spiritual way station between Washington and the New Jerusalem.

To borrow an image from St. Augustine, Christ Church is a visible icon of both the City of Man and the City of God. Because of its cultural moorings, so closely tied to the political life of Washington, its spiritual longings tend not toward the ethereal but gravitate instead toward the pragmatic and mundane. At Christ Church, God's presence is an imminent reality—grace and glory all mixed up with the perplexities and paradoxes of human sinfulness. Or, as Reinhold Niebuhr would probably say, were he still alive, we embody all the ironies of American history. Political power and the gospel sometimes get confused around here. George Washington and Jesus.

For all their differences, however, Trinity and Christ Church share one important quality: neither can depend on the past for its future. Both churches—one a community of eclectic pilgrims and the other a parish of busy practitioners—have become intentional spiritual communities—congregations purposefully remaking their traditions, attempting to create meaningful worship and spiritual practices, engaged in intellectually credible reading of the scriptures, and reaching out to serve the world with near-evangelical zeal. They are spiritually vital places, theologically liberal, growing in numbers and deepening in faith, and they are trying to make the gospel make sense in radically different cultural settings. The transformation is happening more slowly at Christ Church, but it is happening nevertheless.

A generation ago, Trinity and Christ Church were chapels of the establishment where the rich and powerful beseeched God for forgiveness and blessing. Now, these congregations sit on the uneasy edges of the new elite, a class that is largely secular in orientation with little need for the old Protestant mainline to provide comfort or spiritual sustenance. So, unlike their mid-century forebears, who assumed that the mission field was found only in Africa,

Trinity and Christ Church essentially have been forced to become missionary churches reaching out to those who were once their members and to the vast numbers of unchurched people at their doorsteps. The process of that change has baffled, and occasionally blindsided, all of us who have stuck around for the journey.

For Christians, the day of Pentecost, seven weeks after Easter, marks the church's birthday. In Acts 2, Jesus' disciples, themselves Jews, had come together with other Jews to celebrate the yearly religious festival of the giving of the Law. The writer of Acts reports a great miracle of wind and fire that causes Jesus' disciples to speak in "other languages," a spiritual gift referred to as "the gift of tongues." Other Jews at the festival heard the gospel in their own language and were "amazed and perplexed" by the miracle. Others, evidently Gentiles who did not receive the gift, concluded that the Jews were drunk. Despite the cacophonous bedlam, many believed in Jesus and were baptized. About three thousand persons joined the disciples and formed the first Christian community: "They devoted themselves to the apostles' teaching and fellowship, to the breaking of bread and the prayers."

Acts 2 has long been one of my favorite passages in the New Testament. It works particularly well with one of my preferred Bible study routines: read the passage and imaginatively place myself into the text. Who am I in this story? What do I see? What is God showing me? Over the years, I have been a disciple, the Apostle Peter, a member of the crowd, a skeptical Roman, and a newly baptized follower of Jesus. In every case, the confusion of the day is evident. As the participants themselves asked, What does this mean? Whatever character I adopt, however, the text loses none of its tumultuous power. Its enthusiasm and energy carries me to a single conclusion: I wish I had been present that day—bedlam and all—to figure out what it all meant and to witness the birth of the church.

Looking back over the last twenty years of mainline Protestantism, through my participation as a character in the story, I sympathize with those Jews on the day of Pentecost: What does this mean? What does it mean that our churches have lost members and influence, and that we no longer command the respect and cultural power we once did? What does it mean that we find it hard to be in the same room with one another around political issues and concerns about sexuality? What does it mean that there exists a great generation gap in leadership and vision? What does it mean that our liturgies have changed, that women are now ministers and bishops, and that the old ways of doing business have failed? When I look at it from my position in the crowd, it often appears to be babble, people yelling at each other in languages others do not speak. What do the stories of All Saints, Christ Church (Hamilton), St. Stephen's, Holy Family, Trinity, Grace–St. Luke's, and Christ Church (Alexandria), mean? What does my story—played out in the life of those places—mean?

As on the day of Pentecost, it may mean that in the babble of confusion a new kind of mainline church is being born. Not a renewal of the same old mainline: the old WASP establishment mainline continues to die. And insofar as it resists change, it will die. But in those places where tradition is being reworked in innovative ways—where Jesus' followers speak the language of the gospel and old traditions in new tongues—the experience of new birth is evident. All Saints. Holy Family. Trinity. Grace–St. Luke's. Christ Church. "And day by day, the Lord added to their number those who were being saved."

This story is not, however, only a tale of a few successful congregations. I believe, based in both my experience and my academic training, that a new kind of mainline congregation is indeed being born, a new period of American Protestantism has been birthed in the midst of decline. In his essay "Toward a History of American Congregations," Emory University professor E. Brooks Holifield describes four periods of American congregational history: *comprehensive congregations,* 1607–1789; *devotional congregations,* 1789–1870; *social congregations,* 1870–1950; and *participatory congregations,* 1950–present.

Comprehensive congregations, the earliest American model, understood their mission as a call to serve all the people in a geographical community. Devotional congregations, born in the competitive religious environment of the young nation, had to attract members to a denomination by providing innovative and distinctive worship practices. The social congregations of the late nineteenth century returned to the ideal of comprehension, but these congregations could no longer embrace an entire town or city. Instead, they became denominational social homes and initiated a wide array of activities and programs to meet the religious and secular needs of their members. Finally, the participatory congregations of the post–World War II period emerged as full-service centers, providing a new kind of comprehension—one not based on geography, family tradition, or denomination but on personal choice. The congregation became a gathering that invited participation in a variety of programs and worship styles. Hence, the development of church shopping and seeker-oriented churches.

But none of the churches I have attended really fit the description of participatory congregations; they embody a different sort of theological vision. I would like to suggest that some of the mainline Protestant confusion, with its resulting conflict, is the result of an emerging congregational style, perhaps even a new period of congregational history—that of the *intentional,* or the *practicing,* congregation.

The intentional congregation displays some of the characteristics of the participatory model. It is nongeographical, and those who attend choose to do so for a particular reason. Like participatory congregations, intentional churches welcome lay participation, are not clerical or hierarchical, are creative with music and worship, and deemphasize doctrinal uniformity. However, intentional congregations do not draw members primarily because of programs and are not primarily seeker oriented. People come because the church lays out a theologically meaningful (but not dogmatic) vision in worship and Christian formation, giving them the ability to see their work, relationships, and the world with spiritual insight. Intentional congregations draw newcomers because of something transcendent, a connection with God embodied in the spiritual practices of a distinct tradition in the context of a particular community. They are pilgrim congregations—communities that practice faith in the world yet live at some tension with the surrounding culture.

Sociologists of religion Donald Miller and Jackson Carroll have recently described most of the traits of intentional congregations, variously referring to them as "new paradigm" or "posttraditional" churches. Both scholars point out that the new patterns developed first in nondenominational evangelicalism, but they also express hope that if mainline congregations selectively adapt the style, they will experience new vitality.

Indeed, the intentional congregation is not tied to a particular theological position—it may be evangelical or progressive, conservative or liberal. Rather, this congregational ethos emerges from a set of characteristics associated with a group's relationship to the larger culture. The higher the sense of cultural tension, the greater the sense of spiritual journey or pilgrimage. With a clear call to living as a pilgrim, congregations attract members who take faith seriously and engage in distinctive spiritual practices to enrich their journey and deepen their connection to God. This spiritual purposefulness breeds congregational vitality. A committed core of spiritual practitioners will reach out and bring in new members, who, in turn, embrace the practices and continue the cycle.

Although contemporary spirituality is culturally particular and quite distinctive in many ways, this overall pattern is not entirely new in American religious history. In their book *The Churching of America, 1776–1990,* sociologists Rodney Stark and Roger Finke have argued that America's most "successful" religions are those that fit this very pattern. What is new, however, is that the pattern is being appropriated (and, in the process, modified) by mainline Protestants, people who were traditionally cultural insiders.

I believe that the emergence of a pilgrim mentality in the old Protestant mainline is a stunning and perhaps revolutionary change in American religious life. And I think the pattern of intentional churchgoing is far more widespread than most people have noticed. It has taken a while for the Protestant mainline to understand these shifts and the development of this new congregational pattern. But once the reality sinks in, we can expect even greater change in the old mainline.

There are two major reasons for this snail's pace of self-awareness and institutional responsiveness to the change. First, the whole tradition had to experience its loss of establishment power and recognize its distance from the cultural center; second, because mainline congregations tend to have older members, the shift was not obvious until baby boomers began to replace establishment types as leaders in congregations and denominations. Both disestablishment and generational transfer of leadership continue to redefine main-line religion.

Evangelicals, on the other hand, who were already culturally marginalized, demographically younger, and less constrained by denominational hierarchies, adjusted more quickly to the newer social realities and adapted more nimbly. Over the last two decades, their pilgrim sense created faith communities that grew at a rapid rate. In an odd twist of historical fate, American evangelicals, now flush with political power and wealth, find themselves closer to the center (if there is a center) of the establishment than they have been for a century. Evangelicals are now more overtly active in Washington, D.C., than are Episcopalians. As a result of this "success," evangelicals are muting some of their religious distinctiveness in favor of their share of the political pie. Those who were once pilgrims are now pundits and lobbyists.

At the same time, however, mainline congregations are embracing the pilgrim spirituality of the intentional congregation. They are appropriating, reclaiming, and recreating their own traditions in imaginative and innovative ways. Much of this has been an internal challenge, and no sense of the public witness of such mainline congregations has emerged with any real clarity. The mainline public voice has been quiet as these inner processes have been unfolding. Part of the difficulty in identifying intentional congregations is that they engage these tasks of change and renewal without much fanfare. You need to be on the ground—or in the pew—to know what has been happening.

Another part of the difficulty comes from the fact that the specifics of change vary so widely from denomination to denomination. Transformation has happened locally—not as a result of any national institutional network, project, or program. Indeed, these congregations often resist program in favor of discerning God's spirit in community. In the case of my story, the congregations in a single denomination have adapted to the new patterns, based on a highly developed local sense of congregational identity and vocation. Thus, particular practices of intentional faith vary from place to place. While the same impulse guides these congregations, its expression takes different forms.

The overall traits, however, remain generally the same. Intentional congregations know who they are, can live into that identity, interpret it in culturally relevant theological language, engage in practices that engender commitment in their members, and possess a sense of missionary obligation. They cherish and reassert their denominational traditions, but not through links with executive offices or denominational programs. Indeed, they often have ambiguous, or even hostile, attitudes toward official structures and institutions that they view as hopelessly out of touch and behind the times. As a result, their vitality may be seen as threatening to those holding official power in denominations. Local congregations, I suspect, can increasingly expect worried hierarchies to try to control innovation in an attempt to reassert a modicum of authority.

Thus, intentional churches creatively select aspects of their tradition, its history, liturgy, or polity, and establish those elements as the focus of congregational identity and mission. While intentional Episcopalians, for example, eschew their connections to the bishop or diocesan office, they extol the virtues of their congregation, the Prayer Book, eucharistic worship, theological diversity, commitments to outreach and inclusion, and a sense of spiritual freedom. They have interpreted the tradition's grand theological narrative into their local community and culture and find it richly relevant and meaningful. They choose to be Episcopalians because the worship and the spirituality of their particular congregation connects them to God and to others.

Almost all the parishes I have attended have been—or were in the process of becoming—intentional congregations. At All Saints in Santa Barbara, Gethin Hughes purposefully instituted the new Prayer Book liturgy to express a new vision of being church. Empowered by this vision, he renovated the church's sanctuary. And he successfully welcomed and mentored a new generation of college students who simply showed up on his ecclesiastical doorstep. None of this, I am quite sure, was by accident. Rather, it emerged from his clear sense of Episcopalians as a eucharistic people—a sense he imparted to the larger congregation. As a young evangelical, I found that it captured my imagination. It drew together heartfelt faith, vibrant community, and an experiential sense of God in worship. It demanded that I take it seriously, live into it, and embrace its wholistic vision of the world. It was meaty faith.

Christ Church in Hamilton developed a distinct identity of being both Protestant and Catholic, evangelical and sacramental. You had to think about it, study, practice devotional life, and negotiate the tensions raised by its dual commitments. Its distinctiveness drew people and sometimes served as the source of its greatest tensions. St. Stephens in Durham argued over intentionality. There were those who wanted to create an intentional parish versus those who took faith, especially denominational identity, for granted in an older, social congregation mode.

Few congregations are as intentional as the Church of the Holy Family in Chapel Hill. There, Timothy Kimbrough has created a theologically purposeful culture in which every rite of passage, every sacramental action, conveys deeper meaning and passion for living the Christian life. You cannot attend Holy Family without, as my husband, Richard, likes to say, "getting it." Indeed, you cannot join without going through an entire year of prayer, teaching, retreats, and mentoring. Holy Family, as gentle and joyful as it is, is serious church.

For a few years, I had to explore the practices of faith more or less on my own. With the guidance of Michelle Woodhouse, my spiritual director, I found my way back through Christian tradition, its theology and practices, and forward to innovative renderings of that tradition. Writing in my journal, engaging in centering prayer and Christian meditation, reading the mystics, studying the Bible, keeping Lent, walking the labyrinth. I explored theologies that had previously unnerved me. Ultimately, I could embrace parts of these to develop a theological worldview suited for Christian maturity, a bricolage of tradition and practice. Chosen, yes. Eclectic, well, to a degree. At the same time, however, this vision is deeply embedded in historic Christianity and informed theological insight. And, although pursued initially as an individual, I found spiritual fullness only when the new practices were pursued in a place: Trinity—a community of like-minded pilgrims committed to intentional spirituality.

Trinity and Grace–St. Luke's are both intentional congregations. Trinity's intentional identity, as an inclusive church, opens the congregation to ideas and practices unimagined by their forebears. Their use of balanced imagery for God in worship has led them to both alternative liturgies and the renovation of their sanctuary. At Grace–St. Luke's, intentional community flourishes around the worship service itself, Cursillo, Rivendell, and excellent Christian education. Their choice for the new rector, a man formed in small c catholic practices of faith, underlines their shift from the older style of inherited faith to intentional Christian practice.

At Christ Church, several congregations of Holifield's periodization scheme live together in the same building. The ghosts of the comprehensive (our deist founders) and devotional congregations (the nineteenth-century evangelical Episcopalians) still linger in our building as either tourist attractions or architectural relics.

Today, many of the church's elders, that "greatest generation," still embrace the ideal of the social congregation, a number of newcomers under the previous rector helped transform the parish into a participatory congregation, and the emerging congregation is reaching toward the spiritual practice and theological clarity of intentional churchgoing.

Christ Church is more textured than a typical corporate congregation. It is both a big, unwieldy corporate church and a set of overlapping congregations that reflect the distinctive concerns of American Protestantism through its entire history. No wonder it is nearly impossible to understand. Each historical congregation carries particular spiritual and cultural expectations and each envisions itself as a different kind of church—with insights, understandings, histories, hopes, and dreams that often exist at counterpoint.

And Christ Church sometimes forgets that it is living in yet another time of historical transformation—that the church is called to make history and not to provide a safe haven from change for people who fear it. Christ Church has never been a safe haven. It has changed with every wind of change in the nation's history. There are glimmers of a new congregational reality emerging even here. Whether or not we can become an intentional congregation is still up for grabs. Sometimes I think we are too taken by our access to political power and wealth; we are still deceived by the myth that we are in charge. But on my better days, I think we can make it.

For the last two decades, churchgoers, ministers, denominational executives, theologians, scholars, pundits, and critics have been asking the question: What does it all mean? What does all the fuss in the mainline mean? Some people, like Tom Reeves in his blistering jeremiad, *The Empty Church,* think it was only the death throes of an increasingly irrelevant Protestant liberalism. The end of the line for the old mainline. Just as the skeptics "sneered" at the drunken disciples on Pentecost, "they are filled with new wine." They are drunk.

From my place in the story, that of a participant trained to observe, interpret, and narrate, I see something different. New wine, yes. But not the drunken brawl at the night's last call. Rather, the new wine of the Spirit is pouring itself out on the old mainline. The new wine of sensing God's presence through purposeful practice of faith. Some congregations, discerning the sounds of the Spirit, are crafting new wineskins. These wineskins are not the result of some program or church growth technique. They are often creative, local reinterpretations of a parish's identity and sense of vocation, often as individual as the congregation itself. In these places, the old mainline, feeble, sinful, limited, and crippled as it has been, is being remade. It is being born again. A new vitality is making its way across the old mainline landscape, and, for those with ears to hear, it is a time of Pentecost.

Over the last twenty years of churchgoing, I have learned a few things about faith, about hope, and, above all, about love. I still feel afraid occasionally. But I no longer fear the wrath of a vengeful and demanding God. Rather, I fear I cannot begin to comprehend the breadth of God's love. I fear I will not be able to give away enough love—to my family, friends, church, to the oppressed and disenfranchised—before my time is done. Life is too short for all its love, to really understand its transforming power. And I sometimes fear Christians will not rise to the challenge of our times, that we will fail to embody God's love in the world.

As I think about it, however, one lesson stands above all others: it is hard to be a mainline churchgoer. It is not, as some critics claim, the easy road to faith. It is hard being a pilgrim soul in a church learning to be a pilgrim community. Conflict, timidity, injustice, quiescence, institutional dysfunction, and fear of change have been the cup of mainline unfaithfulness. Because of our own shortcomings, we live in congregations where it can be difficult to feel God's presence. I am trying—we are trying—to hear, heed, and practice faith in new ways. But it can be tough to stay with it. For me, for all of us, it has been a strenuous journey.

Looking back, I feel somewhat envious of my evangelical friends, the ones who never felt the need to jump the theological ship of our high school and college years. I still get Christmas cards from some of them—warm and prayerful, some with evangelistic messages like "Jesus Christ was born to die for your sins." There is a kind of simplicity, clarity, and peace to popular evangelicalism that orders life and death in practical, unambiguous ways. Although I occasionally feel nostalgic about it, it also appears completely spiritually predictable. A little boring, perhaps.

My pilgrimage, like that of the mainline, has not been a predictable, smooth path, traveling from victory to victory in Jesus' name. Rather, mainline's rough way has often been hard, following paths overgrown with brambles and thistles, up theological mountains of terrifying heights, and down to the depths of conflict and broken fellowship. Of the true pilgrim soul, John Bunyan claimed "that they have met with hardships in the way, that they do meet with troubles night and day." Fear, doubt, despair, and temptation mark the pilgrims' path. Most days, a vision of God keeps me going, usually visible to me at Sunday morning Eucharist. My girlfriend Julie calls it my mystical streak. But sometimes the fog obscures even that. At those moments in the journey, I find Bunyan's comforting lines written as if for today's mainline pilgrims:

Under such mantles as may make them look
(With some) as if their God had them forsook.
They softly went, but sure, and at the end,
Found that the Lord of pilgrims was their friend.

So, the pilgrimage has brought me to Christ Church where, as a lay person, I serve on senior staff as director of faith formation. When I walk through our graveyard, sunlight dabbled on eighteenth-century tombstones, I wonder if this is the time God will finally forsake us. Or will we, along this pilgrim way, manage to create those new wineskins, to be a community of the New Jerusalem rather than the tomb of the old establishment? Will we succumb to fear or drink the heady wine of Love? Will I? The choice is clear, and the longed-for *telos,* the theological vision of God's culmination, is obvious now. No more establishment churches. No graveyards of dry bones. Only communities of living faith. "And behold," writes Bunyan, "the City shone like the sun, the streets also were paved with gold. . . . The righteous nation that keepeth truth may enter in."

Standing among their gravestones, I think of all those in our history who listened to the Word and heard. Nameless, forgotten parishioners who "found that the Lord of pilgrims was their friend," those who kept faith and, generation after generation, transformed their congregation by making the gospel relevant to their world. Unlike the tourists who throng here, I do not genuflect at the memory of George Washington or Robert E. Lee. As a matter of fact, I find it somewhat painful and awkward that their ghosts haunt our sanctuary, as they are ghosts from a world vanishing from the landscape. A world where some churchgoers misidentified the United States, and its Protestant mainline, as "the righteous nation" instead of God's reign of love and justice.

Rather, I think of the Rev. William Meade, rector of Christ Church from 1811 to 1813, faithful to the point of freeing his slaves, who, in some ways at least, saw past his own prejudices to love and justice. William Meade was an evangelical Episcopalian, one of a number of young, innovative clerics who gathered about "the District" in the early nineteenth century, who reinvigorated Christ Church by wedding it to the evangelical cause. He and his clerical friends had a vision for a new kind of Episcopal Church in a democratic world, one that spoke the language of liberty, freedom of conscience, and heartfelt faith. They recreated Anglicanism in an American mode, adjusting and adapting their tradition to a new culture. By doing so, they helped save an entire denomination from history's graveyard.

Nineteenth-century evangelical Episcopalians had a favorite verse—Revelation 22:17—appearing over and over in their journals, correspondence, and sermons: "The Spirit and the bride say, 'Come.' And let everyone who hears say, 'Come.'"

When I walk into the sanctuary and close my eyes, I imagine the youthful William Meade, eager and enthusiastic, preaching from that verse to his congregation. "Come, pilgrim souls, come, come. Come to the new wine of God's Spirit. Come and drink. Be not afraid. Be changed by the power of God." Then I realize that the Spirit is still calling, even in old places like this: "Come, come, come. Come to the New Jerusalem."

Looking at the sunlight streaming through our windows, I pray, "God, give us faith to recognize that you, the Lord of pilgrims, have led us—have led me—along this way." With God as guide, strengthening us for the journey, maybe we will get there.

BIBLIOGRAPHY

All of the following works provided important background and sharpened my understanding and interpretation of American mainline religion; my ideas were shaped in scholarly engagement with these sources. Although not formally footnoted in the text, most of the quoted material comes from the books here listed. Primary sources—such as parish histories, interviews, correspondence, journals, and sermons—were quoted but omitted from this bibliography.

Ammerman, Nancy, Jackson Carroll, Carl Dudley, and William McKinney. *Studying Congregations: A New Handbook.* Nashville, Tenn.: Abingdon Press, 1998.

Ammerman, Nancy Tatom. *Congregation and Community.* New Brunswick, N.J.: Rutgers University Press, 1997.

Balmer, Randall. *Grant Us Courage: Travels Along the Mainline of American Protestantism.* New York: Oxford University Press, 1996.

Bass, Dorothy. *Practicing Our Faith: A Way of Life for a Searching People.* San Francisco: Jossey-Bass, 1997.

Becker, Penny Edgell. *Congregations in Conflict: Cultural Models of Local Religious Life*. New York: Cambridge University Press, 1999.

Bondi, Roberta. *Memories of God: Theological Reflections on a Life*. Nashville, Tenn.: Abingdon Press, 1995.

Boswell, John. *Christianity, Social Tolerance, and Homosexuality*. Chicago: University of Chicago Press, 1980.

Braude, Ann. *Women and American Religion*. New York: Oxford University Press, 2000.

Brooks, David. *Bobos in Paradise: The New Upper Class and How They Got There*. New York: Simon & Schuster, 2000.

Butler, Diana Hochstedt. *Standing Against the Whirlwind: Evangelical Episcopalians in Nineteenth-Century America*. New York: Oxford University Press, 1995.

Carroll, Jackson. *Mainline to the Future: Congregations for the 21st Century*. Louisville, Ky.: Westminster John Knox, 2000.

Carroll, Jackson, Barbara Wheeler, Daniel Aleshire, and Penny Long Marler. *Being There: Culture and Formation in Two Theological Schools*. New York: Oxford University Press, 1997.

Coalter, Milton, John Mulder, and Louis Weeks. *Vital Signs: The Promise of Mainstream Protestantism*. Grand Rapids, Mich.: Eerdmans, 1996.

Countryman, Louis William. *Living on the Border of the Holy: Renewing the Priesthood of All*. Harrisburg, Pa.: Morehouse, 1999.

Eiesland, Nancy. *A Particular Place: Urban Restructuring and Religious Ecology in a Southern Exurb*. New Brunswick, N.J.: Rutgers University Press, 2000.

Ellwood, Robert. *The Fifties Spiritual Marketplace: American Religion in a Decade of Conflict*. New Brunswick, N.J.: Rutgers University Press, 1997.

Episcopal Church Foundation. *The Zacchaeus Project: Discerning Episcopal Identity at the Dawn of the New Millennium*. New York: Episcopal Church Foundation, 1999.

Fischer, Kathleen. *Women at the Well*. Mahwah, N.J.: Paulist Press, 1988.

Friend, Howard. *Recovering the Sacred Center: Church Renewal from the Inside Out.* Valley Forge, Pa.: Judson Press, 1998.

Gallagher, Nora. *Things Seen and Unseen: A Year Lived in Faith.* New York: Knopf, 1998.

Grammer, Carl E. "Evangelism: Its Past and Future." In *Abiding Values.* Philadelphia: John C. Winston, 1938.

Hoge, Dean, Benton Johnson, and Donald Luidens. *Vanishing Boundaries: The Religion of Mainline Protestant Baby Boomers.* Louisville, Ky.: Westminster John Knox, 1994.

Holifield, E. Brooks. "Toward a History of American Congregations." In James P. Wind and James W. Lewis, *American Congregations.* Chicago: University of Chicago Press, 1994.

Holmes, Urban, T. *The Future Shape of Ministry: A Theological Reflection.* New York: Seabury Press, 1971.

Holmes, Urban T. "Education for Liturgy: An Unfinished Symphony in Four Movements." In M. Burnson (ed.), *Worship Points the Way: A Celebration of the Life and Work of Massey Hamilton Shepherd, Jr.* New York: Seabury Press, 1981.

Howard, Thomas. *Evangelical Is Not Enough.* Nashville, Tenn.: Thomas Nelson, 1984.

Keillor, Garrison. "Episcopal." In Don S. Armentrout and Robert B. Slocum (eds.). *Documents of Witness: A History of the Episcopal Church.* New York: Church Hymnal Corporation, 1994.

Kelly, Dean M. *Why Conservative Churches Are Growing.* Macon, Ga.: Mercer University Press, reprint edition, 1986.

Mann, Alice. *The In-Between Church: Navigating Size Transitions in Congregations.* Bethesda, Md.: Alban Institute, 1998.

McNeill, John. *The Church and the Homosexual.* Kansas City: Sheed, Andrews, and McMeal, 1976.

Mead, Loren. *The Once and Future Church: Reinventing the Congregation for a New Mission Frontier.* Bethesda, Md.: Alban Institute, 1991.

Miller, Donald. *Reinventing American Protestantism.* Berkeley: University of California Press, 1997.

Nicholson, Roger. *Temporary Shepherds: A Congregational Handbook for Interim Ministry.* Bethesda, Md.: Alban Institute, 1998.

Niebuhr, H. Richard. *The Social Sources of Denominationalism.* New York: Henry Holt, 1929.

Niebuhr, Reinhold. *The Irony of American History.* New York: Scribner, 1952.

Norris, Kathleen. *The Quotidian Mysteries: Laundry, Liturgy, and "Women's Work."* Mahwah, N.J.: Paulist Press, 1998.

O'Connor, Elizabeth. *Journey Inward, Journey Outward.* New York: HarperCollins, 1968.

Prelinger, Catherine (ed.). *Episcopal Women: Gender, Spirituality, and Commitment in an American Mainline Denomination.* New York: Oxford University Press, 1992.

Prichard, Robert. *A History of the Episcopal Church.* Rev. ed. Harrisburg, Pa.: Morehouse, 1999.

Putnam, Robert D. *Bowling Alone: The Collapse and Revival of American Community.* New York: Simon and Schuster, 2000.

Reeves, Thomas. *The Empty Church: Does Organized Religion Matter Anymore?* New York: Touchstone, 1996.

Roof, Wade Clark. *Community and Commitment: Religious Plausibility in a Liberal Protestant Church.* New York: Elsevier, 1978.

Roof, Wade Clark. *A Generation of Seekers: The Spiritual Journeys of the Baby Boom Generation.* San Francisco: HarperSanFrancisco, 1993.

Roof, Wade Clark. *Spiritual Marketplace: Baby Boomers and the Remaking of American Religion.* Princeton, N.J.: Princeton University Press, 1999.

Roof, Wade Clark and William McKinney. *American Mainline Religion: Its Changing Shape and Future.* New Brunswick, N.J.: Rutgers University Press, 1987.

Stark, Rodney and Roger Finke. *The Churching of America, 1776–1990: Winners and Losers in Our Religious Economy.* New Brunswick, N.J.: Rutgers University Press, 1992.

Tickle, Phyllis. *Re-Discovering the Sacred: Spirituality in America.* New York: Crossroad, 1995.

Wallis, Jim. *The Soul of Politics*. New York: New Press, 1994.

Webber, Robert. *Evangelicals on the Canterbury Trail: Why Evangelicals Are Attracted to the Liturgical Church*. Waco, Tex.: Word Books, 1985.

Wilkes, Paul. *Excellent Protestant Congregations: The Guide to Best Places and Practices*. Louisville, Ky.: Westminster John Knox, 2001.

Wilson-Kastner, Patricia. *Sacred Drama: A Spirituality of Christian Liturgy*. Minneapolis: Fortress Press, 1999.

Wind, James P. and James W. Lewis, *American Congregations*. Chicago: University of Chicago Press, 1994.

World Council of Churches Commission on Faith and Order. *Baptism, Eucharist and Ministry*. Geneva: World Council of Churches, 1982.

Wuthnow, Robert. *Christianity in the 21st Century*. New York: Oxford University Press, 1993.

Wuthnow, Robert. *After Heaven: Spirituality in America Since the 1950s*. Berkeley: University of California Press, 1998.

ABOUT THE AUTHOR

Diana Butler Bass, an active Episcopal layperson, is a writer and teacher who works as the director of faith formation at Christ Church, Alexandria, Virginia, and an adjunct professor of church history at Virginia Theological Seminary.

From 1995 to 2000, she wrote a weekly column on religion on America for the *Santa Barbara News Press* that was distributed nationally by the New York Times Syndicate. She is a popular speaker on contemporary religion whose credits include numerous radio and television appearances, including the PBS program *Religion and Ethics Newsweekly.*

She holds a Ph.D. from Duke University in Religious Studies. Her prize-winning dissertation, *Standing Against the Whirlwind: Evangelical Episcopalians in 19th Century America,* was published by Oxford University Press. She has taught at Westmont College, the University of California at Santa Barbara, Macalaster College, and Rhodes College.

She serves the Episcopal Church as a member of the General Convention, the denomination's national governing body, and as a consultant to a variety of foundations, boards, and task forces.

Born in Baltimore and raised in Scottsdale, Arizona, she now lives in Fairfax County, Virginia, with her husband, Richard Bass. They have two children, Emma and Jonah. She enjoys spending time with her family, small dinner parties, gardening, wine tasting, and Duke basketball.